Fly Fishing for Pacific Salmon

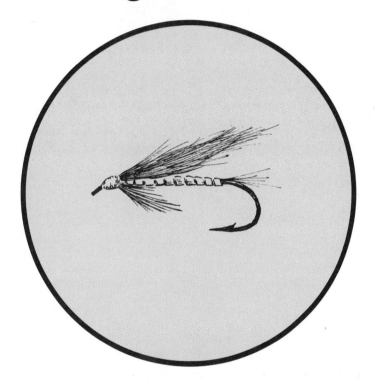

Bruce Ferguson   Les Johnson   Pat Trotter

Foreword by Frank Haw

Frank Amato Publications
P.O. Box 02112, Portland, Oregon 97202
(503) 658-8108

Dedication

To my brother Gordon, with whom I have fly fished in so
many wonderful places.

Bruce M. Ferguson

In memory of my mother, Annite M. Johnson, who helped
me understand the importance of persistence and hard work
to get things done.

Lester F. Johnson

To the newest set of fly fishers in my life: Rena, Adam, Ben
and Diana B., and to the two others who are still extra-
special: Scott and Diana T.

Pat Trotter

Biographies

Bruce M. Ferguson

Since retiring as a forestry and timberlands consultant,
Bruce has devoted full time to improving and expanding
salmon fly fishing knowledge and opportunities in marine
waters. He is a frequent speaker to Northwest fly clubs on
the subject. One of his special projects has been an active
and continuing involvement in Washington's resident salmon
enhancement program in Puget Sound. Bruce is a life member of the Federation of Fly Fishers and is an international
director and co-chairman of that organization's Saltwater
Committee. In 1982 he was recipient of the Conservation
Man of the Year award, presented by the Northwest Council, Federation of Fly Fishers, embracing Alaska, British
Columbia, the Yukon, Washington, and Oregon. He was a
member of the United States delegation in the U. S./Canada
Pacific Salmon Treaty negotiations. An incurable fly fisherman since his youth in New York, Bruce now concentrates his
efforts on Pacific salmon, although he rarely passed up an
opportunity to go after Florida tarpon, Bighorn rainbows,
or Labrador brook trout. *Fly Fishing for Pacific Salmon* is
his first major writing effort. Bruce lives in Gig Harbor,
Washington, on the shores of Wollochet Bay where he is
back at his favorite angling pursuit — casting over surface
feeding coho salmon.

Lester F. Johnson

An artist, art director and writer for twenty-five years, Les has been fly fishing since purchasing a level enameled line and a few flies to use with an oft-repaired three-piece cane rod in 1946. His artwork and articles have appeared in *Field and Stream, Salt Water Sportsman, Western Outdoors, Fly Fisherman, Fly Tyer, Flyfishing* and *Salmon Trout Steelheader*. Les wrote his first book, *Fishing the Sea-Run Cutthroat Trout*, which was published in 1971, and an expanded version, *Sea-Run*, issued in 1979. His angling travels have taken him to northern British Columbia to explore the streams of the Skeena River drainage, to the blue ribbon waters of Idaho and Montana and most of the streams on the coastline from Washington to California. Les lives in Marin County, California, where he is at work on several new projects.

Patrick Trotter, Ph.D.

A scientist by profession, Pat has been an ardent fly fisherman since childhood with a special interest in fly tying and fly fishing history. Pat's column, "From the Flybook," has appeared in *Salmon Trout Steelheader* for several years and his articles have been published in *Fly Fisherman, Fly Tyer, Flyfishing* and *Salmon Trout Steelheader*. He makes an annual pilgrimage to the Deschutes River during the stonefly hatch and prowls coastal streams and bays for cutthroat, steelhead and salmon at every opportunity. Pat is presently at work on another book and has additional writings in the planning stages. A native of Longview in Southwest Washington where his fly fishing interest first blossomed, Pat now makes his home in Seattle, Washington.

David Hagerbaumer

Born in 1921, David has devoted his total energies to outdoor and wildlife painting since 1948. He has published nearly one hundred collotypes, lithographs and etchings since 1963. Added to this are ceramic gamebird models and a limited edition work in bronze called, "The Old Decoy." Known for clarity of detail and accuracy of bird flight, David is recognized internationally as one of America's most respected artists. His painting for the cover of this book certainly reflects his skill and knowledge. David's home and studio is in LcConner, Washington.

Dan Berglund

Dan is a graphic designer, artist and photographer along with being an ardent angler. He is equally at home trout fishing in eastern Washington or steelheading on a coastal stream. While doing research for the illustrations that appear in this book, Dan fished several salmon areas in Washington and Oregon, becoming an addicted salmon fisherman in the process. A clean, crisp style that communicates the message well is the hallmark of Berglund's art. He makes his home near Auburn, Washington.

Foreword

ALTHOUGH I HAVE SPENT A GREAT DEAL OF time in joyful pursuit of Pacific salmon on light tackle, few of my efforts could ever be confused with genuine fly fishing. I am particularly honored that three members of the hallowed brotherhood of fly fishers have invited me to contribute these few words to a book that could add significantly to the improvement and sustained yield of our Pacific salmon resource.

How could this be? *Fly Fishing for Pacific Salmon* describes in detail how to find, lure and take a resource that is already in trouble. But our salmon are a renewable resource and remarkably resilient if we give them the chance they so richly deserve. The future of this fantastic resource will be based upon political decisions and priorities that will be generated at the grass roots level. Wide public exposure to the addictive pleasures of salmon angling and the world of the fish we seek can recruit a most formidable advocacy throughout the fabric of our citizenry that, if properly led, will guarantee the future of this resource. The level of the commitment among those who refuse to accept a future without salmon will be increased by the quality and intimacy of exposure to these great fish. Thus, give me one-thousand citizens who have an ocean bright coho on a fly rod and we will always have salmon!

Most of us know that our salmon stocks can be increased through critical habitat improvement, prudent hatchery production and, as eloquently described herein, by simply allowing adequate numbers of adult fish to spawn. Sustained yields of salmon can also be increased by making wiser use of what now exists.

Salmon have a wide variety of potential commercial uses. For example, prime chinook salmon commands top price for lox, other specialty foods, and fresh fish for the finest restaurants. The same flesh would be excellent if it were frozen or even canned. Further descending the economic scale, our pets, livestock and poultry would thrive on diets contrived from this rich and nutritious flesh; crabs, shrimp and fish would hasten to traps and hooks baited with the succulent red meat, our flowers and vegetables could grow to luxuriance under the influence of its more basic components. But most of these uses, providing the lower economic returns, would be inexcusable and flagrant waste.

Various stocks of Pacific salmon also provide us with some choices as to how we might utilize them for recreational purposes. The value of recreational salmon use is so high that its byproduct alone, manifested in tangible benefits created when anglers spend money, may far exceed any known alternative commercial use. Again, this monetary value is *secondary* to the basic recreational value that we receive in return — just as my meager expenditure near home on Puget Sound is only a token of the importance of the outings to the quality of my life.

If it is wasteful to use prime commercial salmon for pet and plant food, then it appears that we can squander our recreational opportunities as well. In an attempt to remain fully occupied, a biologist observer aboard an ocean charter boat recently recorded the length of time it took for anglers to hook and boat 33 prime coho salmon. Using what could be described as typical gear, the average "battle" lasted thirty seconds! Doubtless, the people enjoyed themselves, but in terms of lasting recreational yield, how could this packaged experience compare with the satisfaction, pleasure and memories resulting from the events culminating in reel-stripping runs from a cavorting coho on fly tackle? It is clear to me who will fill the ranks of those committed to preserving the future of our salmon. It will be those who most fully understand and appreciate what we have. This book will help.

Frank Haw
August, 1984

Library of Congress Catalog Card Number: 85-071263   Printed in U.S.A.

ISBN 0-936608-35-8 softbound, 0-936608-36-6 hardbound

Contents

Acknowledgments

When it was agreed with Frank Amato that *Fly Fishing for Pacific Salmon* was a subject with substance enough for a book, we all looked forward to a one-year adventure. At the outset we didn't clearly see the scope of such an undertaking nor could we have imagined the volume of information that would pour forth from our initial probings. As information accumulated, we soon realized that achieving our goal would entail considerably more effort than had been originally envisioned. The way things turned out, our one-year adventure stretched into an eight-year odyssey.

Our research took us to many of the streams, bays and ocean fishing accesses on the Pacific Coast to try for salmon with our flies and to learn what we could of each place. Every angler should be faced with such a challenge. It was not the fishing, though, however spectacular (or sometimes frustrating) that proved to be the ultimate reward for bending to the task of developing this text. Most gratifying was the opportunity to meet and work with so many exceptional people who shared our enthusiasm for fly fishing and the perpetuation of the Pacific salmon resource. These people — anglers, fly tiers, writers, guides, tackle manufacturers and employees of college fishery schools, state and federal fish and game agencies — all pitched in eagerly to support our effort.

Some of the input we received overlapped our own findings and this was important to us for the purpose of verification. To a much greater extent, the information gleaned from fishing camp conversations, detailed reports and concisely penned vignettes enlightened us to new fly patterns, angling techniques and the timing of certain salmon runs that we would never have known about otherwise. It was this intimate, practical knowledge, some of which had long been held within small, local angling fraternities, that became the mortar of the book.

Without all the people who provided assistance throughout the duration of the project, this book would not have been nearly so complete a work as it turned out to be. How much their contributions enhanced the final product cannot be too strongly stated, so, it is to the following very special individuals that we extend a sincere and heartfelt thank you.

Bruce M. Ferguson
Lester F. Johnson
Patrick Trotter

Mike Foster
Miranda, California

A school teacher for twenty years, Mike lives near the banks of the South Fork of the Eel River with his wife and children. Mike also finds time to operate a fly tackle shop, teach classes for the Fenwick Fly Fishing Seminars and write for various outdoor publications. During the course of this project, Mike provided information on fly fishing in Northern California, detailed accounts on techniques for hooking milling salmon and tied a selection of flies which appear in the colorplates of the Fly Types and Patterns Chapter.

Art Lawn, Project Director
Rowdy Creek Fish Hatchery, Inc.
Smith River, California

An afternoon spent talking with Art Lawn in his small, cluttered office across from the Rowdy Creek Fish Hatchery was a lesson in what people can do if they want something badly enough. Art wanted to save the great fall chinook salmon and winter steelhead of the Smith River. To do so he and other members of the Smith River Kiwanis Club started a campaign to build a private hatchery committed to restoring the Smith River runs through private donations and it is working. Art provided information on the late run chinook salmon entering the rivers of Southern Oregon and Northern California.

James E. Garrett
Sequim, Washington

An ardent fly fisherman who concentrates his efforts on streams draining the Olympic Peninsula in Washington, Jim is an employee of the Washington Department of Fisheries. With his fly rod, Jim takes pink, coho, chum and a few king salmon throughout the summer and fall season using fly patterns of his own design. Information on fly presentation submitted by Jim is incorporated in the Fishing Techniques.

Denny Hannah
Hannah Licensed Outfitter and Guide Service
Port Orford, Oregon

During the course of research there were a lot of hours spent in a drift boat with Denny, or his son, Todd, fishing a variety of coastal streams in Southern Oregon. We tested rods, lines, flies and techniques, counting heavily on the Hannahs' knowledge of local rivers to position us over salmon on a regular basis. Although Denny's camp hosts more conventional tackle anglers throughout the season than fly casters, he welcomed the opportunity to help with our project through his guide service and during long evening sessions giving freely of his experience gained from years of fishing on Oregon rivers. Becoming friends with Denny, his wife Carol (who keeps the camp running smoothly and provides outstanding meals) and Todd has been a marvelous adjunct to the writing of this book.

C. R. "Winnie" Winston
Vancouver, Washington

It is virtually impossible to keep up with everything that is happening on a subject during the course of writing a book. Winnie, a pen pal, acted as my Southwest Washington/Portland, Oregon correspondent, keeping me informed on the salmon fishing in that area. His mailings, stuffed with pertinent newspaper clippings and detailed letters recounting personal observations made while fishing, were eagerly anticipated, enjoyable to read and invariably helpful.

Jack E. Perry
Tacoma, Washington

Sometimes the prototype rods we received for testing arrived as blanks fresh off the mandrels. Jack, a custom rod builder and designer of rod making and fly tying tools, was a great help in quickly turning the blanks into completed rods so we could get onto the rivers and bays with them.

Burt W. Preston
Kirkland, Washington

Involved in the arts for most of his life, Burt made his singing debut as Germont in *La Traviata* with the Chicago Opera Company, went on to teach voice as a full professor at the Chicago Conservatory and became interested in art galleries in 1958. Burt is on the sales staff of Eddie Bauer, Inc., and produces art and wildlife exhibits for the Seattle store. It was at Burt's suggestion that we met with wildlife artist, David Hagerbaumer, who provided the watercolor for our book jacket.

LFJ

Dr. R. L. Burgner

Dr. Burgner is Director of the Fisheries Research Institute at the University of Washington. In this capacity, he provided me with a wealth of background data on life histories including migration routes for all salmon species. Of equal importance, he put me in touch with many other knowledgeable people in this field.

Errol Champion

Errol is a past president of the Federation of Fly Fishers, indicating his enormous devotion to the resource. He explored and developed flies and fishing techniques suitable for saltwater coho, chinook, pinks and sockeye around Juneau, Alaska, where he makes his home. He has shown infinite patience and generosity over the years in sharing his knowledge and fly patterns with me.

Jim Darden

Jim is a member of the Fourth Corner Fly Fishers. When he moved to Bellingham, Washington from eastern Washington, nobody told him he couldn't catch chinook salmon on a fly in salt water. As a result, he developed a unique deep water system which he shares with us in the book.

Kurt Fresh

Kurt is a biologist for the Washington Department of Fisheries specializing in marine ecology. Based on his knowledge in this field, he developed the tables in the book outlining salmon feed by species in different marine environments and contributed the basic marine ecology concepts discussed in the text. This important information can become a basis for continuing fly design and technique development for salmon at different stages in their life history.

Frank Haw

Now retired from the Washington Department of Fisheries, Frank, in his role as originator of the Puget Sound resident salmon delayed release program, has provided recreational and commercial fishing to hundreds of thousands of Washington fishermen. His contribution to the book has been enormous. He has never failed to arrange for or provide information, support or constructive criticism as the book evolved over time. His foreword reflects his enthusiastic approach to light tackle saltwater fishing in which he is an unparalleled guru.

David R. Hurn

David retired as Assistant Director, Fish and Wildlife Branch, Ministry of Recreation and Conservation, British Columbia. He developed flies and fly fishing techniques for "feeder" saltwater salmon over a timeframe of many years from his home on the southern end of Vancouver Island, B. C. The book is richer for the inclusion of quotations from his correspondence and his fly patterns which he so generously provided.

Bill Ludwig

Bill owns a pharmacy in Tacoma, Washington, and has been a long-time member of the Puget Sound Flyfishers. He is also a long-time friend and constant fishing companion. Bill showed amazing tenacity of spirit in his willingness to fieldtest various techniques and theories in all kinds of weather, including the proverbial wind, sleet and snow. His photographs of salmon feed and fishing scenes complement the text.

Bert and Mel Nelson

This is a father and son team, owners of Kitsap Bait Sales, Port Orchard, Washington. A tour of their modern processing facility clearly identifies the scope of their business. Catching live specimens of a number of the baitfish species needed for the book's photographs presented a real problem. However, Bert and Mel put their expertise, time and equipment at my disposal for this purpose and accomplished "mission impossible."

Bill Nelson

Guide extraordinaire for April Point Lodge, Quadra Island, B. C., Bill is a charter member of the Federation of Fly Fishers and an early developer of saltwater fly fishing for feeding coho, chinook and pinks. In addition to guiding me during the early stages of the book data collection process, he has kindly shared his proven flies and techniques for inclusion in the final product.

Barry Thornton

A school principal in Comox, British Columbia, Barry was the founding chairman of the Steelhead Society of B. C., its president for several years and a past director of the B. C. Wildlife Federation. He has authored a book, *Steelhead, the Supreme Trophy Trout*, and numerous magazine articles. For the book, he has graciously shared his beach and feeder coho fishing experiences, as well as his flies.

In addition I would like to thank the following individuals for their very substantial contribution to the development of the book: Dave Allen, Westport, Washington charterboat skipper; Norman Parks and Percy Washington, National Marine Fisheries Service; Dr. Kenneth Chew, University of Washington College of Fisheries; Kendra Daly and Gayle Heron, Department of Oceanography, University of Washington; Bob Trumble, Washington Department of Fisheries, all for their instruction concerning the life histories of both the salmon and their feed. Tom Fredrickson and Lloyd Morrell, for zooplankton flies and techniques; Mike Cellers, Mike Dieker, Warren Peterson, Garry Sandstrom, Brian Steel, Harold Van Riper, and Dr. David Wands for baitfish flies and techniques; Al Allard for beach fishing flies and techniques; Lee Hendrickson for his zooplankton photography; Narrows Marina and Westport Seafood for access to their live baitfish for photography. Pete Bergman, Dick Geist, Ed Manary, Duane Phinney and Lloyd Phinney, retired or with the Washington Department of Fisheries; Don McDermid, B. C. Wildlife Federation, for their constant flow of information on salmon management and economics.

BMF

1.

General Introduction

FLY FISHING FOR SALMON – PACIFIC salmon! Why would anyone want to write on the subject? Twenty years ago very few anglers were doing it, let alone considering it material for a book.

Fly fishing for Atlantic salmon is so well-established on both sides of the Atlantic Ocean among angling enthusiasts that it is generally regarded not only as the sporting way to go, but in many instances, the only legal way. The taking of Pacific salmon on cast flies is not in the same category at all. Even though it is well-known to coastal river fishermen, its saltwater and estuary participants are just now moving out of the oddity stage.

Throughout the world, catching an Atlantic salmon on a fly is considered to be a lifetime angling experience. The price of an Atlantic salmon trip, both in effort and money, is also a long-remembered experience. On the other hand, with much of our Pacific salmon angling, the cost is not nearly so prohibitive. Yet, if you cut through the haze of tradition and literature, there is a great similarity in the experience itself. The taking of salmon and most other sizable gamefish on flies requires an enormous amount of patience and persistence

As is the case with all sea-run fish, you must first be in the right spot at the right time with the right water conditions in order to intercept the run. Then you may have to cast for hours – or days – to enjoy even a solitary strike. Unless you just happen to like casting, you will keep at it mainly in anticipation of the reward. When a salmon finally hits and you are suddenly on the other end of the aerial acrobatics and screeching runs of a beautiful, silver-sided fish, you'll experience a rush of exhilaration that will let you know that all the preparation and effort to reach this moment was worthwhile. After the angling experience, there remains the pleasure of preparing your catch for a repast that in itself can be wonderfully memorable.

What makes the Pacific salmon so attractive in comparison to Atlantic salmon is that there are so many more of them to start with. For residents of the West Coast of North America, salmon are available from San Francisco, California throughout most of Alaska. All five species will take a fly and the annual runs are counted in the millions. In spite of the ongoing depredations of civilization on their numbers, there are still huge numbers of salmon, including substantial populations within easy fishing range of big cities.

Perhaps the major act of faith for a fly fisherman to embrace is that Pacific salmon will take a fly with any degree of consistency, but getting one to strike may require considerable effort. However, if thousands of people will do exactly the same thing for Atlantic salmon every year, why not for Pacific salmon? Most of it is a matter of attitude. Historically, Pacific salmon have been regarded as food fish, not gamefish. Even the sport fisherman on an offshore charter boat views his catch essentially as something to be boated quickly so he can be sure of a dinner or two.

We have written this book in an effort to help change these attitudes. It is about fly fishing for all five species of Pacific salmon. It contains "how to" information used by anglers in Alaska, British Columbia, Washington, Oregon and California. It includes fly patterns, tackle and duffel necessary to do the job, insights into the life and wanderings of these beautiful, ocean-roaming fish, and, of course, the techniques for actually catching them. But, beyond this, the real theme of our book is a viewpoint and a challenge.

Fly fishing is, at its best, a way of life that when tied to the pursuit of gamefish like Pacific salmon, can approach its pinnacle in producing sheer delight in accomplishment. Our chosen sport is going through another surge of popularity and probably won't peak for a long time, if ever. Just as with water skiing, tennis or jogging, the techniques of fly fishing are being taught everywhere, from college campuses to tackle manufacturers' schools, and a blossoming market is bringing about rapid improvements in rods, lines, reels and attire. But, from a more detached point of view, we can see that something very important — perhaps most important to fly fishing — is being passed over, namely *sportsmanship!*

In a fast-developing society where growing numbers of people have more leisure time than ever before it is vital that we learn to educate ourselves to preserve the aspects of our sport that are the very heart of the experience. Sure, it is fun to catch the most fish, biggest fish and the most glamorous species, but it is not fun to venture out onto your favorite water only to have unthinking fellow fly fishermen behave with a total lack of ethics or even lawlessness. There is no reason that fly fishermen cannot be the front runners in restoring and developing a workable code of ethics that can be taught along with angling techniques. Fly fishing is a glorious sport and we owe it to ourselves to keep it so.

Finally, it is our hope that all who read this book will look on it as a beginning. We have only begun to unravel the mysteries surrounding the catching of Pacific salmon on flies. More work is needed on saltwater migration routes, feeding areas and understanding the effects of tides at different times of the day and year. Angling techniques and fly patterns for taking all five species, but especially pink, chum and sockeye salmon, remain as open-ended assignments for the future. Finding answers to the many remaining questions is an exciting task that we would like to have you undertake with us, and as discoveries are made, we'd like you to pass them on to your fellow fly fishermen so that they may benefit from what you have learned, then build on it and convey it, along with their own findings, to yet others.

Coho salmon taken near a small Puget Sound estuary in early September. Flies are typical attractors that are used when the salmon are holding just off the rivermouths and up into tidal pools. BMF photo.

2.

A History of the Fishery

"FIFTY FOUR-FORTY OR FIGHT!"
That was the American rallying cry back in 1845 when the U. S. and Great Britain stood eyeball-to-eyeball over the location of the border between Canada and what would in time become the Oregon Territory. Those were tense times in the Pacific Northwest. One wrong move, one diplomatic misstep, and the region would have been plunged into war.

One British warship captain, an outspoken Scotsman named Gordon, took a dim view of the whole affair.

"I would not exchange one acre of the barren hills of Scotland for all I see around me," the disgruntled Gordon expostulated. "What a country, where the salmon will not take to the fly!"

How wrong he was!

Oh, he and his cronies had tried. They had fished the rivers with traditional Atlantic salmon methods that had worked so well back home, but without success. Looking back, it's not so surprising. We have long since learned that Pacific and Atlantic salmon are quite different fish. They're not even of the same genus. So how could Gordon be expected to know that the traditional methods of Scotland simply were not suited to the sulky, nonfeeding ways of the Pacific salmon once they return to fresh water? And it never occurred to him to cast his flies in the salt, where the fish *do* actively feed.

But perhaps it's just as well. If Gordon had been successful, he might have participated more willingly in the border dispute. On the other hand, since he wasn't, a tradition of sport fishing for Pacific salmon with the fly had to wait a few years.

THE FLY IN SALT WATER

In 1876 a ship of the U. S. Coast and Geodetic Survey sailed into Baker's Bay at the mouth of the Columbia River and dropped anchor under the bluffs near the new military post, Ft. Canby. Its mission was to chart the rivermouth. But its captain, Cleveland Rockwell, was a fly fisher and the silver salmon were showing in the clear, salt water of the bay. How could he resist?

He couldn't. Rockwell himself later described his historic encounter in the pages of *Pacific Quarterly*, Vol. X, No. 4, October, 1903:

Equipped with a good two-handed English salmon rod of ash, with a lancewood tip, one hundred yards of braided line, and the best flies, all furnished me by a valued friend, I left the vessel's side, alone in my dinghy, to try for silverside salmon.

No salmon had ever been known before to take a fly . . . and I had very little hope of success. I had but a few hundred yards to pull from the vessel before arriving near the steep and rocky shore of the bay, and, laying in the oars, I took my rod and commenced casting. Though an old hand with an eight-ounce trout rod, I found a two-handed rod an awkward thing. However I soon succeeded in making a cast far enough from the boat to hook a salmon. What a thrill of excitement accompanied striking the hook into the solid tongue of that first salmon — and how my heart rushed up into my throat as the alarmed fish made his first frantic rush for liberty! . . .

The salmon and I fought it out . . . all around the harbor, and half the military post was down on the shore to see the fun; and when I finally thrust the gaff into its shining belly and lifted it into the boat, a cheer went up . . . which, with the salmon thrashing around in the boat, made me feel quite proud of the adventure. He weighed twenty-five pounds.

The genial and enthusiastic lighthouse keeper at the Cape became much excited and expressed the profoundest regret that he had lived there ten years and never knew that salmon could be caught with a fly. He came aboard to examine my tackle, and I supplied him with a few flies.

In a week every rooster on the military post presented a most forlorn appearance; necks and tails had both been plucked to make salmon flies.

Many a salmon have I taken from the sparkling bay under Cape Disappointment since that day, but the lively adventure with my first salmon remains an episode of supreme pleasure.

Rockwell's account indicates that for a time the residents of the bay at the mouth of the Columbia enjoyed the fly casting sport. But it didn't last. Gradually the more serious business of making a living and putting food on the table prevailed. Pacific salmon had always been taken for food and commerce. The fly rod gave way once again to the nets and the baits.

Fly fishing became a game for gentlemen sportsmen — those few individuals who could afford the time and expenditure for equipment to travel long distances in pursuit of their sport. Such men visited the Northwest from time to time and left accounts of their exploits in libraries and letters.

Sir Bryan Leighton visited the east coast of Vancouver Island at the turn of the century. In a letter dated December 31, 1905 and quoted in Hodgson's *Salmon Fishing*, Sir Bryan wrote, "Of salmon on the Pacific coast we find six varieties — the king or spring salmon, the coho, the steelhead [they still didn't know much about fish classification at the time], the humpback, the dog salmon and the sockeye. Only the first three will take a lure, and I have caught the coho on the fly only." He went on to say, "The coho I have many times caught on a fly in the estuary of a river. I found that the coho took any silver bodied fly and that no. 4 or no. 5 was the best."

Another early writer was Sir John Rogers, who came all the way from Egypt to troll for kings at Campbell River. But often for a change of pace he would anchor his boat off a point where he knew the fish would pass and cast a fly for cohos. He took a great many fish in this way and was copied by other anglers who saw the success he was having.

Thus by 1919, when A. Bryan Williams published his book, *Rod & Creel in British Columbia*, it was a "pretty well acknowledged fact that the coho salmon will take the fly readily and the spring salmon occasionally if it is presented to them properly."

The way to do it, Williams wrote, was to "choose shallow water, or even anchor your boat out on the line of a run of cohos when they are swimming in schools near the surface," or to place yourself off the mouth of any small creek up which the fish go to spawn.

"Use a double-handed fourteen foot rod at least," Williams recommended. Then he added, "It need not be an expensive split cane; a good greenheart will do quite well. For salt water a plain enameled line is good enough, as you seldom need to make long casts and salt water soon ruins a silk line. Most of your flies should be tied on 5/0 hooks. Few patterns are needed; the Jock Scott, Silver Doctor, Silver Wilkinson, and Durham Ranger are as good as any."

Williams observed, in 1919, that while a few men always used a fly and others did occasionally, the sport had not really been followed up as it should. The idea of the salmon as anything but a food fish, to be boated in the most efficient manner possible and hauled off to the table, was a hard one to get across. And nothing had changed 15 years later when Roderick Haig-Brown published *The Western Angler*. Haig-Brown wrote that while quite a few fishermen could claim a long-time habit of spending September and October with a fly rod in some bay where the cohos school and feed, the development of the sport had been quite slow. About the only change to be noted was that fishermen had largely put aside the standard Atlantic salmon flies in favor of patterns with silver bodies and various combinations of white, red, yellow, and brown bucktail. These flies were usually tied on 2/0 hooks and had nearly uniform two-inch long wings.

About 1935 or 1936 there was a tremendous improvement in coho flies as anglers became more and more aware of the candlefish, herring, and other baitfish that salmon actually feed on, and they tried to tie flies to match. Polar bear hair was now commonly substituted for bucktail and

Jim Teeny, originator of the Teeny Nymph, picking a color that will entice a sockeye salmon into striking. — David Tye photo

the wing was extended to three or more inches. These new, longer flies proved themselves quickly.

Roderick Haig-Brown lauded the change. "The old bucktail fly was a dead, ugly creature, dull of color, without luster or any illusion of translucency," he wrote. "Polar bear hair is superior in every way . . . There is very little doubt that in nearly all conditions it is more attractive to the fish than is bucktail."

By this time, too, American anglers had spread the sport to the Puget Sound country. Places like Possession Bar, Bush Point, Point No Point, Steamboat Island, Double Bluff and Elliot Bay came to be as well-known among the fly fishing fraternity as the Campbell River and Cowichan Bay.

It is even likely that one of those American anglers led the move to the more realistic polar bear streamers. The story has been told several times how in 1936 Letcher Lambuth of Seattle set up a glass tank in his basement workshop to study the appearance of live baitfish under simulated underwater illumination. He equipped the tank with a light source and filters, filled it with salt water containing enough plankton to give it the same optical characteristics as water in which cohos would normally feed, then observed live candlefish and herring in the tank. By drawing streamer flies through the tank under the same lighting, he arrived at combinations that matched the baitfish quite closely. The resulting flies, of polar bear, quickly became standards and are used to this day.

But while Lambuth and his friends were experimenting with close imitations, another trend was developing that led to an almost wild proliferation of patterns. It was known even then that salmon would generally take a trolled fly better than a cast fly and as previously pointed out, catching salmon always had been more closely identified with food on the table than with sport. It was perhaps inevitable that fly fishermen would revert to the more efficient method of fishing their flies. Thus bucktailing — trolling a long bear hair or bucktail streamer in the wake of a fast-moving boat — was born.

Somebody noticed that one color of trolled streamer would sometime catch fish when another color would not. "This was enough," reported Roderick Haig-Brown, "to arouse an intense interest in any and every fly that differed from the others before it. Yellow flies appeared, scarlet flies, blue flies, purple flies, mauve flies — flies of every shade and color were towed through the water, and nearly all of them took fish at times." The late Roy Patrick once attempted to catalog just the most effective ones and even then he came up with 22 separate patterns!

Saltwater fly casting for Pacific salmon enjoyed perhaps its widest popularity and greatest number of practitioners in those mid-1930 years. There are many interesting stories. For instance, Mrs. Mickey Sherman of Tacoma, who fished with her brother, Dr. J. A. Brewitt, a dentist, recalled how they would rent a boat at Point Defiance and row out to catch the tide. The in-tide would take them down to Crab Point. Then they would catch the big eddy that would carry them back. And all the while they would be casting for salmon. Sometimes they would take a cabin on Mud

This tidal pool on the Klamath River in northern California, calm and serene in August, will be alive with salmon and salmon anglers in September and October. LJ photo.

Bay near Olympia, and in the evenings when the tide was coming in and the salmon were working close inshore, they would go out in a boat and cast toward shore. The other anglers would laugh at them, but fascinated all the same, would come out in their own boats to watch what they were doing.

But World War II came along and when it was over the interest was never quite the same. There was a brief resurgence, but one by one the old-timers passed on and few younger anglers seemed interested enough to take up where they left off.

The sport still had its chroniclers, however. One of these was A. J. McClane, angling editor of *Field & Stream* at the time, who visited the Campbell River area about 1947 to make a movie for the Canadian Tourist Board. An article based on his experiences appeared in the May, 1950, issue of *Field & Stream* magazine. Incidentally, that film was still available the last time I checked and could be obtained for showing by contacting *Field & Stream*. It is well worth viewing.

The postwar years saw much of the technology developed for warfare introduced into everyday life. This included some major changes in fishing tackle. The old 14-foot, two-handed salmon rods yielded to shorter sticks of powerful fiberglass and the old enameled lines gave way to nylon. A. J. McClane described the tackle he used for salmon as being the same as what he used for bass fishing, that is, a 9-foot, 6-ounce rod outfitted with a GAF torpedo-taper line. This would be about a 9- or 10-weight outfit by today's standards. With this outfit, McClane could cast a big fly a long way and shoot line out fast to cover the swiftly moving salmon, just like the old-timers had done with their double-handed rigs.

But the postwar years also brought some bad things. Those were years of rapid growth, especially in the Puget Sound region, both in numbers of people and industrialization. We now know that the runs of salmon that provided the bulk of the sport for those prewar anglers were fish that spent much of their saltwater lives within the confines of Puget Sound. The metropolitan area streams in which these fish were spawned bore the brunt of the region's growing pains and the good runs all but disappeared. The large run of silvers that appeared off Whidbey Island in the Double Bluff area in midsummer became a thing of the past. Likewise, some excellent fishing in Elliot Bay, at Seattle's backdoor, dwindled to nothing. No wonder then that fly casting for salmon in the salt became a near-forgotten art.

But fly fishing in all its phases has experienced unparalleled growth in the last 15 to 20 years. In many sections of the country salt water is accessible but good trout streams or lakes are not. So the new generation of fly rodders is taking to the salt to pitch feathers and fur in ever-increasing numbers. In the process, all along the Pacific Coast from Alaska to the Bay Area of California, little groups of anglers are discovering anew that Pacific salmon will indeed take the cast fly. They have in their hands tackle more advanced than the pioneers of the sport even dreamed of. And in some states, far-thinking fishery managers are trying hard to bring the old runs back. The stage is set, it seems, for an upsurge that could surpass even the heyday of the mid-'30s.

THE FLY IN FRESH WATER

The efforts of Captain Gordon and his friends aside, the pursuit of Pacific salmon with the fly rod in fresh water had its beginnings on the streams of northern California and southern Oregon by anglers more intent on catching cutthroat and steelhead trout than salmon. In fact, many of these anglers considered hooking a salmon an annoyance. This reflected their bias toward traditional stream fishing, but more importantly, the most accessible waters were trout streams. With the exception of Humboldt and San Francisco bays, Californians had no protected bays within easy reach of available transportation. Similar constraints faced Oregon anglers who were, during this period, still years away from daring launches through the surf at Cape Kiwanda in specially-designed dories.

One of the earliest reports of deliberate fishing for salmon on a fly in fresh water is datelined Sacramento City, February 3, 1850[1], just five years after Captain Gordon's disparaging remarks about the Pacific Northwest. But the first sport fishery of any real importance dates back to 1860-1870 when the Western Pacific Railroad started a line of service up the Sacramento River Valley. With this transportation spur opened, it wasn't long before small towns and resorts sprang up to serve vacationing San Franciscans arriving to enjoy the interior valley weather and the excellent fishing along the Sacramento River and its many tributaries. In those days the small feeder streams were fished with fly tackle for trout and steelhead while the main Sacramento was worked with spoons for salmon.

The prestigious California Anglers Association was formed in San Francisco in 1890. It was made up primarily of transplanted eastern or European fly fishermen who favored nearby Papermill and San Mateo creeks, the Russian River, and many other excellent streams within easy commute of San Francisco. Their catch consisted mainly of steelhead and salmon smolts, called, erroneously, "trout." While these streams all held fairly strong runs of salmon, the fish of importance was certainly the strains of small, highly energetic steelhead that arrived in good numbers from late winter through spring.

Meanwhile, several hundred miles to the north on Humboldt Bay stood the little town of Eureka. Located not far from the mouth of the Eel River amid stands of virgin redwoods, Eureka was a bustling town on its way to becoming the logging and lumber center of the state. As logging firms cut roads into the Eel River Canyon, local anglers testing the water discovered that it fairly teemed with sea-run cutthroat trout, steelhead, and salmon. When word of this fishing hit San Francisco, the first trips to the Eel were hastily planned and expedited.

It was no small task to travel to the Eel from San Francisco in those days. By stagecoach, the first stop was Sherwood, thence northward another 105 miles to Dyerville on the Eel, where there were a few boat liveries and lodgings for the infrequent vacationing anglers from San Francisco. When steamships started the San Francisco to

---

[1]Special thanks to The Museum of American Fly Fishing for calling attention to this early account.

Eureka run some years later, the trip became considerably less adventurous, if not less nauseating. The trip was worth every bump or every wretching heave of seasickness, though, because the salmon and steelhead fishing was spectacular.

John Benn was among the first anglers to make the trip to the Eel during the summer of 1890. Totally smitten with the area and the fishing, Benn, upon his return to San Francisco, promptly sold his business and holdings, went back to the Eel, and purchased a home near the small town of Scotia. Here Benn learned the fly tying art and became the first of many great Eel River tiers. Though his patterns were specifically dressed for sea-run cutthroat and steelhead

Mike Foster, Miranda, California, fly tier, angling instructor and writer, hefts a large late run chinook taken on a fly from the South Fork of the Eel River. LJ photo.

trout, he soon discovered they would also take coho salmon with regularity and even the occasional chinook. If there is a time to pinpoint for the conception of a fly fishery for Pacific salmon in fresh water, it would have to be during the years John Benn spent on the Eel. Prior to Benn's success with flies, it was pretty much a common opinion that salmon could only be taken efficiently with spoons or bait.

As Benn's legend grew and attracted an ever-increasing flow of fly fishermen to the Eel, the primary fish sought was still the summer steelhead. It was anglers using stout casting tackle and spoons who would go after fall chinook that began showing in September. Fly fishermen, still under the influence of eastern and European techniques, usually fished steelhead with small, brightly dressed wet flies. It must have been a sight to behold when a gentleman angler would suddenly find himself contending with a 40-pound chinook salmon that had grabbed his No. 10 Professor and chugged off across the pool. Most of these encounters ended with the salmon parting the gut leader with a casual shake of the head.

The California angling camps on the Klamath, Trinity and Eel rivers were well established and approaching world renown in the early 1920s when word leaked out about Oregon's Rogue River and the Umpqua a bit further north. The Rogue's salmon pools started a few miles above Gold Beach, while challenging steelhead lies were found in the swift slicks of the upper river. The summer steelhead of the North Fork Umpqua drew a nearly frantic following of anglers who would arrive annually at Steamboat to stay at Major Mott's camp.

The Rogue and Umpqua were great rivers and they attracted great anglers. They were the rivers of Al Knudson, Polly Rosborough, Clarence Shoff, Clarence Gordon, Zane Grey, and President Herbert Hoover. They still remain high on the list of ardent fly fishermen including present-day greats like Dan Callaghan, Jack Hemmingway, and Ernest Schwiebert.

While angling success for steelhead and sea-run cutthroat continued to improve during the early years, coho and chinook salmon remained enigmas. For the most part, anglers fly fishing specifically for salmon played out an exercise in frustration as they watched big, bright salmon calmly finning in the depths of clear pools while their deftly cast patterns drifted in vain over them.

Fortunately, enough of those early anglers got lucky and others developed techniques to hook salmon in numbers to keep the effort greased and going. If, in those days, some fish had not been taken from time to time, it is not difficult to imagine the entire Pacific Coast salmon fly fishery being totally defunct by the early 1920s. Fly fishermen, then as now, were a persevering lot and even a rare success could keep them casting diligently for weeks. Through these efforts, knowledge continued to grow.

Unlike their angling brethren on the Rogue and Umpqua, Eel River fly fishermen were not content to fish solely for summer or early autumn steelhead. By 1930, they were working its pools and drifts into November and December. If summer run fish would take a fly, they insisted, so would the larger fall and winter steelhead. Their assumptions proved correct as heavily weighted bucktails and optics began accounting for impressive numbers of big steelhead.

Deep-drifting heavy flies not only took steelhead, but attracted coho and big, late-run fall chinook with increasing regularity, making the years around 1930 very significant.

Just as the anglers of the late 1800s and early 1900s blazed the trails to the banks of Pacific Coast streams, the angling brigade of the 1930s moved the salmon fishery forward several notches toward the sport we are familiar with today. The anglers of this period read like the "Who's Who of Fly Fishing," for they have written important angling literature, developed angling techniques and successfully scoped the baseline of tackle requirements that remain valid to this day. Naming just a few of these individual contributors — Roderick Haig-Brown, Enos Bradner, Clarence Gordon, Syd Glasso, Ken McLeod, Mike Kennedy, Jim Pray, Lloyd Silvius — sets the imagination afire with thoughts of great streams and great fish. All devoted steelheaders, these angling greats also supplied the provocation that led to taking salmon on flies in rivers.

The next important development is credited to Ken McLeod of Washington, and Californian Myron Gregory. Independent of each other, they were working on splicing short sections of heavy fly line to small-diameter running lines. Gregory's focus was on finding the right combination to attain record distances from the platform during fly casting tournaments. McLeod was intent on designing a line that would drive a fly across the wide, swift Northwest rivers he fished. Both men were tremendously successful. Gregory became a tournament casting champion and McLeod put many winners into the *Field & Stream* record books.

Ken McLeod soon discovered that the longer casts he was getting with the "shooting head" fly line caused a problem of what to do with a rather unwieldy length of running line. He decided he needed some sort of casting platform, so he devised a canvas container to hang from his neck about waist height for storage of running line as it was stripped in. This allowed Ken to make long casts and accompanying long drifts without his line becoming tangled around his boot-straps or in the rocks. This container of McLeod's became the "shooting" or "stripping" basket and it gained immediate acceptance among Washington anglers.

The '30s and early '40s saw most serious West Coast salmon and steelhead fly fishermen outfitted with high quality tackle since they had found that cheap rods soon took dreadful sets and the horror stories about reels exploding into a scattering of screws, springs and spindles under the strain of a big fish were becoming increasingly common during an evening bourbon around the campfire. Stout, superbly-built, split bamboo rods from Orvis, Leonard, Powell, Winston and other great shops became the order of the day. These rods of 9 to 10 feet could be cast with one hand, drive heavy lines and weighted flies long distances, or negotiate a shot-laden leader through a deep pool.

Many reels were used but if one captured the fancy of West Coast anglers, it was the Hardy Model Perfect 3-7/8 inch. Its strong, three-piece construction, left side palming plate, and beautiful whining song when checking a running fish all contributed to its totally justified popularity. Even today, an original Model Perfect 3-7/8 inch in reasonable condition will command a handsome sum from almost any West Coast angler who has an opportunity to bid for it.

The single remaining problem for salmon fly fishermen was that even bead-headed optic patterns or flies heavily weighted with fuse wire could not always be counted on to sink deep enough in the pools to get in front of bottom-hugging fish, especially chinook, with regularity. This was a particularly frustrating facet of the fishery and just about every stratagem was attempted to overcome it. Silk lines were soaked overnight so they would sink readily. They also weighed a ton and cast miserably, putting tremendous strains on prized bamboo rods. Some manufacturers attempted to braid lines over wire cores, but this proved to be marginally successful as the wire would soon break in several places and start poking through the braided surface. Shooting heads were varnished in another attempt to add sinking weight. But for all practical purposes, none of these notions worked very well, and angling proficiency for Pacific salmon remained limited by the fly lines available — lines which simply weren't adequately designed to fit the needs of the West Coast angler.

For the most part, the history and evolution of salmon angling on Pacific coastal rivers was slow and steady from the 1870s on up to around 1950. The pioneering spirit and visionary nature of the anglers involved was the primary driving force. The steady growth of the region provided access to the rivers and without access there is no fishery. But equipment, lines, reels — with the exception of fiberglass rods coming on line after World War II — remained quite static for 75 years.

Then in 1953 a small fly line company named Scientific Anglers, Inc., located in Midland, Michigan, undertook development of a synthetic fly line formed over a braided solid core. Under the guidance of Leon Martuch, they discovered that not only could they manufacture a line with excellent casting properties that would float all day without dressing, but they could also make one that would sink — not by soaking up water but by having a greater specific gravity than water. Viewing the Pacific Coast as a prime place to experiment with such lines, Martuch rallied a team of the region's angling notables (including Ken McLeod and his son George, Enos Bradner, Myron Gregory, Karl Mausser, Forrest Powell and John Walker to name just a few) and the field test was launched.

Within a few years, big steelhead and salmon began showing up in the *Field & Stream* contest like never before. George McLeod took a world record 29-pound steelhead on a fly from British Columbia's Kispiox River using the new Wet Cel line. A few years later, Karl Mausser broke McLeod's record with a 33-pound fish from the same river. Salmon of 50 pounds and over were taken with increasing regularity from California's Smith River, Oregon's Chetco River, and Washington's Kalama River — all by fly fishermen using the new sinking lines. The Wet Cel, as it was called, was a genuine innovation. Since 1953, the continued development of fly lines by Scientific Anglers, and other companies like Cortland and Orvis, has given anglers a range of lines from very slow sinking to a super-fast rate once thought possible only with irksome lead-core shooting heads. There are no longer many rivers too deep or too swift for today's well-equipped salmon fishermen.

From the mid-'50s to the present there have been continuous breakthroughs in equipment technology. Ultra-transportation systems have made the world's most remote niches of fishing water accessible to the angler with the dollars to get to them. Now even the deepest salmon pools can be efficiently dredged with flies. But, sadly, salmon, especially big chinook salmon, are becoming alarmingly scarce. And it must be noted, if with considerable regret for the romantics in the ranks, that we are now in a time frame where the main thrust of the fishery is driven not by vision and pioneering spirit, but by technology. The world's waters and fish stocks are being competed for and coveted as never before. It is a time when we must take care not to get swept up in the hype of it all but must keep a close eye on the hands that are on the throttles of technology. The gratifications of the moment must be curtailed if the fishery is to be strong in the future. Indeed, these are times when what we do must be tempered with conscience, sensitivity, and yes, even today, with pioneering spirit and vision.

Going through the fly patterns used for Pacific salmon angling proved to be a major effort. Authors (left to right) Johnson, Trotter and Ferguson making final determinations on patterns that will appear in color plates. Dan Berglund

3.

Salmon Life Histories

THE FIVE SALMON SPECIES NATIVE TO THE North American Pacific Coast not only look somewhat alike, but their spawning, feeding, and migratory habits are similar as well. It is nonetheless vital for the fly fisher to understand the unique differences that exist between the species and major strains of each species in order to pursue the sport successfully. This understanding is also necessary as the basis for intelligent participation in decisions that will insure the future of the resource. This chapter covers the highlights so that a general understanding can be achieved. It is not intended to be an in-depth, scientifically probing analysis.

The most widely accepted theory on the origin of present-day species of Pacific salmon goes back to pre-glacial times when the genus *Salmo* was distributed around the entire northern section of the northern hemisphere. The best evidence now suggests that development of the genus *Oncorhynchus* from the original *Salmo* stock took place in what is now the Sea of Japan about six million years ago. The parent *Salmo* was an anadromous fish, meaning that it migrated to fresh water at maturity in order to spawn successfully. The newly evolved *Oncorhynchus* was also anadromous. Its evolution into the several species now known and the distribution of these species into what is now thought to be their native range is believed to have occurred during the subsequent periods of fluctuating glaciation that geologists call the Pleistocene Epoch.

All Pacific salmon die after spawning, perhaps an evolutionary survival trait to provide nutrients to the rather sterile nursery streams for sustaining the developing baby fish prior to their ocean migration. Steelhead trout of the Pacific Coast, Atlantic salmon and sea-run versions of the other trout species are also anadromous, but do not all die following spawning. Why the difference, no one really knows.

All Pacific salmon have comparable life cycles. Spawning adults travel to freshwater spawning beds located anywhere from just above tidewater to thousands of miles inland. The homing instinct of salmon remains one of nature's greatest marvels with most fish returning to the identical sections of gravel from which they themselves were born. Still, considerable straying does occur, which characteristic undoubtedly greatly aided colonization in new river systems following glaciation. Depending on species and particular strain, they arrive from July through April, although most stocks of all species spawn in the fall.

Each species has its own preferred spawning habitat. Some use small gravel, some large; some spawn in fast, relatively deep water, others in shallow, relatively slow moving water. Even lake beaches are commonly used, especially by sockeye salmon. All require clean, well-oxygenated water, and unsilted gravel.

Pairing occurs with aggressive males fighting for the female of their choice. This accomplished, the female builds a nest in the gravel. Using her tail, she scoops out a depression, clearing it of silt, sand and smaller gravel. This is repeated until a saucer-shaped depression is created. Moving so her vent is directly over the nest or redd, and with the male swimming alongside, the two release eggs and sperm together. The sperm, having performed its job, is swept away in the current downstream, while the orange-red fertilized eggs settle to the bottom of the redd. Now the eggs must be covered. The female moves upstream from the redd, and again using her tail, she loosens the gravel which drifts down with the current to cover the eggs. This process is repeated until all eggs have been deposited and covered. She continues to guard the redd until, close to death and too weak to maintain her position in the current, she drifts downstream and dies, as will spawning males. The entire process from spawning to death consumes less than two weeks.

After wintering in the gravel, the *alevins* hatch, and after absorbing their egg sacs, become *fry* that wiggle free and begin their independent feeding. Only five to ten percent survive to this point. Freshwater life for these juveniles varies by species and strain from a few days to three years. During this time, they feed on varied organic matter and grow rather slowly. Their stream position is determined in large part by size, and a definite pecking order exists in any given stretch. As expected, the larger species and larger individuals occupy the best food producing paths.

As length increases to about two inches, the fish become known as *fingerlings* or *parr*. Eventually, the time arrives for the fingerlings to move out into the estuaries and salt water. This occurs in the spring, at which point they undergo another change. The dark backs and barred sides or parr markings give way to a greenish back and silvery sides, felt to be another survival adaptation so the fish will be less conspicuous to predators upon reaching salt water. In addition, they acquire the extraordinary ability to switch from living in fresh water to living in salt water. While undergoing these changes and working their way downstream to the sea, they are called *smolts*.

After spending a few weeks in the rich estuary feeding area, adapting to salt water, the young salmon, which have experienced a growth surge in the food-rich estuary environment, begin their ocean migration. Generally, they move northward, traveling within 25 miles of shore until they hit the main feeding grounds in the Gulf of Alaska where the stocks spread out and intermingle in the ocean pastures. Depending on species, with some variation within species, they spend from a few months to several years in this environment, gaining rapidly in weight. Their movement is generally counterclockwise, following the prevailing ocean currents.

There are some strains that do not follow this pattern, however. Many stocks important to fishermen from California to Washington never reach the Gulf of Alaska in their northward journey, and some of these move south, sometimes a thousand miles or more, to develop into mature fish. Others are satisfied to treat the inland sea areas from Puget Sound through the Inland Waterway in Alaska as home base for their entire saltwater existence. Most of these strains are believed to migrate only short distances within their particular part of this "inland" arena. This latter group is unusually important to the fly fisherman as it allows a year-round fishery, relatively protected from the offshore weather.

Feeding habits in salt water vary somewhat by species in regard to the size of food they require to sustain themselves as they gain in weight. Feeding also varies with respect to geographic location and the availability of food. Generally, feeding behavior is tied to the presence or absence of squid, various baitfish (such as herring, anchovy, smelt, candlefish and pilchard), crab larvae, euphausids, amphipods and copepods. Attention to the specific feeding details for each species plays an important role in aiding the angler to develop patterns and presentation methods that will attract salmon.

The foregoing presented an overall view of all Pacific salmon and their habits. A more in-depth focus on the individual species follows.

CHINOOK — *Oncorhynchus tshawytscha*

Chinook salmon are also known as king, tyee, spring, blackmouth (immature), and grilse (immature, less than three pounds). They are the largest of the salmon species, weighing about 18 to 20 pounds and less than 40 inches at maturity. However, chinook have been taken commercially up to 126 pounds (53 inches) at Petersburg, Alaska, and to 92 pounds, also in Alaskan waters, by sport fishermen.

Chinook are the least abundant of the salmon species by a wide margin, yet they are the most sought by sport fishermen. Still, the 1976 commercial and subsistence catch was 3,743,000 and 1,031,000 sport-caught for a total of 4,774,000 chinook taken in North America that year.

Chinook life spans vary, with the spread being three to eight years. Ignoring precocious males (or "jacks" which mature at two or three years), most survive four years, with five years common in Alaska.

In salt water chinook are identified by black spotting on the back, dorsal fin, and upper and lower tail. They are greenish-blue to black on the back, shading to silver on the sides. They have a blackish mouth in the lower jaw at the base of prominent, sharp teeth. The male spawner is blackish, while the female spawner is brassy.

Chinook spawning grounds in North America range from San Francisco Bay in California, to Alaska's Wulik River, which empties into the Arctic Ocean. The bulk of the spawning takes place in relatively few major rivers. For instance, in Canada, 50 percent of the spawning occurs in 14 rivers, even though spawners use 260 Canadian rivers.

In the United States, major production occurs in the Sacramento River (California); the Columbia River (Oregon, Idaho and Washington); and the Copper, Nushagak, Kuskokwim and Yukon rivers (Alaska).

Chinook enter North American streams almost year-round. The Columbia River has a spring run that enters the river from February through May; a summer run arrives from June through July; and a fall run from August through September, with some into October. The Sacramento River has not only a spring and fall run, but also a winter run from November through February. In general, the more southern rivers have multiple runs, but moving north these are reduced to a single fall run in rivers like the Yukon in Alaska.

Of particular interest to freshwater anglers is the fact that spring and summer strains generally are traveling to the headwaters of large river systems and retain their saltwater vigor and appearance during much of their extended upstream migration, whereas the fall runs typically begin to darken and lose their vigor and flavor in the estuary even before entering fresh water.

Actual spawning generally takes place from August to December, depending on run timing. Chinook spawning grounds vary from the main stem in large rivers to small tributaries, but the grounds do have certain common characteristics. Of these, the stream underflowing large gravel to sand with alternating pools and riffles is most important. Spawning nests (or redds) mainly occur at the lip of a pool, as it becomes a riffle providing a maximum of the all-important underflow, thereby providing necessary irrigation of eggs.

Fry emerge in spring and if born close to the ocean, may spend a few days to a few months in fresh water before smolting and moving to salt water. These are called "ocean" type and are more characteristic in the southern part of the range. The "stream" type, on the other hand, are generally born far upriver and spend a year or longer in fresh water before smolting. This type occurs throughout the range, to the exclusion of the "ocean" type in the northern sections. Smolting and migration peak for both ocean and stream types in spring, but can occur at anytime of the year.

Les Johnson with a chunky chinook salmon that fell to an Orange Comet pattern, size 8, fished on a downstream drift.

Chinook smolts are three to six inches in length. They spend the summer in the estuary and with the fall freshets, head out to sea. During this time they grow to about eight inches, feeding primarily on a diet of crab larvae, insects, some baby fish and sand fleas.

At sea, chinook generally move north with a few important exceptions. Generally, they remain in the coastal areas during their first year, gradually moving northward to offshore feeding grounds in the North Pacific Ocean and Bering Sea. From what is now known, chinook in their final year appear to head generally southeasterly by midyear in the return journey to their North American spawning rivers.

Of all the salmon species, chinook are known to occur in the greatest range of water depths. They have been taken with surface gillnets as well as commercial trawl nets working the bottoms. Along the coast they have been found in depths up to 350 feet, generally preferring depths greater than 60 feet. This feeding characteristic makes them a more difficult fish to take on a fly in salt water, although as chinook approach their spawning rivers in coastal areas, they tend to hug the shorelines in kelp beds found at the edges of dropoffs.

Of special import to the saltwater fly fisher is the strain of "resident" chinook which remain for their entire salt-water existence in the protected inshore waters of Puget Sound, the Strait of Georgia, and Alaska's Inland Waterway. Some of these are natural wild fish, while a much larger percentage, at least in Puget Sound, are hatchery fish whose migratory instincts have been killed by being held in hatchery ponds an extra few months. In all other respects, hatchery fish exhibit the same habits as their ocean-going relatives, although they are generally somewhat smaller at maturity. They, too, prefer deeper water and feeding close to bottom.

COHO — *Oncorhynchus kisutch*

Coho are also called silver, hooknose, northern, blueback and grilse (immature fish under three pounds). Adults average six to 12 pounds, but the largest coho of record is a 31-pounder taken in 1947 off Victoria, British Columbia. Its length was in excess of 38 inches.

Coho are somewhat more abundant than chinook, but not as plentiful as the pink, sockeye and chum species. Coho are the backbone of the sport catch. The 1976 commercial and subsistence catch in North America was 9,977,000 fish, which, when added to the sport catch for that year of 2,072,000, totaled 12,049,000 coho salmon.

The coho life span is predominantly three years from British Columbia south, while in Alaska four-year survival is common because of a freshwater juvenile residency of two years rather than one. Early sexually maturing males (or jacks) spawn and die a year earlier than normal.

Coho are identified by black spotting confined to the back and upper tail. They are metallic blue on the back, shading to bright silver on the sides and belly. Their mouth is whitish or greyish along the lower gum line with prominent, sharp teeth. Male spawners have bright red sides with bluish-green backs and heads. Female spawners are not as brightly colored.

North American coho distribution is reported from as

far north as the Nome River in western Alaska, and as far south as Monterey Bay, California. However, coho are most plentiful from Oregon to central Alaska. They spawn not only in the many tributary streams and headwaters of major rivers, but also in a great variety of small, coastal streams. However, they seldom spawn more than 150 miles inland. An exception occurs on the Yukon River in Alaska where coho move upstream over 1,100 miles.

Although there are "early" and "late" runs of coho, the fish tend to assemble in coastal waters in late July and August, entering their spawning streams with the fall freshets, normally from September through November. Some runs tend to feed and stay bright longer in proximity

Pat Trotter with an ocean run coho salmon taken on a fly at Neah Bay on the northwestern tip of Washington State. BMF

to their spawning rivers than do their more "urgently" arriving brethren. Also, the later runs are larger due to a longer feeding period in the ocean. Runs traveling to tributaries of the headwaters of long, large rivers hold brightness and general body condition for a longer time after entering their home river.

Actual spawning occurs mainly from October through January, but has been reported as late as March. As with the other salmon species, coho select highly-oxygenated water which usually occurs in riffles. Spawning gravel must be free of silt. Following the standard spawning procedure previously described, the eggs incubate for 40 to 100 days or more, depending on water temperature. Fry emerge from the gravel in about three weeks, which event can occur from March to late July.

Coho fry tend to school initially close to their emergence site, but as they begin to grow, disperse and take up individual feeding stations, establishing their "territories" which they guard very aggressively. As a general rule, their freshwater residence lasts at least a year and in the case of the more northerly stocks, two years. Smolting and downstream migration takes place from April to August, depending on geographic location, smolt size and water flow. Main migrations take place at night with the silver, three- to five-inch smolts schooling up in the estuaries and inland waters. They remain here for several months before heading out into the ocean.

The coho diet during this period consists of crab larvae, amphipods, euphausids, mysids, and fish larvae. The salmon move to more open marine water when they reach about eight inches in length.

The migratory or "ocean" group of coho generally work northward and may travel as far as a thousand miles before turning south toward their home spawning streams 18 months to two years later. While in salt water, they grow faster than any other salmon species, with recorded ocean growth from 1.76 pounds in April to 8.80 pounds in September of their final year, or well over a pound per month! They are reported to prefer feeding and traveling in the top 30 feet of water, resting close to the surface at night and deeper in the daytime. Coho hold well out from the coast on their return trip, feeding and growing rapidly. The more northerly strains of salmon apparently leave the Gulf of Alaska, heading south in late June, and have been known to travel as far as 30 miles per day, averaging 16 over long distances. Some other major stocks remain for their entire oceanic life in coastal waters, traveling both north and south to reach spawning streams.

A non-migratory, or "inshore," type of coho occurs in the protected waters of Alaska, British Columbia and Puget Sound. These fish provide the largest share of fly-caught salmon. Although there are historical wild races, the majority of these fish are now produced artificially by holding the smolts in hatchery ponds for an extended period. As is the case with resident chinook, the shorter saltwater existence and reduced feeding opportunities tend to result in smaller spawning adults, with an average weight of four to six pounds. Migrations do occur to capitalize on feeding opportunities, but are confined to a relatively small arena. The coho's general use of the top 30 feet of water coincides with the fly fisher's interest in fishing close to the surface.

PINK – *Oncorynchus gorbuscha*

Pink salmon are also known as humpback or humpie salmon. They attain a length of 30 inches and a weight of 12 pounds. However, the average fish is much smaller, between three and five pounds.

The pink is the most abundant of all the salmon, without question. Even though the bulk of the fishery is commercial, it is a readily available and increasingly popular sport fish. Significantly, major runs occur almost exclusively in alternate, odd-numbered years in Washington and western Alaska. In the remainder of Alaska and British Columbia, there appears to be a more balanced run size between odd and even years.

The North American commercial and subsistence catch of pink salmon was 35,154,000 fish in 1976, and the reported sport catch was 93,000, yielding a total overall North American catch in that year of 35,247,000 fish.

Life span is virtually always two years. Because of their short life, there are no early maturing jacks.

Pinks, in their ocean phase, have metallic blue backs, shading to silver on the sides. They have several large, black, oval spots on the back and tail. Teeth are small and weak. Scales are much smaller than on other species. The spawning male develops a pronounced hump at the shoulders. Its sides and back turn brownish while its lower side and belly become very white. Spawning females do not develop the hump or hooked jaw of the male.

Pink salmon are found in North America from central California's Russian River throughout Alaska and eastward along the Arctic Coast to the Mackenzie River. However, the main spawning distribution is from the Puyallup River in Washington's Puget Sound up to and including the Mackenzie River in Canada's Northwest Territories. Spawning occurs mostly in the lower parts of rivers, sometimes even in tidewater. There are, however, some strains that make runs well over 100 miles upstream.

Pinks enter coastal waters on their spawning migration from June through September throughout their range. They enter fresh water from July to October. Spawning takes place shortly thereafter. Pink salmon lose their brightness either shortly before leaving salt water or shortly after arriving in fresh water due to their quick ripening and characteristic spawning a short distance above salt water.

Spawning itself typically takes place in September and October utilizing the method basic to all species. The eggs, which are buried in clean gravel, hatch from December through February after an incubation period of 90 to 150 days. Fry emerge from the gravel in April and May and move directly downstream, traveling at night to avoid predation. If the spawning stream is short, fry may arrive in salt water the same night they started downstream. At this point, they are only an inch or so in length. In the estuary, the juvenile pinks form large schools and remain there for several months, feeding on copepods, other zooplankton, and fish larvae.

Beginning in July and continuing into fall, juvenile fish migrate rapidly northward in a narrow band along the coast, which may stretch for almost a thousand miles. They travel at an estimated ten miles per day during this time. While wintering at sea, they continue to move and feed in a gen-

erally southward direction in the Gulf of Alaska, turning northward in their final spring and summer before their homing migration.

Time in the open sea is approximately 12 months, following the several months they spent as juveniles in the more protected estuary salt water.

Research conducted on the open seas indicates pink salmon prefer surface water feeding. Most appear to feed and travel in the top 30 feet of water, but may be found up to 75 feet below the surface. Most active feeding occurs at dusk.

As is the case with chinook and coho, there are some strains of pink salmon which remain as "resident," non-ocean migrating fish in inshore saltwater areas with their entire life span confined to Puget Sound. These fish tend to be somewhat smaller than their more plentiful ocean-run relatives, but as a tradeoff they are present on a year-round basis.

SOCKEYE – *Oncorhynchus nerka*

Sockeye are also known as red salmon and blueback. A landlocked strain is known as kokanee or silver trout. Sockeye are the most streamlined of the salmon, and adults are normally from five to seven pounds. They can attain a length of 33 inches and a weight of 15 pounds. Stocks from the Columbia River are smaller, averaging only three to four pounds.

In North American waters, sockeye are the second most abundant salmon species (behind pinks), and most are taken by commercial and subsistence fishermen. In 1976, the commercial and subsistence take was 18,481,000, while the reported sport catch was only 28,000. Although freshwater fisheries on "bright" fish are important in Alaskan rivers and in Lake Washington located in Seattle, Washington, the notable exception to the modest sport catch is the non-migrating kokanee which is a popular sport fish in lakes from California to British Columbia. Although they are small (seldom exceeding 16 inches or about a pound), the annual catch of kokanee is in excess of 1,000,000 fish per year. This figure is in addition to the 18,507,000 total for all anadromous sockeye caught, as reported above.

Sockeye have a life span of from three to eight years with four and five years most common. Jacks mature one year earlier. The more northern runs tend to be the five- and six-year-old fish, while the southern range produces more four-year-olds.

In salt water, sockeye are a metallic, greenish-blue on the back with fine, black specklings. There are no large spots. They have silver sides, shading to white on the belly. Teeth are small and not prominent. Male spawners are a brilliant red overall, except for the head, which is olive-green. Female spawners have the same coloration, except for some runs which exhibit green and yellow blotches on their bodies.

Spawning populations of sockeye occur from the Sacramento River in California through the Yukon in Alaska. However, the bulk of the fishery occurs between the Columbia River and Bristol Bay, Alaska. Most spawning occurs in major river systems, with the Bristol Bay area the most productive and the Fraser River system in British Columbia the second in importance. Other major systems are central Alaska's Cook Inlet, and the Chignik, Copper and Karluk rivers; and British Columbia rivers and Smith inlets, as well as the Skeena and Nass rivers.

Adults enter their spawning rivers between May and October, with the bulk moving into fresh water from July through September. Some of the larger river systems have early runs (from July to early August) and late runs as well (from September through October).

Spawning may take place only a mile or so above tidewater, but mainly occurs considerably more distant — up to 700 miles or more. In almost all cases, spawning takes place in rivers which have lakes in their headwater regions. Actual spawning occurs in the gravel of feeder streams entering the lake, in gravel areas of the lakeshore fed by springs, or in the outlet stream to the lake.

Fry emerge from the gravel in April and May and proceed to the lake where they reside from one to four years (generally one to two years) before smolting from April to June, and traveling downstream on their seaward migration. Sockeye smolts are three to five inches at this point. On entering salt water, they move along the coast during their first summer in a rather narrow belt during which time they feed actively on fish larvae and crustacean zooplankton, including copepods, amphipods, euphasids and crab larvae. However, by winter they have become widely dispersed and have moved well offshore in the North Pacific and Bering Sea. They will make feeding migrations — north and west in the summer, and south and east in the winter, during their one- to four-year ocean residence.

At sea, they can be found at depths up to 200 feet, but more normally are nearer the surface in 50 feet or less. As they approach the inland waters on their return trip, they travel at a rate of 30 miles per day, continuing to feed during this time. Sockeye do not appear to linger in coastal waters on their way to their spawning streams, with some major stocks completing 80 percent of their migration within 15 days. For the fly fisherman, this means he needs to know individual run timing and be there when one is happening.

CHUM — *Oncorhynchus keta*

Chum are also known as dog or fall salmon. They can attain a length of 40 inches and a weight of 33 pounds. However, the average size is six to ten pounds.

Of the five species of Pacific salmon in North America, chum are of average abundance. Regarded as primarily a commercial and subsistence fish, the total North American chum catch in 1976 was 9,107,000. The sport catch was only 16,000, yielding a total catch of 9,223,000 chum salmon in 1976.

The chum life span varies from two to seven years, but more commonly from three to five years.

In salt water, they have metallic blue backs with occasional black speckling. They do not have black spots on their bodies, fins or tails. Teeth are not prominent. Spawning males develop vertical reddish or dark streaks against an olive background. Females have the same markings, but not to the same degree.

Distribution in North America is greater than for any of the other species, occurring more or less continuously from the Sacramento River in California through Oregon, Washington, British Columbia, Alaska and east to and including the Mackenzie River in Canada's Northwest Territories. They tend to spawn a short distance from salt water in small coastal streams and larger rivers, but some strains also spawn well upstream, as in the case of the Yukon River in Alaska, nearly 2,000 staggering miles from the ocean. There are both early and late runs, but in general, spawning occurs earlier at the northern end of the range than at the southern limits of distribution.

Because most stocks spawn so close to salt water, chum tend to assume their spawning colors and lose their brightness early, in many instances even before they enter fresh water. They are, therefore, not much of a prize to the fly fisherman unless he nabs them when they first arrive in coastal areas and are still actively feeding. They are truly spectacular fighters at such times. The later runs generally produce larger fish, sometimes up to 20 pounds or more.

Actual spawning takes place from June through January, depending again on specific strains. Fry emerge from the spawning gravel the following spring and move downstream immediately, usually at night. When traveling long distances, they feed on insect larvae. Regardless of river length, all fry reach saltwater estuaries no later than midsummer, but most appear to arrive there in April and May. In any event, chum salmon do not have a freshwater residency period, with the exception of the time it takes them to migrate downstream.

Once in salt water, the young fish school and remain in coastal areas for the next several months (within 20 miles of shore), during which time they feed on copepods, amphipods, euphausids, crustacean larvae, fish larvae, and insects, a diet the maturing fish retain. By fall and early winter, they move out to sea, at which time they are about eight inches.

North American stocks of chum spend the bulk of their lives in the Gulf of Alaska. They seem to inhabit deeper waters than coho, sockeye and pink salmon, with offshore depths of 200 feet recorded, although they approach the surface levels at night. Later, as they approach their spawning rivers, they are commonly found at depths of 50 feet or less. By July the bulk of maturing fish are on their way from North Pacific feeding grounds, with the exception of the very early runs, which have already departed. Since there are so many stocks and run timings, there is no mass exodus as is the case within the more concentrated runs of spawning sockeye. Growth is rapid during final migration.

Summing up, it can be seen that each salmon species as well as stocks within the species has its own distinguishing characteristics. Salmon vary in terms of their life span, their size, their diet, depths at which they feed, migration routes (especially toward maturity), size of individual runs, and run timing. These variables are all signficant to the salmon fly fisherman. To be successful, he needs to learn the distinguishing traits of each salmon species.

4.

Salmon Feed

ANY FLY FISHERMAN WORTH HIS SALT IN the last five to ten years has become intimately acquainted with almost all of the insects and baitfish to be found in the freshwater environment. He is literally done-for at any gathering of his fishing friends if he can't rattle off the Latin names of 20 or 30 bugs and instantly identify the life stages to boot. Except for a very few oddballs, those fishing salmon in salt water, especially those *fly* fishing for salmon in salt water, have relied on the following generalization: *Salmon eat baitfish that have silver bodies and dark backs, or they will strike at something bright-colored out of curiosity or anger.*

With the exception of candlefish imitations developed in the 1930s by Letcher Lambuth and Roderick Haig-Brown, salmon fly patterns have mainly been developed by trial and error. The following chapters attempt to set the stage for a more biologically-based development of fly patterns and fishing techniques based on extensive stomach analyses which were performed to identify what each salmon species actually feeds on and how these organisms look and act while alive in the water. The discussion is by no means complete, but is nonetheless a serious attempt to get a movement started in this direction.

Although the diet of juveniles in fresh water and marine estuaries was touched upon in the chapter on Salmon Life Histories, the organisms comprising the diet of salmon of catchable size (arbitrarily identified as 12 inches and over, depending on species fishing regulations), in salt water are isolated for special attention because of their direct influence on salmon during their active feeding and growth periods.

Salmon habitat ranges from pure, fresh water in streams, to pure, ocean salt water. In between, there is a vast range of habitats. Some key ones have been selected to group the organisms associated with each. The importance of this

The Pistol River in southern Oregon cuts a channel through the sand bar at its mouth to reach the Pacific and open the way for salmon to forge across into the tidal pool at high water. LJ

to the fly fisherman is that there are different feeding characteristics associated with each habitat.

Some salmon, depending on where they were spawned, can progress through different habitats during their development. For instance, a salmon from southern Puget Sound would go through the entire range of possible habitats, whereas a salmon spawned in a small, coastal stream would pass through only a small marine estuary before directly entering the ocean. Some resident strains do not go to a pure oceanic habitat at all; they are pure "inside" fish.

The following flow chart and accompanying definitions may help to focus on these relationships more clearly. Obviously, the flow works in reverse as the salmon head for their natal streams, although they normally phase out feeding as they progress through the marine transition zone on the return trip.

EXAMPLES:

Fresh Water —
Sacramento River, California.
Nisqually River, Washington.
Fraser River, British Columbia.
Yukon River, Alaska.

Freshwater River Estuary —
Sacramento River delta, California.
Nisqually River delta, Washington.
Fraser River delta, British Columbia.
Yukon River delta, Alaska.

Marine Transition Zone —
San Francisco Bay, California.
Puget Sound, Hood Canal, Washington.
Strait of Georgia, British Columbia.

Sub-oceanic —
Strait of Juan de Fuca, Washington.
Alaskan inland waterway.

Oceanic —
Gulf of Alaska.
North Pacific Ocean (northern California to Alaska).
Bering Sea, Alaska.

Since the marine transition zone provides so much of the fly fishing on resident salmon, it has been further broken down to identify more specific areas. These are:

Littoral or Intertidal Zone — The area between high and low tide.

Shallow Sub-littoral or Sub-tidal Zone — From low tide to 35 feet deep. This important area often includes eel grass and kelp beds. Eel grass is associated with gently sloping sand and mud flats, while kelp beds are normally associated with sharp dropoffs and strong currents.

Nearshore Pelagic Zone — Any open water area from low tide to 70 feet deep.

Offshore Pelagic Zone — Any open water deeper than 70 feet.

"Pelagic" means inhabiting open water, and in the case of marine organisms, living free from the bottom and near the surface. Thus, salmon, which are essentially an open water fish at catchable size, are considered pelagic, and most of the organisms comprising the salmon diet are pelagic as well.

MARINE TRANSITION ZONES

WATER SURFACE — HIGH TIDE

TIDE RANGE   WATER SURFACE — LOW TIDE

35 FEET

70 FEET

BOTTOM

LITTORAL OR INTERTIDAL

SUB-LITTORAL OR SUB-TIDAL

NEARSHORE PELAGIC

OFFSHORE PELAGIC

SALMON FEEDING HABITS

The following tables and illustrations depict the organisms eaten by each of the five Pacific salmon species at different life stages. Asterisks indicate the most important items in the diet. Salmon of catchable size feed in all saltwater habitats, depending on time of day, time of year, and location of prey, but they tend to feed in the habitats listed as they grow to the sizes indicated. In other words, as they get bigger, they need more nourishment to sustain them, which translates into either greater quantities of food of the same size, or larger food. By and large, the organisms comprising the diet of salmon fall into three major categories, namely, baitfish, zooplankton, and squid. The more important members of each category are identified with highlights from their life histories.

A Summary of CHINOOK Salmon Feeding Habits

| Marine Transition Zone[1] | | | | |
Shallow Sublittoral	Nearshore Pelagic	Offshore Pelagic	Suboceanic[2]	Oceanic[3]
3-8 inches	3-8 inches	Greater than 4 inches	All sizes[5] (Greater than 3 inches)	All sizes[5] (Greater than 3 inches)
May-September	**May-September**	**Year-Round[4]**	**May-September[6]**	**Year-Round[6]**
Crab larvae*	Crab larvae*	Fish (herring)*	Fish (herring, sand lance or candlefish, smelt)*	Fish (anchovy, herring, smelt, sand lance or candlefish, pilchards)*
Insects*	Insects	Euphausids	Insects	Euphausids
Fish	Fish	Hyperiid amphipods	Crab larvae	Crab larvae
Gammarid amphipods	Gammarid amphipods	Squid	Amphipods	Squid
			Shrimp larvae	

* Especially important food items.
1 Puget Sound, Hood Canal and Strait of Georgia.
2 Northern Puget Sound, Strait of Juan de Fuca and Alaska bays.
3 Gulf of Alaska, Bering Sea, North Pacific Ocean (Northern California to Alaska).
4 Supports a population of "residents" that occur year-round.
5 Includes fish migrating through (generally larger) and fish from more local rivers (smaller).
6 Availability in sport fishery will be subject to regulations.

A Summary of COHO Salmon Feeding Habits

| Marine Transition Zone[1] | | | | |
Shallow Sublittoral	Nearshore Pelagic	Offshore Pelagic	Suboceanic[2]	Oceanic[3]
4-8 inches	4-8 inches	Greater than 6 inches	Greater than 4 inches[5]	Greater than 4 inches[5]
April-July	**April-July**	**Year-Round[4]**	**April-August[4]**	**Year-Round[6]**
Crab larvae*	Crab larvae*	Fish (herring, sand lance or candlefish)*	Fish (herring, sand-lance or candlefish)*	Fish (herring, anchovy, pilchard, smelt)
Amphipods[7]	Euphausids	Euphausids	Amphipods[7]	Euphausids
Fish eggs and larvae	Amphipods[7]	Crab larvae*	Crab larvae*	Squid
Mysids	Fish	Amphipods[7]	Mysids	
			Isopods	
			Insects	
			Euphausids	

* Especially important food items.
1 Puget Sound, Hood Canal and Strait of Georgia.
2 Northern Puget Sound, Strait of Juan de Fuca and Alaska bays.
3 Gulf of Alaska, Bering Sea, North Pacific Ocean (Northern California to Alaska).
4 Supports a population of "residents" that occur year-round
5 Includes fish migrating through (generally larger) and fish from more local rivers (smaller).
6 Availability to sport fishery will be subject to regulation.
7 Includes both hyperids and gammarids.

A Summary of SOCKEYE Salmon Feeding Habits

Marine Transition Zone[1]				
Shallow Sublittoral	Nearshore Pelagic	Offshore Pelagic [4]	Suboceanic[2]	Oceanic[3]
Not commonly found in this habitat.	3-8 inches	3-8 inches	Data not available	All sizes
	April-September	**May-September[5]**		**Year-Round**
	Euphausids	Insects		Copepods*
	Shrimp	Amphipods		Euphausids*
	Fish larvae	Crab larvae		Amphipods*
	Calanoid copepods	Euphausids		Crustacean larvae
				Fish
				Squid
				Crab larvae

* Especially important food items.
1 Puget Sound, Hood Canal and Strait of Georgia.
2 Northern Puget Sound, Strait of Juan de Fuca and Alaska bays.
3 Gulf of Alaska, Bering Sea, North Pacific Ocean (Northern California to Alaska).
4 Data not available from Puget Sound. Strait of Georgia data were used instead.
5 Especially abundant, May-July.

A Summary of CHUM Salmon Feeding Habits

Marine Transition Zone[1]				
Shallow Sublittoral	Nearshore Pelagic	Offshore Pelagic	Suboceanic[2]	Oceanic[3]
1.5-4 inches	2-6 inches	3-8 inches[4]	2-6 inches[5]	All sizes[5]
March-July		**May-August[4]**	**April-September**	**Year-Round**
Harpacticoids*	Calanoids*	Amphipods	Harpacticoids*	Copepods
Larvacea	Euphausids	Euphausids*	Gammarid amphipods	Euphausids
Calanoids*	Amphipods[6]	Crab larvae*	Calanoids*	Pteropods
Euphausids	Larvacea	Fish	Crab larvae	Fish
Amphipods[6]	Crab larvae	Copepods	Mysids	Squid
	Harpacticoids		Insects	Crustaceans (unid.)
			Fish eggs and larvae	

* Especially important food items.
1 Puget Sound, Hood Canal and Strait of Georgia.
2 Northern Puget Sound, Strait of Juan de Fuca and Alaska bays.
3 Gulf of Alaska, Bering Sea, North Pacific Ocean (Northern California to Alaska).
4 Some chum may remain in Puget Sound and form a "resident" population and grow substantially larger than 8 inches.
5 Includes fish migrating through (generally these are larger) and fish from more local rivers (smaller).
6 Includes both gammarids and hyperids.

A Summary of PINK Salmon Feeding Habits

Marine Transition Zone[1,4]				
Shallow Sublittoral	Nearshore Pelagic	Offshore Pelagic	Suboceanic[2]	Oceanic[3]
1.5-4 inches	1.5-6 inches	Data not available	All sizes[6]	All sizes[6]
February-June	**March-July**	**March-August[5]**	**March-September**	**Year-Round**
Calanoids*	Calanoids*	Amphipods[7]	Calanoids	Fish
Harpacticoids*	Harpacticoids	Crab larvae*	Harpacticoids	Euphausids
		Euphausids*	Gammarid amphipods	Amphipods[7]
		Larvacea	Barnacle larvae	Squid
			Larvacea	Copepods
			Insects	
			Fish eggs	

* Especially important food items.
1 Puget Sound, Hood Canal and Strait of Georgia.
2 Northern Puget Sound, Strait of Juan de Fuca and Alaska bays.
3 Gulf of Alaska, Bering Sea, North Pacific Ocean (Northern California to Alaska).
4 Juveniles are present almost exclusively in even-numbered years.
5 A small number of pinks may be "resident" in Puget Sound and consequently found available to the sport fishery.
6 Includes fish migrating through from other areas (generally larger) and fish from more local rivers (smaller).
7 Includes gammarid and hyperid amphipods.

BAITFISH

Body shapes of baitfish range from moderately deep (herring), to moderately slender (the various smelts, sardines and anchovies), to very slender ("candlefish" or sand lance). Almost all exhibit prominent pearly eyes with black pupils; dark, bluish-greenish or brownish to black back spots, shading to silver on the sides and bellies. Post-larval length varies from about two to 12 inches, but at this stage most appear in the three- to nine-inch category.

Baitfish comprise a limited portion of the diet for chum, sockeye and pink salmon, but supply a substantial portion of the maturing coho's diet and the bulk of the chinook salmon diet.

Herring

Pacific Herring — *Clupea harengus pallasi.* These fish are bluish-green to olive on the dorsal surface, shading to silver on the sides and belly. They have a prominent, pearl-colored eye featuring a black pupil. Sexually mature specimens are from six to 12 inches.

They spawn in shallow water, generally from February through June. These baitfish travel in large schools, with the juveniles (usually 1½ to 4 inches) living in relatively shallow water from May through October. They move to deeper water in the fall. These herring have a lifetime aversion to light and are found on the surface only at dusk, night and daybreak unless forced to the surface in "balls" by predatory diving birds and feeding salmon.

Herring are found from San Diego, California, to northwestern Alaska, and are a major food in the diet of chinook and coho salmon, especially as one- to five-inch juveniles.

These fish tend to swim in large schools, spreading out to feed. When under attack from the side or below, juveniles jump and scatter. When frightened, they all dart simultaneously at the same speed, without pausing, anywhere from a few feet to 30 feet away from the perceived danger point, thus creating a hole in the school, but otherwise becoming a more concentrated school. As the danger passes, the hole disappears. When crippled or sick, and therefore prime salmon prey, herring swim aimlessly or flutter erratically, rising, and then sinking between flutters.

Anchovy

Northern Anchovy — *Engraulis mordax.* These baitfish are a metallic bluish-green on the dorsal surface and silver on the sides and belly. They have a pronounced pearl eye with black pupil, a very large mouth with gillcovers that flair out as it swims. From above, it looks like a silver dime. Anchovy are usually four to five inches with a maximum of nine inches.

They spawn in inlets or offshore in surface waters year-round. These fish move offshore in winter and return in spring. They prefer the bottom in the daytime and surface at night.

Anchovy occur from Cape San Incas in Baja, California, to the Queen Charlotte Islands in British Columbia. They,

Resident Puget Sound salmon of this size are often evident in good numbers during the spring season. BMF

too, are a preferred food in the diet of chinook and coho salmon.

As do herring, anchovy exhibit a strong schooling tendency whether in open water or along beaches; they can frequently be seen in surface waters in the daytime. The silver flash of their gills as they feed in unison is unmistakable. When frightened, these baitfish dart away and down, leaving an open area commensurate with the size of the attack. The darting motion covers at least three feet and is very fast. When feeding, the individual fish motion is one of pronounced undulation, like that of a belly dancer, and involves the whole body.

Sardine

Pilchard or Sardine — *Sardinops sagax.* Dark metallic blue or green on the back, shading to silver on the sides and belly. Round, black spots occur along the upper part of the sides. Prominent pearl eye with black pupil. These rather slender fish do not normally exceed a foot in length. They spawn 100 to 300 miles offshore, mostly in April or May. The young move inshore where they tend to school near beach areas. They migrate north in summer and south again in the fall, with the largest and oldest fish migrating farthest north to the west coast of Vancouver Island. Smaller fish move north to Washington and Oregon. Distribution is from Baja, California, to southeastern Alaska. Sardine are a good source of food for chinook and coho when available, although the numbers of this once abundant baitfish have declined steeply since heavy overfishing in the mid-forties.

Smelt

Surf Smelt — *Hypomesus pretiosus.* Light olive-green to brownish on the back; sides and belly silvery and iridescent with a bright reflecting band along the side. Large pearly eye with black pupil. These are slim fish, and attain a length up to 12 inches in California waters, but only eight inches in British Columbia. They spawn on moist beaches most of the year. Three- to five-inch immature fish have been taken in the Strait of Georgia in April and June. They occur from Long Beach, California, to Prince William Sound, Alaska, and are among the preferred items in the diet of chinook salmon.

Smelt are straight-line swimmers when under attack. They leave the area at high speed, essentially using their tails only for movement. These baitfish do not ball up or school when under attack, but scatter as individuals. They are seen in shallow water only on spawning runs at high tide.

Whitebait Smelt — *Allosmerus elongatus.* Pale greenish, almost colorless, with a sharply-defined silver stripe along each side. Eye is distinct, with black pupil against pearl backdrop. These slender fish grow to a length of nine inches. They spawn in the ocean, and the juveniles remain translucent until they are some three inches long. These baitfish are found from San Francisco, California, to southern Vancouver Island in British Columbia on the Strait of Juan de Fuca.

Capelin — *Mallotus villosus.* These baitfish have olive-green backs merging to silver on the sides and belly. These slim-bodied fish achieve a length of five inches in the southern part of their range, and up to eight inches in the northern range. They, too, have prominent pearl eyes with a black pupil. Spawning occurs on fine gravel beaches at high tide in late September and early October. They are found in North America from the Strait of Juan de Fuca, British Columbia, throughout Alaska.

Eulachon, Candlefish or Columbia River Smelt — *Theleichthys pacificus.* Bluish to bluish-brown on the dorsal area, shading to silvery white on sides and belly. The eye is rather small, pearl with black pupil. The body is slender. Maximum length is about nine inches. They spawn in freshwater rivers from March to May, with distinctly separate stocks of fish. Distribution is from the Russian River in California, to the eastern Bering Sea in Alaska. The name "candlefish" was given to this coastal fish as it was used extensively by the Indians as a source of oil. Dried, and with a wick added, the fish were burned as candles.

Sand Lance

Pacific Sand Lance or Candlefish — *Ammodytes hexapterus.* Gray or green dorsally, iridescent sides and silver belly. The eye is relatively inconspicuous. These are a very slender fish, ranging in maximum size from eight to ten inches, and frequently seen as immatures of four to six inches in shallows and along kelp beds where they are a seemingly preferred diet item for chinook, coho and maturing pink salmon. They are an offshore fish as well and an important one for fly fishermen to imitate. They are eel-like in appearance and their swimming action is snakelike. These baitfish have the unique ability to bury themselves quickly in the sand. Distribution is from southern California to Alaska's Bering Sea. When present, they are a frequent diet item of chinook and coho salmon.

Sand lance travel in a loosely-knit school with two to three fish per cubic foot; they are usually observed feeding along shorelines. They travel in the same direction or hang stationary in the current. Feeding individuals move with a corkscrew, darting action, one to two feet at a time. When frightened, they dart in a straight line down at a 45-degree angle or greater.

SQUID

Squid come in a great variety of species from very small to the giant squid of maritime legend. Obviously, in order to be considered feed for salmon, they have to be small enough for a salmon to eat, and not the other way around. Therefore, when considering squid as an important food item for salmon, we are discussing either those species under about eight inches in length or the juveniles of larger species when the juveniles are in this size category.

Squid occur throughout the entire range of feeding salmon, with some species found at very great depths, while others are more surface oriented. However, most species tend to approach the surface at night. Sockeye, pink, chum, chinook and coho all include squid in their oceanic diet as do toothed whales, porpoises, sea lions, seals, sea birds and many other kinds of fish, not to mention man. Squid themselves feed on other mollusks, crustaceans and fish, depending on size and species. They grasp prey with the suction cups on their tentacles and bring it to their mouth, which is a strong, horny beak. Food is torn into small pieces before being eaten. Squid grow rapidly, have short life spans, and die after spawning.

Of special interest to the fly fisher is the squid's rather unusual means of locomotion. All swim by water-jet propulsion. They are able to swim in either direction with equal ease and amazing speed, matching that achieved by the most active fish. Its two fins or wings allow the squid to hover or glide by slow undulation. When frightened, the wings and jet combined can produce dazzling speed in a straight line for considerable distance. There does not appear to be a pulsing action, but rather one of smooth, and if necessary, rapid acceleration.

Another point of interest is the squid's ability to change color rapidly by means of chromatophores imbedded in its skin. They can lighten or darken the hue, or change color completely to match the background, or as a reaction to various stimuli. The basic color of squid is translucent grayish-white with dots of this color scattered across the body; like all members of their family, they have the disarming ability to eject a black, inky cloud when frightened — the original "smoke screen." In all, this ancient marine animal is fascinatingly different from what is normally seen in salt water, and worth observing in its own right. Squid are important as food for salmon and well worth developing as flies. Sport and commercial salmon trollers, both offshore and inshore, have used the familiar Hootchies, with their long, rubbery tentacles in various colors as a mainstay for taking fish, fully recognizing the squid's role in the salmon diet.

A single species has been selected for description and illustration. (See Color Plate.)

Squid – *Loligo opalescens*. This squid has a maximum total length of under 14 inches, with the largest specimens in British Columbia not over eight inches. The body is a tube-like mantle with a large, stabilizing fin on one end and a pair of prominent, pearly eyes with black pupils on the other, beyond which extend a number of short tentacles. The eye cover is iridescent greenish-yellow on top. Body color is milky translucent with a faint bluish tone and fine, brown spots. These can change within seconds to darker colors, or when the animal is excited, to completely different coloring in small, iridescent spots of red, brown, orange, yellow or mottled gold.

The *Loligo* is the second most important squid in world commercial operations and is distributed from Cedros Island, Mexico, to the southern part of the Gulf of Alaska on the Pacific Coast of North America.

It spawns at ages one to four, but is typically three at

Bonaparte gulls homing in on euphausids, an important item in their diet. Fly fishermen watch for feeding Bonapartes, knowing that when they are feeding from the top, salmon are gorging on euphausids from below. — Bill Ludwig photo

sexual maturity. Spawning takes place in ten to 115 feet of water in protected bays throughout the year, but usually occurs from April through July, with spawning in the northern end of the range earlier in the year, and into winter in the southern end. Death typically results after spawning. The colorless young are dispersed by the ocean currents. Juvenile growth in shallow water is rapid, where they become an important salmon food. Young squid feed primarily during daylight hours in 60 to 150 feet of water. However, in collecting live specimens to photograph for this book, squid were taken on an overcast day no more than 50 feet from shore in less than ten feet of water along a beach in Puget Sound, Washington. Toward evening they move toward the surface, and feed actively on moonlit nights. They are definitely attracted to light at night.

Swimming behavior is the same as that described for all squid. Because of the *Loligo's* affinity for living relatively close to shore in protected, shallow water, and its importance in salmon diet, this species is especially important to imitate in fly patterns and retrieves.

This prime 8-pound chinook salmon was taken just before dark in Puget Sound by Bruce Ferguson on a tube fly fished deep with a fast sinking shooting head. — Dave Ferguson

ZOOPLANKTON

This broad group of salmon prey is defined as "passively floating or weak swimming minute animal life." Individuals range in size from about 1/16 of an inch to two inches with most between 1/8 to 3/4 inch. Characteristically, they have prominent, dark purple to black eyes and transparent bodies with a variety of tints depending on species and background. These hues range from milky-white to pink, yellow, orange, red, green, gray, brown, and even purple. Many species collect in tide rips and eddies in large clouds of massed individuals, but may appear at other times as well-separated individuals. For some, habitat is close to shore between the kelp or eel-grass and the intertidal zone. Most, however, dwell in the offshore environment in the top 25 feet of water and right under the surface at night and early morning. Since zooplankton generally dislike bright light, they tend to descend to lower levels during daylight hours. They are primarily small crustaceans, but include the larval forms of large crustaceans and fish.

The zooplankton discussed in the following section comprise a large part, but far from all, of the diet of salmon. These "beneath notice" diminutive animals form the bulk of the diet for sockeye, chum and pink salmon, and are a preferred diet for coho when available in sufficient quantity. Only chinook salmon feed on zooplankton to a lesser degree. In fact, sockeye, chum and pinks do not even have prominent teeth since there is so little need for these salmon to grip larger pieces of food.

Salmon are basically opportunistic, looking for the most food for the least effort. Because of this, free-floating zooplankton, especially when massed in large groups called swarms, present an attractive food choice, and fish seem to zero in on this situation in preference to other available food.

A striking example of this occurred one August day on Puget Sound. My friend, Bill Ludwig, and I had headed out on a dead calm dawn in front of my house in southern Puget Sound, anticipating catching a couple of maturing resident coho by means of a slowly-trolled cut-plug herring, a light sinker and lightweight monofilament spooled on a standard fly reel attached to a fly rod — a deadly method when you are not able to see signs of salmon on the surface. As an afterthought, we threw our fly casting gear in the boat. Nothing happened with our trolling, even though there were numerous euphausids on the surface being frantically fed on by thousands of visible herring, both favorite foods for silvers feeding heavily the last few months before spawning.

Suddenly, we spotted a few large boils in the midst of this frenzied activity: salmon! In came the trolling gear, and out came the fly gear. There was as much activity in the boat putting rods, reels, lines and flies together as there was in the water. Running the outboard up to casting range of the fish only served to put them down, so Bill volunteered to row quietly into range instead. This produced nothing, using the usual fast-stripping motion, even though the fly was perfectly placed ahead of the moving salmon.

Inadvertently, I stopped stripping while looking down at my box of flies to consider a pattern change, thus allowing the fly to sink in a fluttering way. As I mentally decided on the next fly, I looked up and resumed my retrieve. Instantly, I was hooked to a wildly-jumping five-pound silver, a glorious sight indeed. By the time it was netted, the "rise" was over, so there was no further opportunity to repeat the technique successfully. But two important observations were gleaned from this exciting experience. The first was that my fly, a streamer pattern with good action in the water, when allowed to sink, looked like a wounded baitfish and, therefore, and easy meal that a salmon would not have to chase. The second observation came when I opened the silver's stomach and found it filled with 3/4-inch milky-white translucent euphausids, and *no herring*. The implication was that the euphausids made an easier meal to catch in quantity than the fast-moving herring, even though the salmon almost had to push the tightly-packed feeding herring out of the way to get to the euphausids. Either that, or coho actually find the euphausids more pleasing to their palates.

Whatever the proper analysis for this experience is, the importance to the fly fisherman cannot be overstated, and perhaps the principal "new" thought in this book is the development of techniques and patterns that are successful for each salmon species when they are actively feeding on zooplankton.

The theory is even proposed that the acceptance of "small" flies by salmon and steelhead on their freshwater spawning runs is keyed to their very recent feeding on marine zooplankton rather than their "memory" of feeding on insects much earlier as freshwater fingerlings and smolts.

The enlarged color photos, descriptions and capsule-form generalized life histories of significant zooplankton forms included herein hopefully will help to unveil some of the mysteries of the sea. (See color plate.)

CRUSTACEANS

Crab Larvae

Dungeness – *Cancer magister*. These larvae are basically transparent with a reddish-brown to brownish cast. Eyes on stems are an iridescrent bright blue. The larvae have a roundish appearance and prickly feel. Seen under a microscope, the quarter-inch specimens clearly show all the detail illustrated. The sixth, or megalops, stage of development is important as this is when the major feeding by salmon occurs. During the earlier five stages, or zoea, the organisms are only about 1/32 of an inch and perhaps not large enough to be of interest to salmon.

The free-floating megalops stage, which lasts about a month, appears from April in Oregon to September in British Columbia, within a half mile offshore. This stage occurs in Puget Sound in late May and early June. Megalops are mostly found in the top six feet of water within five miles of shore. As the larvae develop into adults, they drop to and remain on the bottom where they assume "normal" crab posture, at which stage they are no longer a viable salmon food.

The swimming action of the larvae is smooth and continuous in a straight line at a rate of perhaps six inches per second. Although the larvae of other crab species are important, the dungeness was selected for description because it

is the most commly known and widely distributed. It ranges from the tip of the Aleutian Islands in Alaska to the southern tip of Baja, California, in Mexico.

Dungeness larvae are a substantial source of food for both chinook and coho when available, and to a lesser extent to the other three salmon species.

Shrimp Larvae

Coonstripe – *Pandalus danae*. These larvae are transparent with iridescent reddish spots visible under a microscope. Spot coloring can apparently be changed at will. Other species are also transparent, but with spotting and antennae color variations including pink, yellow, brown, and orange-red. To the unaided eye, these colorings give an overall pastel hue of the colors noted. In the free-swimming stage, they are from one-third to one-inch with general appearance similar to a mature shrimp with the same prominent antennae but more slender body proportions.

Larvae are present from March through May in all species reviewed. Although research data indicate they are found at depths from 25 to 200 feet, it is our belief that they rise closer to the surface at night and early morning when light conditions are poor, and retreat to the depths noted during daylight hours. As the larvae mature, they move toward bottom, finally taking up residence there as adult shrimp.

Swimming action is slowly forward in a continuous fashion. When frightened, they scoot backward in short, fast jerks. Coonstripe shrimp are found from Sitka, Alaska, to San Francisco, California, in 60 to 200 feet of water on sandy or gravelly bottoms as adults. A number of other species have overlapping distribution and occur in generally deeper water. The larvae is an identifiable chinook salmon food.

Euphausids: Krill

There are 11 genera and 85 species of krill which is a common name applied to all euphausids. The largest resides in the Gulf of Alaska and measures close to four inches. The best known is the antarctic krill, which is over two inches. Krill are a major food in the diet of the baleen whales of the world. It is fortunate that krill are so abundant as a single whale will eat 1.5 to four tons per day! Virtually everything in salt water preys on krill: squid, fish of all kinds, penguins, albatrosses, puffins, seals as well as whales. And almost anyone who has traveled on salt water at night has seen them, probably without recognizing what he was seeing, for krill are frequently observed as flashing sparkles of light as a boat cuts through the water, or as an anchor is dropped over the side. They are the lightning bugs of the sea. A number of species swarm on occasion — that is, they form large, tightly grouped masses near the surface which, in general appearance, looks like the Milky Way.

Of the large number of krill species, one which occurs most abundantly in the salmon range is described here in more detail.

Euphausids: *Euphausia pacifica*. Individuals of this species vary in length from about 1/8 inch to a maximum of slightly less than one inch. They appear as tiny shrimp with slender bodies and more legs. They are a milky-white translucent color overall, with tiny color spores above the legs, which may give them a faint pinkish cast. Locally, they are known as "shrimp spawn."

This euphausid is distributed from southern California to the Aleutian Islands in Alaska, and is the most abundant species in Puget Sound. It is found in larval form in surface waters both day and night. However, the mature forms tend to react negatively to light and are found at or near the surface primarily at dusk, night and at daybreak. In Washington, they have been observed on the surface during late fall and winter months in midday. Otherwise, they are reported to descend to depths of as much as 200 feet in inland waters, and over 1000 feet offshore in California and Oregon.

Spawning takes place in California on a year-round basis. with the majority occurring from May through July. Oregon coastal waters produce spawning in late summer and early fall.

The northern range of ocean spawning is in late May and June. In Washington's Puget Sound, with which we are most familiar, spawning is at its peak in April and May, declining in summer, with a lesser resurgence in the fall. Populations decline from late fall through February. The life span is reported to be a single year throughout its range, except in Alaska, where it is two years.

Euphausids of this species glide along, head first, using a rapid leg action. They can hover in place, proceed at a fast, steady pace in any direction, or move in short "darts." They also are capable of a corkscrew swimming motion with the diameter of the corkscrew from two to six inches. When frightened, they appear to snap their abdomens and scoot backward from three to eight inches, actually jumping out of the water when pushed.

All five salmon species feed actively on euphausids whenever they are available, both in inland and open ocean waters. When on this feed, especially when the euphausids are at or near the surface, salmon can be readily persuaded to take a fly.

Copepods

With some of the largest of these small crustaceans being only 1/5 of an inch long as adults, it is understandable why so few outside the research field, or recent graduates of a marine biology class, are aware of the importance or even existence of these animals. In fact, there are some 4,500 copepod species, and they form a vital link in the aquatic food chain as the initial consumers of microscopic plant life. They are reported to be the most abundant group of crustaceans and even of plankton in general. One estimate states that in a single year a little over ten cubic yards of water in the Baltic Sea produced nine billion of these organisms.

More inhabitants of the sea feed on copepods than any other animal. This ranges from baleen whales to the tiniest fishes, and most certainly includes sockeye, pink and chum salmon, the primary planktonic feeders of the Pacific

salmon. Coho and even chinook feed on copepods to a lesser degree, especially as juveniles.

Although, as salmon food, most attention is devoted to the free-swimming, pelagic calanoids, it is worth noting that copepods have developed a number of parasitic species. Among these, the familiar sea lice are most well known. Salmon, therefore, cannot only eat copepods, but at the same time, in a sense, they can be eaten by copepods. Such is the intricacy of nature.

A generalized life history of a typical, abundant species of calanoid copepod is presented here in more detail.

Copepod – *Calanus plumchrus*. Adult length is about 1/5 of an inch. This species, like other calanoids, has a single, very long antenna on each side of its head, in which there is a single, inconspicuous eye. The body is colorless, unless the animal has stored pigmentation from ingested plant food, in which case red, orange or gray-green coloration and easy visibility may result.

Calanus plumchrus are distributed from Oregon to the Bering Sea in Alaska. They are abundant in the spring and summer, as adults, in surface waters when they spawn. The developing juveniles live in deeper waters throughout the colder months, and then rise to the surface again in warmer months to feed on microscopic plant food.

They are excellent swimmers, tending to hang upright in the water, settle, then move upward in a short, body-length pulsing movement. When frightened, this copepod moves from several body lengths to several inches in any direction at a speed hard to follow with the naked eye. The overall appearance in this situation is a quick, darting motion. Their long, prominent antennae are important in facilitating either motion.

Amphipods

There are some 3,600 different species of amphipods. They are predominantly marine but have numerous freshwater forms as well. Some are pelagic and free-swimming, which are of primary importance to salmon, while others, in fact, most, tend to creep along the bottom or among aquatic plants. Most are bent in shape, having curved backs, and in general resemble fleas, to which they are totally unrelated. The freshwater scud, familiar to trout fishermen, is an amphipod, as is the sand hopper or sand flea of marine beaches. The largest known species is a deep-water variety almost five inches long, but the bulk of marine pelagic forms are only about a tenth of an inch in length, making up for their small size by their vast numbers.

Amphipods comprise the food staple for a good many fish, and are reported as a portion of the diet of baleen wahles. Herring and mackerel feed heavily on them as do tuna and arctic penguins.

Man rarely consumes them, but they have been known to save men's lives. In a recorded report, the ill-fated Greeley Expedition to the Arctic in the early 1880s included 25 men. In March of 1884, in desperation, when their larder was nearly depleted, they constructed a net with an iron barrel hoop ring, and a bag made from sacking. With this, they snared as many amphipods as they could. Although between March and June 23rd of that year, most of the expedition died from starvation, seven were rescued and owed their lives not only to their rescuers, but also to the amphipod diet. It was estimated that some 1500 pounds were caught and devoured in that time period.

More relevantly, sockeye, pink, chum and coho consume amphipods as an important part of their diet.

The pelagic forms eaten by salmon are of two types: gammarid and hyperid. Gammarids have inconspicuous eyes, while hyperids have large heads and large, dark eyes. They are generally transparent with pastel hues of pink, orange, green or violet. Powerful back muscles can be straightened suddenly, causing a rapid hopping or darting motion which thrust carries these animals several times their body lengths. Amphipods also "zoom" in erratic curves or circles. They commonly lie on their sides when at rest, in their characteristic "flealike" position.

Barnacle Larvae

Adult barnacles that are found firmly attached to rocks, shores, boat bottoms, sea turtle shells and even whales, as well as virtually any other underwater marine surface, go through a series of developmental stages as free-swimming larvae. It is during this stage that the larvae are a recognizable salmon food. Less than a tenth of an inch in size, these minute, three-sided, colorless, transparent crustaceans are nonetheless fed on by salmon, especially pinks.

FISH LARVAE

The larval forms of many fish species provide nourishment for salmon when available. They are generally colorless, transparent, and with prominent dark eyes. Size is small, up to an inch or so. The larval forms are weak swimmers, moving forward with quivering undulations, and are therefore attractive prey for all salmon species, especially for juveniles or small, immature fish.

CONCLUSION

The overviews of representative marine salmon prey species presented in this chapter hopefully provided the fly tier with many new insights into the tremendous potential for tying patterns of interest to Pacific salmon. If nothing else, you'll turn a few heads at the next meeting of your fly fishing club when you report that you hooked a nice sockeye on a No. 16 copepod imitation in the near-pelagic zone of your favorite bay.

Frisky little coho leaps high in an effort to shake the hook. Action took place in Hale Pass, Puget Sound, Washington.
— Bill Ludwig photo

5.

Finding the Salmon –
Where and When

LOCATING SALMON IS A BIG PART OF THE game. In fresh water, on their route to spawning beds, they tend to lie in the same spots year after year. Once identified, these holding spots can be counted on to produce consistently. The trick is to pinpoint when they'll be at a given location, as the fall freshets urge salmon on to their final destination.

In salt water, locating salmon is more complex. Fish are moving constantly in search of food and migrate over enormous distances in this pursuit. Different species have different depths at which they habitually search for favored diet items. Tides, winds, time of year and time of day are all factors to be considered.

Rather than attempt to pinpoint each likely spot throughout each species' range, the basic conditions and water types that tend to put you in the right place at the right time are described. Your personal salmon fishing diary, given careful entries over time, will reveal your local area's secrets.

SALT WATER

With all the variables involved, fly fishing for salmon in salt water becomes an intense, fast-paced, three-dimensional hunting expedition rather than a leisurely outing on the salt. Many stream-bred fly rodders are overcome by the huge expanses of water, either believing that there is a salmon under every wave or that they're on an impossible needle-in-the-haystack mission. In both cases, the challenge is soon abandoned out of frustration and the fly fisher misses out on some of the best angling available. There is no question that confidence is a basic requirement as is persistence. Those who hang in there soon learn to recognize the productive water and to arrange their trips to take advantage of the most favorable conditions. It's not that difficult, although there is a learning curve, and the rewards can be well worth the effort.

Salt water has a character all of its own. Neither river nor lake, it is a combination of both and then some. Thanks to the continually changing tides and winds, the salt is never quite the same two days – or even two hours – in a row. It has a mysterious underlying and elusive restlessness about it. Maybe that's why is is so compelling.

Where fish are located is, therefore, never an absolute, nor for that matter is when they will be in any specific given spot. The search is part of the fun, but it can also become very frustrating if locating fish comes about only by accident. Here are some thoughts on how to improve the odds.

WHERE THEY ARE

Points of Land

Salmon are no different than any other animal. Those which survive learn to feed themselves the easiest way. As the tide flows past a point of land or around an island, it tends to create an eddy on the "downstream" or "downtide" side. Feed, whether weak-swimming zooplankton, or strong-swimming baitfish, collect in such areas, providing readily available nourishment for foraging salmon. Look for these spots and try them, remembering that when the tide changes, the location on the reverse side of the point will hold the feed as long as the land has the same characteristics both ways.

Tide Rips

For offshore ocean fishing, there is most of the time no other indicator of fish location except in the rips. Here again, two or more currents working at different speeds will create a slower moving face that tends to concentrate salmon food. If there is accumulated drift material on one side, often the other side is clean and a fly cast along this edge will remain debris-free and in the fish zone. Of course, there are rips and then there are rips. When the wind blows in one direction and the tide moves in the opposite direction, you can end up with a monumental chop on the water. If you've ever tried to stand up in a small, open boat, using both hands to cast a fly, and at the same time tried to retain

The saltwater fly caster always anticipates action along the edge of a tide rip. Easily recognized where smooth and choppy water forms a distinct line, the strong, converging currents that make up a riptide sweep baitfish and crustaceans into the flow where they become easy prey for feeding salmon.

your balance, you know what I mean when I say this situation is not what we're looking for. It's even worse on a charter or head boat where you're forced to brace your body against the rails for balance. These always seem to catch you in mid-thigh, and a day of fishing in this sort of rip will not only leave you jarred to your boots, but find you black and blue in a line across your thighs — definitely not something you will want to do everyday, no matter how masochistic your nature. Besides, these strong, violent rips don't usually hold the fish. What you are really looking for, ideally, is a barely discernible or modest rip line with little or no wind to blow you off course. Oftentimes you will be able to see swarms of zooplankton and/or schools of bait in these areas — a good sign salmon are nearby.

The edges of kelp beds like this one are good spots to find feeding salmon in salt water. LJ

Kelp Beds

Kelp is usually associated with fast-moving currents close to shore and dropoffs. Salmon have learned that kelp is beneficial in two ways. First, it provides cover for them, and second, schools of bait are concentrated in these locations by the strong-moving currents, thereby providing a ready meal for the salmon. A fly cast between the kelp and the beach, particularly when bait is seen breaking the surface, is most often productive near high tide, while one cast alongside or out from the outer edge of the kelp is more often taken on the lower end of the tide.

Water Depth

Feeding as well as migrating salmon often follow a shoreline. Although they sometimes can be found breaking into baitfish in as little as a foot of water — a scene almost guaranteed to make you fumble a too-eager cast — generally, salmon seem to prefer holding in six to 30 feet or more in these locations during daylight hours.

In the winter of 1982-83 in southern Puget Sound, for some unexplained reason, most of the herring of the year (two to four inches long) elected to jam themselves into virtually all of the shallow bays in the area rather than seek deep water as was their normal habit. Most old-timers in the region could not remember a similar situation in decades. Obviously, this was a gift from heaven for the fly fisher, and it wasn't at all unusual to see the heavily-trafficked marinas full of eager fly fishers at daybreak, bundled up to the ears in heavy, waterproof clothes and even millar mitts, casting in and around the moored boats.

Herring were so thick they would form solid black masses with holes in the schools around the dock pilings. From time to time extra holes would erupt in the black mass. Salmon and bait would scatter in the pale, icy, early morning air. Much time was wasted casting and retrieving just under the surface while those in the know fared much better by letting their flies sink close to the bottom before retrieving. They had observed that the salmon, by and large, were

Anglers are always watching for baitfish dimpling on the surface, a sure sign that salmon are not far away. BMF

roaring up from the depths, stunning their prey, returning to the bottom and picking up the cripples as they floated down below the general level of the healthy, uninjured herring. Instead of being at the surface, in fact, the coho and chinook present were 20 to 30 feet down.

Feeding salmon — in areas accessible to fly fishers — are usually present in the top 40 feet of water, and they seem reluctant to move up or down from their selected feeding level of the moment by more than five to ten feet. Chinook salmon are the exception. Although often found near the surface, they're a bottom-loving creature, more often found at depths far beyond the range of the most patient fly flinger. Basically, if you find the feed level, you find the fish — a truism for all salmon species. This holds for all marine areas — not just along shorelines.

Surfacing Fish

When out on the salt, salmon that show themselves on the surface are usually easier to catch than those taken fishing "blind." Many people, however, never see these fish merely because they don't comprehend what they are looking at. Small, immature silvers and pinks jump frequently. As these fish increase in size, they tend to show their dorsal fins and tails more in a slow roll when near the surface. When chinook and coho are frantically feeding on bait, they will slash at it and frequently explode on the surface. And in the fall, as all species impatiently hold off the rivermouths for the water to rise while adapting to the brackish water, they will sporadically jump and roll.

Salmon almost always are moving, and a casual observer may surmise that there are many more fish present than is actually the case. Someone, whose name is long forgotten, did me a great disfavor when I was just attempting to unravel the mysteries of this fishery. His comment was that if you saw a salmon jump, there are at least a hundred more

in the school with him. That remark, along with a long background of stream fishing for resident trout, where a fish stayed put in his lie, retarded my observations of what was really going on for an extended period of time.

Finally, and fortunately, I was shaken out of this concept by my equally avid fly fishing brother, Gordon, on a fishing trip to the Queen Charlotte Islands off the northern coast of British Columbia one September many years ago. I was fruitlessly casting a monstrous fly with an equally monstrous glass rod, while Gordon had sensibly brought his ultra-light spinning outfit and a Mepps spinner. In the gray light of an overcast early morning, fitted out in a 12-foot, fast-leaking aluminum rental rowboat, we were witnessing numerous large, hooknosed coho rolling and jumping. I was casting intently with increasing frustration, while brother Gordon took in the scene. Finally, in all his wisdom, he said he thought maybe the salmon that jumped was the one we should fish for, and of course, for it to take, we would need to get the lure in front of it. He promptly flipped his Mepps spinner in front of the next fish that rolled in range and immediately had a hookup that when boated after a spirited fight, turned out to be a 12-pound coho.

After this magnificent demonstration, my brother gallantly volunteered to keep the boat afloat while I tried in vain to match his performance with my flies. Advice came thick and fast as he bailed constantly with his boot (we had forgotten a bailing can), but it didn't help. I couldn't break the habit of casting directly to where I had seen the fish. But just to prove his point, some might say to rub it in, he duplicated his earlier accomplishment with another 12-pound fish before the bite was over.

Being a slow learner, it took me some time (years) to realize that not only was there probably only the sighted fish present when it surfaced, but that it was traveling at considerable speed. A fly cast with the customary false casting could not be propelled in front of the salmon with anywhere near the same speed as a lure attached to mono-filament spinning line. Therefore, compensation must be built into the fly fishing technique to match that of the successful bird hunter who is so completely versed in the rule of leading a fast-moving quarry.

More about technique later, but suffice to say that there's nothing in my knowledge of fly fishing to match the excitement of casting and hooking fish that you first see on the surface. With this in mind, we soon learn to spot other signs of fish working, even on a wind-swept surface.

Sea Birds

Diving, circling, screaming concentrations of marine birds have been a well-known clue to the location of pelagic game-fish throughout the world. It is no different with salmon. In Washington's Puget Sound country where I make my home, certain birds are even identified with specific types of feed. The dainty Bonaparte's gull, with its black head in summer and white head with gray patch in winter, is a dead giveaway to the location of concentrations of zooplankton and small baitfish. Their very call of "ere-ere" compels you to rush over to see what's going on. They may be present by the hundreds and even thousands. A careful look into their midst may show salmon boiling or finning on the surface, sharing the bounty with the Bonaparte's. Even if nothing is evident on the surface, there are generally salmon not far under the surface.

In the same area, winter provides the familiar herring balls. Here, the murres, auklets and pigeon guillemots which fly as easily under water as above, herd the hapless herring into tightly-massed, revolving balls. These frequently can be seen with a portion above the water surfaces — for all appearances in the sunshine, a replica of the multi-mirrored surface of ballroom lights of a past era. To complete the scenario and to provide the visible key to baitfish location, screaming glaucous-winged and other large gulls hover and dive on the balls, picking off whatever herring they can. The predominantly white coloration of the adult gulls makes them plainly visible for long distances. Salmon are usually in close attendance under the herring balls. A word of caution is in order, however. Roaring into these birds full throttle with your boat will invariably put the fish down. Don't do it if you hope to catch salmon. Instead, motor to within casting range on one side of the birds. When working out of my aluminum cartopper, I break out the oars at this distance and row quietly into position. I almost always take a fish or two before they move out of range. You'll be happily surprised by the difference in results.

Migration Routes

Just as in fresh water, salmon migrate along accustomed and predictable routes. It is normally on their return trip from the ocean feeding grounds, when the fish are full size and still feeding voraciously in anticipation of spawning, that the fly fisher will be looking for them on these routes. Inquiring locally at marinas and tackle shops as to usual run

Typical Puget Sound resident cohos taken in September near an estuary. BMF

timing will provide clues as to when these routes are productive. And, of course, the well-kept personal fishing diary should stand to reveal this information.

Rivermouths and Estuaries

As the various runs near their natal river or stream, there is a period of time when they must adapt themselves biologically to fresh water. Depending on species and run timing, they may also hold off the rivermouths awaiting the fall rains to raise water levels to allow them access to their spawning beds. These "waiters" will normally flush in and out of the estuaries with the tide. On short coastal streams, they frequently change from bright silver to pronounced spawning colors during this period. On rivers where there is considerable distance to travel before reaching the spawning grounds, this color change may not take place until they are well on their way upstream. In any event, while milling around in salt and brackish water, they will be concentrated for a period of from several days to several months. The salmons' feeding urge is winding down at this point, but they will still take a well-presented fly. Jumping and rolling will often give away their presence.

WHEN'S BEST

No matter how well you learn *where* to look for salmon, it's not of much value without knowing *when* to be there.

Light Conditions

Anyone who does his saltwater fishing between 10:00 a.m. and 4:00 p.m. to insure a full measure of creature comforts, having made that choice, must then resign himself to the fact that he isn't going to catch many salmon on a fly. One of the old rules of thumb that still seems to apply is: *50 percent of the salmon are taken in the first hour of daylight, 25 percent in the last hour and the remaining 25 percent are brought to net over the entire remainder of the day.* So, even if you hate to get up in the dark, if you really want to score consistently, you'll be on the water when it's just light enough to string a rod. By full sunup, most of the fast action is over.

In the evening, the reverse is true and you'll want to be leaving the fishing grounds with your running lights on. There's a reason for this. Zooplankton, which comprise so much of the food supply, seem to exhibit a negative reaction to light. They are closest to the surface in darkness or dim light. Baitfish and salmon forage where the food is, and so tend to be close to the surface, at the same time. Besides, in the poor light they aren't as vulnerable to attack from above.

As the day progresses, and the light increases, the entire food chain seeks deeper water — in many cases, deeper than the fly fisher can readily sink a fly. Keeping this in mind, it logically follows that a cloudy, overcast or foggy day will extend the time near-surface fishing is productive. For the same reason, winter fishing is more often productive longer into both ends of the day due to the less intense light at that time of year. Summer fishing, by contrast, generally calls for the most discipline. If you arrive 30 minutes late in the

morning, you may have missed *all* of the day's action. Since salmon are feeding by choice under the safest conditions available, it also follows that anything approaching a full moon in a cloudless sky at night invariably moves the salmon to do their feeding then, under the cover of semi-darkness. Daybreak fishing the following morning is usually a bust. The salmon's appetite is already sated.

Tides

No serious fly fisher would think of going out on the salt without checking his tide table or chart. The reason is that salmon seem to be triggered into feeding by certain tidal conditions. Slack water on the actual tide turn, either high or low, is generally unproductive. The two hours just prior and after this slack period seem to produce the most consistent results. Here again, there's an explanation. Moving water tends to collect food in a more restricted area, so salmon are expending less energy to get the next meal. Extreme tides, however, can produce such heavy currents that the fish become too scattered.

There are always exceptions to any rule. When fishing for salmon hanging off the estuaries, an extreme low tide will be a major factor in producing success. The significant drop in water level tends to flush these fish, en masse, back into the salt. Estuary mouths normally have an extended sand spit on one side and a steeper bank on the other. The water is forced to move in and out through a narrow channel. This means that if you take a station in the slot, all of the fish present are forced to go past your fly twice — once as the tide falls, and again as it rises. The odds for success are greatly enhanced by these forced concentrations of salmon.

Wind

A howling gale may present a fishing opportunity for a fisherman set up for trolling with a downrigger. Not so for the one casting a fly. With the exception of a light riffle on the surface to permit less demanding presentation, the less wind the better. A flat water surface allows a much clearer picture of surface activity over a much greater area. Besides, pleasure and accuracy in casting is derived in inverse proportion to the intensity of the wind. So check the weather forecast, and given a choice, select light and variable wind (0 to 5 mph) conditions. If for no other reason, consider your companion's and your own safety. High waves in strong winds can capsize a small boat in very short order, and a vagrant fly blown off course just as you're leaning into your cast can bury itself with unexpected severity into various tender parts of your anatomy.

Time of Year

Coho are especially suited to the customary modes of the fly fisher. They exhibit accelerated growth in their final year and modify their feeding habits in order to get the most weight gain for the least effort. Until coho reach about two pounds, they concentrate their efforts on the abundant, slow-moving zooplankton. At this time they are readily taken on the fly, and are most visible mornings and evenings on the surface. If more food is available, coho grow more rapidly, and close out this phase at an earlier date. As they become larger, and perhaps faster swimmers, they switch to baitfish as their principal fare. This will remain their staple until they spawn unless they're able to find dense swarms of euphausids and other easily caught zooplankton as an apparent diet preference.

For resident salmon in Puget Sound, the zooplankton-phase fishing starts in November and lasts until the change-over, which occurs most generally in June. Farther north, in the Straits of Georgia, the switch in feed occurs earlier due to a more abundant food supply. From then until spawning in the fall, the baitfish diet prevails, with fish showing less frequently on the surface. In September and October, they generally appear at the rivermouths. There is a great variation in run timing for coho as well as for the other salmon species. It is wise to learn the specifics for local streams and keep accurate personal diaries. If you're early or too late, like fishing in the bathtub with the plug pulled, nothing much is going to happen.

Summing up, the time to go salmon fishing is when you can take the time, and where to go is where you have ready access. But, given a choice, the more of the variables of where and when you can plan to have in your favor *before* you take off with fly rod in hand and eye on the horizon, the more likely you are to get into salmon.

FRESH WATER

Fly fishing for salmon in fresh water is simpler, yet sometimes more frustrating than the saltwater pursuit. It is a game where locating the quarry — even spotting dozens of the brutes holding in a clear pool — is pretty predictable, while enticing them to a fly often proves dreadfully difficult. Once in fresh water, salmon (although they will hit lures, anchovies, herring, roe or flies when conditions are right) have essentially stopped feeding. Their sleek bodies, fat and firm from foraging in the rich pastures of the Pacific, will now serve to sustain them from first entry into fresh water through spawning. Since they are not actively seeking food but do at times go on a vigorous bite, success can range from fast and furious to none at all, or, somewhere in between.

Pacific salmon home in on a variety of streams from short, coastal creeks tumbling only a few miles from a mountain source to long rivers where the spawning gravel is several hundred miles inland. In any stream, the best fishing is over bright, energetic fish which dictates that you intercept them early in the run and in the lower reaches of the river whenever possible. Also, the odds for success are considerably better on a small- to medium-size stream than on a major river like the Columbia or Sacramento. On large rivers, the bank angler is at a definite disadvantage in covering water as some pools are extremely deep and difficult to work with a fly. Conversely, on small streams of relatively short length, a day of fishing — either driving from place to place or boat drifting — allows you to cover most of the productive pools, thus enhancing your prospects of locating concentrations of salmon.

While the tremendous diversity found in saltwater angling is not as evident in freshwater fishing, neither is the latter such a simple undertaking that it should be approached casually. We must know where salmon hold in a river, for random casting is rarely productive. Finding the heaviest-hit hot spots on a river isn't difficult because areas surrounding them often look like used car lots, jammed solidly with motor vehicles of every description. We all fish these hot spots, hopefully during the week when they aren't elbow-to-elbow, but it is even more important that we locate the less desirable, little known, or, perhaps undetected riffles and pockets that often hold a few salmon that haven't been subjected to a lot of angling pressure. Working the off-the-beaten-trail places can provide a few additional holes in the punchcard and maybe a bit of serenity and solitude as a bonus.

Alaskan sockeye salmon put on an aerial display for this lucky fly fisherman. — David Tye photo

A freshwater stream — a small to medium-size one in particular — does not compare to the vast expanse of open water that challenges the saltwater angler. This is not to say, however, that a river does not hold its own unique mystique. Bordered by douglas fir, hemlock or redwood, and dappled with alder or myrtle, a clear-flowing stream, alive with a fresh run of chinook or coho on a misty, fog-shrouded morning, is personal, intimate and quietly exciting.

Tide Pools

After salmon have made the transition from salt to fresh water in natal stream estuaries or just outside the sand bar of a river flowing directly into the ocean, they will move into the river, usually resting for a few hours to several days in the tide pools. The tide pool section of a stream begins with an initial, quiet lagoon, then may have one or more additional, smaller pools upstream that are affected by the rise and fall of the tide. A river emptying directly into the

though, the most attractive aspect of tide pools is that they will hold at least a few good salmon everyday of the season.

How long salmon hold in tide pools differs from river to river and even within fish of the same run. Early returning fish that are weeks away from spawning may not move upstream for several days. Other salmon may be showing spawning colors while still in salt water and be much closer to spawning ripeness. This urgency will cause them to push through the tide pools and upstream at a faster pace.

Tide action affects the flow of a stream's lower section and the water depth of the tide pools. On a low tide, lagoons and tide pools may be nearly pure fresh water. On the flood tide, they will be almost entirely salt water in the lagoons and brackish water in the upper pools influenced by tidal action. Salmon tend to move upriver through the tide pools on rising or high water and hold up during falling or low water. They may, in fact, be temporarily trapped during times of low water in the tide pools of some small streams, unable to move until the next high tide. It is during the falling and low water periods that salmon are quite

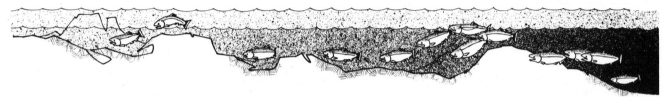

Large rivers usually have enough flow to allow salmon to move in almost anytime. They may hold in lower pools for several days waiting for a freshet to raise the river so they can move upstream.

Pacific Ocean will often have a tide pool running parallel to the beach for some distance before cutting through the sand bar at the mouth and spilling into the sea. A stream feeding into a protected bay like Puget Sound or Hood Canal will more often simply broaden out, sometimes dividing into many fingers that wind through the estuary flat to open water.

vulnerable to the fly, which is not to say, however, that a moving salmon won't strike. A substantial rain freshet, adding depth and volume to a stream, will result in salmon moving rapidly through the tide pools regardless of the tide, pausing only briefly on their way to the upstream lies.

Locating salmon in tide pools isn't difficult in that they occasionally break water and will seek out the deepest sec-

Salmon entering small coastal streams or rivers in areas having extreme tide fluctuations must sometimes wait for a high tide in order to get over sand bars into the tidal pools. The following out tide will often trap them for several hours until the next rise of water when they can again move upriver.

Depending on the size and character of a stream, and provided it hasn't been brutally urbanized, its tide pools may be surrounded by grassy flats and a scattering of tenacious trees; or it may be barely above the upper limit of a sandy beach or extend well up into the scrubby, wind-sculpted coastal conifers. There is a definite pulse beat attached to the tide pools of a river in that they are resting areas for flocks of migratory waterfowl and a variety of resident sea birds with the intertidal (the area between low and high tide) and supertidal (the area above high water) zones providing habitat for muskrats, weasels and other small wild creatures. For those carrying heavy-duty fly rods,

tions to hold in provided there is no other cover available. If a pool is located on a sharp bend, salmon will be schooled under the bank that has been carved out by heavy currents or seasonal spates. Tide pools often contain large logs or uprooted trees that have drifted downstream during winter floods and have become imbedded solidly into the mud banks. Next to and below every such log, tree or stump, a deep slot or hole develops that will attract salmon. During low tides it is common for salmon to school at the head of a pool awaiting the high water that will allow them to ascend to the next pool. Other fish may allow the increased stream flow or low water to push them down toward the tailout of a pool where they will school up until they feel the push of the tide turn to signal them upstream.

The opportunistic fly fisher commences working the tide pools while the main run of salmon is still schooling in the estuaries or offshore and continues to give them attention from time to time throughout the season. It is truly a rare day that tide pools are barren of fish during a major run and it is not uncommon to find them stacked with chinook and coho salmon. On small, coastal rivers, canny anglers will walk the beach watching for pods of fresh fish to splash through the riffles on a rising tide, wait for them to settle into the tide pools and begin casting from shore or an anchored boat.

Middle River

In the middle reaches of a salmon river there is yet another transformation. This is the part of a stream that many anglers consider prime fly casting water. It is here that the stream is traveling a course through a valley floor with nearly every bend forming a sloping, rocky beach on one side and a green, holding pool on the other. The pools can be comfortably waded and backcasts can be made without fear of sacrificing a pattern to the willows.

Every pool and slot in the midsection of a river rates attention since they nearly all will hold good numbers of

Salmon will hold in fairly shallow pools and runs if there are large boulders to buffer the current and break up the surface water to provide overhead cover. Sometimes it is difficult to work a fly in this type of holding water.

Lower to Middle River

Above the tide pools, West Coast rivers take on a different appearance. Most will have at least some public access or can be reached by hiking well-marked paths through the private lands of understanding people. These lower to middle stretches are often bordered with a heavy growth of willows or alder and the underbrush can be a nearly impenetrable tangle of berry brambles, nettles and devil's club. In other spots along the middle stretch, the underbrush barrier may not be nearly so menacing.

salmon. The best spots may be worth sitting on for several hours since they are likely to be stacked with both adult salmon and active, precocious jacks. Heads and tailouts of pools will continue to carry the greatest concentrations but the entire length of a pool should be worked with a variety of patterns and techniques before moving on to the next spot.

Some of the salmon in midriver will be wearing the first flush of spawning coloration and a few will have head and flanks vividly splashed with spawning hues. These fish are still vigorous — at times taking a fly eagerly — and have

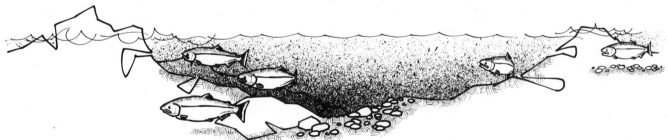

The head and tailout of classic, deep pools are favored by holding salmon. The midsection begins to hold fish as the run peaks, crowding pools throughout the river.

Salmon holding in the lower to middle stretch of a stream are generally found in deep slots along a bank, behind a current-breaking jam of down timber or around large boulders that offer respite. As always, the head and tail of any pool are worth a few casts and big bends that form green holes are prime salmon lies. While salmon prefer water a bit slower than that steelhead readily hold in, it is not prudent to pass up good steelhead drifts since they will attract salmon from time to time. It is never a good idea to dwell at an average spot for more than a short time, though, if there is an unattended honey hole just around the bend.

ample strength to test tackle. Each day, as the spawning urge intensifies, signaling them further upstream to eventually find spawning gravel, brighter, but rapidly darkening, salmon are arriving from the lower river to settle in prior to the final leg of the journey.

The Upper River

In the uppermost reaches, right up to the angling deadline, a river changes character again, primarily due to the quickening rate of fall from its high country source. Short, deep pools are followed by long, granite-sided chutes and whirling eddies. Interspersed throughout the upper reaches are shallow, gravel-bottomed runs. The spawning ritual begins here and continues well up into the headwaters and small feeder creeks. By season's end, the gravel runs will be choked with salmon, the kype-jawed bucks fighting over ripe henfish already busy digging redds in which to deposit their eggs.

Spawning salmon can be wheedled into grabbing a fly, particularly the males due to their combative nature, but they are thin, nearly spent, with barely enough strength remaining to complete the vital spawning process before dying. They are better left to propagate the runs. Besides, at least in Washington, such fishing is illegal.

Late in the season the persistent fly fisher — and one must be persistent to take salmon on the fly — is back to the lower river, even down to the tide pools. Chilling wind and rain squalls will be coming in off the ocean now, one after another, marking the onset of winter. It is here, where the river season began more than two months earlier, that it will end. Bundled in woollens, pile and raingear, the dedicated angler will punch cast after cast through the gray, imposing weather, hoping that a lot of perseverance — and a little luck — will result in one last hookup with a bright, battle-ready, late-run straggler fresh in from the Pacific.

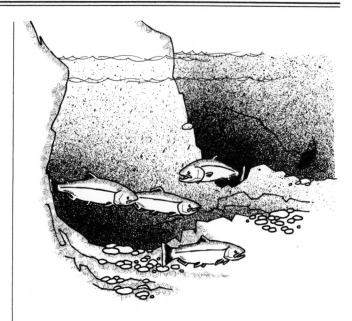

Salmon like deep pools but are often very difficult to move to a fly.

Obstructions such as tree roots and boulders deflect the water on the downstream side providing resting areas for salmon.

6.

Fishing Techniques – Casts and Retrieves

FINALLY, LOCATING FISH DOESN'T END THE contest. Too often, this is where the real frustration begins. Whether in fresh or salt water, there are special techniques that have been found to work much of the time, all wrung from countless hours of patient, but determined experimentation. Others wait to be discovered. For coho, chinook and pink salmon, some real, solid methods have been developed to get them to strike, while for chum and sockeye in salt water, much remains to be learned.

To the great benefit of the purveyors of fly tying materials and finished flies, most of us have a knee jerk reaction to the situation where salmon are jumping all around us, and yet refuse to take an interest in our most valiant efforts to hook them. We conclude that it just has to be that we're using the wrong fly. Wrong! That could well be the case, of course, and there's considerable space in this book devoted to the subject, but more than likely, the technique is at fault.

Our objective is to throw some light on the best of these techniques and launch you toward a more rewarding search for hookups.

SALTWATER ANGLING TECHNIQUES

Because of the constantly moving quarry and size of the arena, some rather highly-specialized techniques have evolved for taking salmon during their saltwater phase.

Approaches

Approaching deep chinook holding water in a motorboat at high speed is not a matter of great concern in terms of spooking the fish. Furthermore, some veteran lure and bait fishermen swear that surface-running coho and pinks are attracted to the air bubbles and spinning blades of the propeller, and they troll at relatively high speed with a short

line to take advantage of this concept. But when the case is casting to surface-feeding fish, nothing can put them down faster than the noise and vibration of a gas or diesel motor, especially when it is running at high speed in calm, shallow water. This creates a real problem, because most of the time surfacing salmon are moving faster than you can row a boat to keep in range. However, there is a good way to turn this to your advantage.

Upon spotting a pod of working fish some distance away, determine their direction of travel, start your motor, and make a wide circle, coming in well ahead and preferably upwind from them. Cut your motor and either row into an intercepting path or simply wait for the salmon to approach within casting range. As the fish move, or you are blown off course, "fine tune" your position with the oars. Repeat the process when the fish have passed you, and are well out of casting range.

Open salt water is usually as clear as a mountain lake. A fly fisher standing in a white, high-sided runabout may not realize how readily visible he is to his intended catch of the day. I used to have just such a boat, an 18-footer, with a white canvas top to boot. In order to keep from tangling my line, I stood on a large Igloo cooler, letting the fly line rest on top of the canvas canopy. Except under very subdued lighting, I kept wondering why the salmon always seemed to be surfacing just out of my casting range. It wasn't until I borrowed a friend's 12-foot aluminum cartopper that I noticed I was suddenly able to cast that extra 20 feet to get in range of the fish — or was it just maybe the fact that my profile was lower and I could approach the fish closer, without scaring them off. When I watched another friend regularly taking salmon at close range while casting seated in a canoe, the answer was obvious. My casting hadn't improved. My profile was just less threatening to the fish.

Carpeting in the bottom of your boat will also allow more frequent in-range casts, simply because it deadens the noise and allows a closer approach.

There is no question, if you keep in mind that your quarry is basically skittish and lives in clear water that carries sound readily, you'll catch more fish using techniques that offset these characteristics.

Casts

There are basically two specialized casts developed for this type of fishing, namely the *coho cast* for surface or near-surface feeding and waiting salmon, and the *lob shot* for deep-water fishing.

Coho Cast. As pointed out earlier, surface-feeding coho and pink salmon are almost always moving salmon — fast moving salmon. If you can't row fast enough to keep up with one, it stands to reason, you can't expect to have your fly in front of the fish if you insist on casting to the rise. If the fish can't see the fly, he can't strike it. Thus, the coho cast was born of necessity. The firmly entrenched trout fisherman has a hard time adjusting to it. The really classic caster is a pleasure to watch. He carries an almost full line in the air and after many false casts, presents his fly delicately on target. He never hurries, because his intended catch isn't going anywhere. Nor does he regularly have to cast long distances. The ancient quote that most trout are caught within 30 feet of the fisherman is probably reasonably accurate — for trout. For surfacing salmon, neither the 30-foot cast, nor the leisurely approach to casting, will collect many fish. It's an entirely different ball game.

The caster first must strip all the line he intends to cast from his reel onto the indoor-outdoor carpet in the boat under his feet. He then stretches his line to eliminate the inevitable coils, being careful not to step on it, thereby damaging his line. More importantly, he can avoid the frustration of thinking 80 feet, only to cut his cast short at 20 feet. With even a slight wind blowing, it is amazing how that line will take on a life of its own and actively crawl underfoot.

A salmon jumps or swirls. Instantly, the angler stands and starts his cast. One, two, or at most three false casts, using a double haul to increase line speed, and then he shoots his cast. When the fish broke water, he noted one of four indicators of direction the fish might be traveling in. If the fish showed a dark back, he knew the fish was going away from him. If it showed a white belly, it was swimming toward the boat. If it leaned to the left, it was moving in that direction and if it leaned to the right, it was probably headed that way.

Whatever direction is indicated, the fisherman presents his fly at least ten feet ahead of where the fish showed. If his retrieve fails to produce a strike, he roll casts to clear the water and repeats his cast 20 feet on the other side of the rise. If he still hasn't scored, he looks for the next fish to show. A delicate presentation isn't necessary. What counts is the speed of getting the line out. I like to think of the cast in terms of a bullfrog flicking his tongue out to snatch an unsuspecting fly from midair — fast and deadly.

And then there's the 30-foot myth for distance. Only under the failing light of evening will salmon be taken with such a short cast. The successful coho cast requires the caster to be comfortable with at least a 50-foot achievement. If he can produce 100 feet, so much the better. This sounds harder than it is. Constantly seeing fish break ten feet farther than you can reach automatically tends to stretch your ability. Practice does the rest.

Wind is the almost constant companion to this style of fishing, so it's necessary to learn to place your cast where you want, in spite of the wind. From a drifting boat, a cast with the wind is simple and ego building, because it goes so far with so little effort. The hitch is that no matter how fast your retrieve, you're always drifting over your line and therefore can't get any action in your fly. It is far better to cast at right angles to, or directly into, the wind, so that you are retrieving against a tight line. To do this requires throwing a tight loop — low to the water to get "under" the wind. Believe it or not, it works. Again, practice is the key to improvement, if not to perfection.

The coho cast is usually made with a full line rather than a shooting head. My favorite is the 20-foot sink tip or wet belly. This gives you the ability to lift the line off the water while at the same time getting the fly well below the surface. For some reason or other, salmon seem to strike more readily below the surface than on top, even if they're showing themselves by jumping, finning or swirling. A ten-foot wet tip presents the fly closer to the surface, and is also quite popular. There are times when a floating line works best, and certainly provides the most excitement watching the "V" of a following fish and the swirl of the strike. This line is most effective when fish are in shallow water a few feet deep as in the case of "waiters" in the fall off the rivermouths, or when fish are staying on top finning and feeding in a limited area in the rips.

Going the other direction, when fish are not showing, there is still the need for distance, but instead of leading the salmon, you need to get to their feeding depth. Sinking lines (Nos. 2 and 3) as well as the No. 4 or hi-speed, hi-d sinkers provide an array of choices. It's not at all unusual to try several different lines while searching for the fish. With two people fishing out of the same boat it's very useful to have one with say a wet-tip line and the other with a No. 3 sinking line, to bracket the depth. Many are the times when at midday fish are to be had with a hi-speed, hi-d line and that same evening, the wet-tip takes all the salmon. It's nice to have a full range of lines with you and to experiment until something produces — kind of like having a quiver full of arrows at your disposal.

Lob Shot. It would be difficult to think of successful deep water fly fishing when the salmon are feeding on baitfish without acknowledging the priority ranking of lead core, deep water express, cannonball and other such extra fast sinking shooting heads. Their development opened up a whole new world of deeper water to fly fishers, including those searching for salmon. Chinook are notorious for holding close to the bottom, and the other species frequently are down there too.

The lob shot is nothing more than a cast developed to handle these lines with efficiency. They are generally attached to a hundred feet of 25-pound soft monofilament and then to the micron backing. False casting to any extent can be hazardous to your health as anyone will attest who has been hit in the back of the head, driving home his forward cast with one of these heavyweight lines.

A normal shooting head is 30 feet long. However, if you use an 8-weight outfit like I do, you'd break the rod, casting the full head. Instead, the procedure is to cut off enough weight of line to balance your rod. Generally, this is one or two weights higher than your rod calls for. In other words, for an 8-weight rod, use a head section for a 9- or 10-weight rod. For a 700-grain, deep-water express I use only 12½ feet of the 30 feet. Therein lies the beauty of the lob shot. For short heads, no backcast is involved at all.

on a windy day. An outing with this kind of casting can reduce a normally composed fisherman into a driveling idiot. The only saving grace, and the one that needs to be constantly kept in mind to avert total frustration, is that fish caught are usually big, making it all worthwhile.

My friend, Jim Darden, from Bellingham, Washington, has had much to do with development of this type of deep water fishing for chinook. He moved from the dry eastern Washington climate with its lake fishing to the northern end of Puget Sound some years ago. Since nobody told him it couldn't be done, he enthusiastically worked out a system that has had a high rate of return. His cast is the lob shot,

Steep dropoffs and ledges can be very productive, especially for chinook salmon. To reach the fish, long drops with extra-fast sinking or lead-core shooting heads are required. Saltwater fly casters who master this technique often use depth finders to locate such spots and consistently take chinook salmon from depths of 90 feet — or even deeper.

The procedure for the caster is to strip off as much head and monofilament as he can cast on the carpeting in the bottom of the boat. Next, he stretches the monofilament to eliminate the coils. Now he flips the head and several feet of monofilament back of him and lets it hang in the water. He comes forward slowly with the rod and makes a forward haul on the line, releasing it at the point of maximum power. The whole works should fly through the air and land farther out than he ever thought he could cast. That is, if he made sure he had all the coils out of the monofilament, and he wasn't stepping on the line. Being much lighter in weight than fly line, the monofilament has a habit of tangling around anything sticking up in the boat, or that failing, around itself. This characteristic is only aggravated

except that he uses lead core and with more line makes a backcast *very carefully* before shooting it off into the horizon. The part that is unique is his way of getting to the right depth. His portable fish finder shows him how deep the bottom is and having an engineering background, he figures out the time it takes for his shooting head to get to that depth, with a knowledge of the sink rate, and some allowance for wind and tide. An alarm stop watch does the rest. Although it is more normal to fish at depths of less than 40 feet, he is undaunted by depths of twice that. Of course, this may mean casting as far as he can, which is very far indeed, and then stripping out additional line so no drag exists until he begins his retrieve. The wait for the line to settle to the bottom may take several minutes to achieve.

Jim Darden, Bellingham, Washington, with large chinook taken from 90 feet of water. Jim uses a countdown system and a sinking shooting taper to take salmon from deep saltwater slots. BMF

In other words, he stands up, casts, sets his stop watch, strips off extra line, sits down and waits for his alarm to go off.

This type of cast gives you lots of time to relax and appreciate your surroundings — sea lions, cormorants, murres, and even clouds rolling by. It does put your fly where the fish are, too.

Retrieves

To consistently catch salmon on flies you will want to start thinking like a salmon — what triggers it to strike — how the zooplankton and baitfish act when they're either frightened or crippled — and then making your fly consciously behave that way. This means mentally "seeing" your fly under water as you retrieve, doing the things you want it to do to imitate the actions that tease, or infuriate, the salmon into striking.

Confidence that what you're doing will produce, incredibly enough, has a lot to do with success. Just to cast your fly out and retrieve it in a routine fashion doesn't hold a candle to the hard concentration and anticipation of a strike that quite frequently puts a fish on your line.

Zooplankton Retrieves. When salmon are either actively feeding on zooplankton in winter and spring or are in their "waiting" period off the rivermouths in the fall, they seem particularly susceptible to the same type of retrieve. This has been fine-tuned over time, but its "birth" seemed more like a short series of revelations for me.

The first of these came about on a beautiful October day when I was out fishing for waiting coho with my old friend, Al Allard, off a shallow rivermouth in southern Puget Sound. Standing side by side in his boat, anchored just out of the outgoing tidal current, we cast repeatedly. I was watching Al out of the corner of my eye to try to learn something about his retrieve. He was using a dry line, a 9-foot leader tapered to 6-1/2 pounds, and a sparsely-tied, long-winged Royal Coachman bucktail on a short-shank No. 6 hook. I had on a shorter-winged Polar Shrimp of the same size. Otherwise, my outfit was a duplicate of Al's. Both of us were apparently retrieving in the same way, but, from my perspective, there was something terribly wrong. *He* was catching fish after fish, while *I* couldn't tempt the first strike. Finally, in total frustration, I told Al, "Give me your fly. You've caught enough fish for one day, anyhow. I need to see if that's what's making the difference."

Fortunately for me, Al was very generous, and did exactly as I asked. Armed with his "killer" fly, I cast out and started my retrieve with great confidence, expecting a strike at any instant. Nothing. Again, and again, I repeated the process with the same result. Once more, I ate humble pie and said "Al, I'm not doing something you were doing. Watch my retrieve and tell me what's different."

As he looked more carefully at my maneuvers with the fly, he spotted the key.

"Shorten up your strip to six inches to a foot in length, make it snap at the end of the stroke and move it. They like a fast moving fly."

I thought I'd been doing these things, but apparently not emphatically enough. Anyhow, using the revised retrieve, I was into six big coho, one after the other, before the bite was over.

Thereafter, I had great success with this retrieve, but had a hard time accurately describing it. One evening the following spring, I was out on the water with Frank Haw and his wife, Angela, trying to show them how it was done. The fishing was good, but the correct retrieve was critical to success. My explanation to Frank wasn't getting across, when Angela, a registered nurse, broke in and said, "Frank, it's just like shaking down a thermometer." Never have I heard it described so well before or since.

Two variations have added to the retrieve's effectiveness. The first of these I've named the "amphipod hop." Live amphipods, in a saltwater aquarium, were observed to swim in a short hopping or jiggling motion. Since they form an important part of the saltwater diet of cohos and pinks, it seemed reasonable to believe the fish would be attracted by a similar action on the retrieve. They were. While continuing a normal zooplankton retrieve without slowing down, merely add a rapid side to side twitching of the rod tip. This is a little tough to master, since it's like rubbing your stomach and patting your head at the same time. But, it works. I use this most often as an extra teaser when I see a salmon following close behind my fly, but not hitting it, or when I feel repeated tugs but no strike, indicating the fish is nipping on the tail of the fly without grabbing it. A large percentage of these salmon will climb all over the fly shortly after the amphipod hop is started.

The second variation is especially good when visibility is

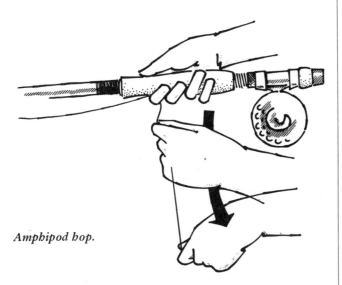

Amphipod hop.

poor, such as in roily water, at daybreak, or just before nightfall. In these cases, salmon can usually be seen jumping or finning, but won't take the fast moving fly. The answer, many times, is to make several strips about half normal speed, pause, letting the fly settle, and then repeat the process. Most often, the strike comes just as you begin to strip after a pause. When you think about it, there's a good reason why this is so effective. In the limited visibility, it's much harder for the salmon to spot the normally fast moving fly. By giving them more time to zero in on their prey, they're much more likely to see and attack your offering.

Humbleness is reportedly great for building your character. With this prospect in mind, I want to reveal a major annual blank in my understanding of what works for surface feeding cohos and pinks in May and June. At this time of year the fish are still feeding heavily on zooplankton and range in size from two to three pounds. During the early morning hours with little or no wind to ruffle the surface, it is not uncommon to see a hundred or more fish dimpling, finning or just plowing along under the surface, indicating their presence by the "V" wake created by their movement. Euphausids, amphipods, and crab larvae appear as large clouds in and around the light tide rips. This is a rare opportunity for the fly fisher to really show his talent.

However, most often such occasions are marked by total failure. The feeding process is so easy for the fish they just can't be bothered chasing a fast moving fly. To date, limited success has been achieved using a 12-foot or longer leader tapered to about four pounds and a short-shank No. 6, 8 or even 10 fly. The approach and cast is made very carefully, as it would be to a spring creek brown trout. Parallel to and close to a minor tide rip is a good place to work. The fly, instead of whipping through the water with blinding speed, should be inched along much as you would fish emerging chironomids or mayflies in a freshwater lake.

Undoubtedly, a way to take fish routinely under these circumstances will reveal itself in the near future, but we're not there yet.

Baitfish Retrieves. Important as zooplankton are in salmon diets, there's no substitute for baitfish when it comes to putting on weight. Chinook spend most of their saltwater existence in the pursuit and capture of small fish for feed, while the other species, in varying degrees, use baitfish to fill themselves out as they close in on maturity. For coho and pinks, this means by the time they've hit the three-pound mark.

Baitfish of all kinds can move with amazing speed when frightened, so it's logical that the salmon, in their role as efficient predators, would seek out the slower, weaker or otherwise crippled members of a school. The retrieve that is going to work best, therefore, needs to emphasize the irregular and erratic movement of a wounded specimen, rather than rely on a steady or regularly repetitive motion which would imitate a healthy and difficult meal to catch.

In June and July it is common to see herring and sand lance of the year in dense schools along the shorelines. These will be only an inch to three inches in length. Salmon frequently locate these schools in early morning and evening, charging into them in water sometimes only a foot deep. This again is visible casting and retrieving with a high degree of excitement attached to it. It is easy to forget that a delicate presentation and retrieve can sometimes be required to produce in such thin water.

Barry Thornton, of Comox, British Columbia, probably best known for his involvement with steelhead, has nonetheless done his share of saltwater salmon fly fishing. Several years ago, he and his son put in a glorious several days off Quadra Island discovering the wonders of this type of fishing in water so shallow the trollers didn't dare work it. The bottom was blackened by schools of small herring, readily visible in the gin clear water. Pods of eight- to ten-pound coho were driving through the bait. Barry, using a 20-foot sink-tip line, a 16-foot leader tapered to six-pound test and a small "Pink Minnow" fly, cast ahead of the scattered herring. His retrieve was short, continual four- to six-inch strips alternated with a brief pause after several strips. The strikes came as he resumed his stripping and the fight was on. Numerous heavy-shouldered coho fell for this retrieve before moving on in their southerly migration.

By late July and early August the salmon are feeding heavily on the fast growing herring and sand lance. Dave Hurn, of Sooke, British Columbia, has fly fished the waters off Vancouver Island for many years, and describes the situation during this timeframe as follows:

"Evidence of the feeding fish is commonly given by the

Ferguson preparing his 12-foot boat for a salmon excursion in Puget Sound. LJ

frantic scurries of driven herring marked by the equally frenzied activity of gulls, terns or diving birds. At first glance, there is no apparent pattern to the outbursts of the harried herring. Casual observation suggests that the salmon, cruising at depth, encounter a group of herring, take up attack pattern, slash, feed, and move on. This, I believe, is rarely the case. More often than not, there is a layer of herring dispersed several feet thick over an area up to an acre or more, and the predatory salmon pack, sensing feeding opportunity with escape depth, move upwards, cutting out and cutting up the herring. Constantly cruising, taking advantage of surprise, the movement of the coho may be marked by the successive locations of herring boils, enabling the angler to reasonably guess in what direction the fish are moving.

The impatient angler may be drawn in by the challenge of surface slashing salmon and tend to place a fly hurriedly to the herring boil and "bucktail" by hand. While occasionally successful, the method suffers poor odds, for the slashing fish are few, moving upwards and downwards very fast and there are too many real herring present.

What is really happening below? The boils of herring are being created by a few fish whose method is to drive and confine a group of herring to the surface, and by rapid and violent thrusts, injure and stun as many as possible in that brief flurry at the surface. The injured herring drop from the pack, twitching, arcing and whirling, to be consumed by the feeder salmon below. For every fish which is in attack there are five to ten fish beneath which, without haste or gymnastics, clean up the drifting, crippled herring.

Anticipation of the likely next herring boil and the presentation of the fly to that area is the game.

A fast sinking line is essential for there is *never* time to move the boat. The cast should be made to account for the stream of the tide, and mended to a depth which seems beneath the herring. At first it is sloppy: slack line to the sinking fly. Then as the line pulls full, the fly is worked. Twitch, pause, short draw, pause, twitch, draw, pause, and so on. The line should be fingered or inched rather than hauled, all the while keeping the fly at below-herring depth.

The take of the fly is not a mad, rod-rattling strike, but rather some subtle hint of change which tells you to firmly and fully draw out the slack to set the hook. Most fish are hooked deep in the mouth, in the gill arches, the base of the tongue or even in the soft of the throat. In the first few seconds, you will only know you have a fish — most likely a coho but very occasionally a feeder chinook, a rockfish or a small lingcod which sometimes attend the coho pack."

For this action, Dave uses a fast sinking line, a seven- to nine-foot leader tapered to a four- or six-pound tippet. His flies are shown in the pattern section of the book in some detail, but are essentially the size of the baitfish being imitated.

Bill Nelson, a charter member of the Federation of Fly Fishers and a saltwater salmon fly fisher for over 30 years, resides at April Point, British Columbia. In conjunction with Warren Peterson, owner of April Point Lodge, he and others at the lodge provide a fly fishing guide service for the several species of salmon in those waters. So far as I know, it is still one of the very few in existence oriented specifically to feeding salmon rather than milling fish in the estuaries or spawners on their upriver journey.

"A day on the water in their company is worth five years of fishing on your own." This comment came from my notes covering a notable September fishing trip made in 1977.

Using a No. 4 shooting head with a six- to ten-foot leader testing ten pounds at the tip to turn over the four-inch long flies tied on 2/0 or 3/0 hooks, Bill retrieves in different ways to fit the circumstances.

For surfacing herring he lets the fly sink below the bait-fish and uses a strip retrieve, slowly if zooplankton are also showing, and faster if there's a herring boil.

When tied up to the kelp, fishing the tidal current, he dead drifts his fly into the down current swing. At this point, he starts with a couple of fast pulls to get the fishes' attention, followed by long, medium speed pulls.

I had only to watch Bill and Warren perform using these techniques to realize I was not in the company of amateurs. They had absolutely no trouble taking coho from four to seven pounds during my stay. My only regret was that I couldn't have remained longer to see if some of their expertise couldn't be absorbed by osmosis. As it was, enough of it rubbed off so that I caught several nice fish, both feeder chinook and coho in the same size range.

Farther north, Errol Champion, former president of the Federation of Fly Fishers, now residing in Juneau, Alaska, fishes from June through September for maturing coho, pinks and sockeye. Fishing at depths of three to 15 feet with a fast sinking shooting head, a leader of just 4½ feet tapered to a ten-pound tippet and flies from No. 4 to 1/0, he allows his fly to sink to the desired depth before begin-

ning his retrieve. For his most frequent catch, the pinks and coho, he uses a fast, erratic strip of various lengths. In contrast, the few sockeye taken responded best to a dead drift or short three-inch strips. For these, a fly of hot pink chenille, with a hot pink or white wing, was preferred over the standard bucktail used for the other species.

The following excerpt from a story by Errol published in *Alaska Magazine* several years ago illustrates how well his technique can work.

"I cast my fly about 70 feet toward a school of salmon that was cruising between our pram and shore. It sank two to three feet and after half a dozen strips of the line, the rod tip jerked, the slack line snapped tight and the Hardy reel immediately sang of a running fish. For the next 20 minutes I battled the coho, before bringing it alongside.

That afternoon provided some of the best fishing Jerry and I could ever expect. Together we hooked, landed and released more than 30 coho and pink salmon. The coho ranged from seven to 14 pounds, and the pinks from four to seven pounds. Nearly every cast produced at least one strike and often we missed the first fish to have a second strike on the same retrieve. Many salmon threw the fly on their first or second run. By night we were exhausted and after a quick snack, crawled into our sleeping bags."

Deep water retrieves for chinook are not noticeably different, except normally slower. The big thing is to get down to the right level and make it erratic. A strip from six inches to a couple of feet at medium speed, ended with a snap of the wrist with occasional pauses thrown in to let the fly flutter down, will provide enough unusual behavior to the fly to bring about takes. If fishing really deep water, bring

Anglers fishing a beach on Vancouver Island, British Columbia. — Gary Strodtz photo

Oregon anglers launch these rugged and highly specialized boats right through the surf to get at the salmon offshore. BMF

it in about 40 feet, then let it back out, retrieve 40 feet and repeat once more before bringing it to the surface. This will provide a lot more time for the fly to work in the strike zone.

Late this winter, after listening to Jim Darden describe his chinook techniques at a Saltwater Salmon Fly Fishing Seminar we put on in Tacoma, Washington, my special fishing comrade, Bill Ludwig, and I decided to try it all out. From our navigational charts we had selected an area close to home in southern Puget Sound with water depth of about 30 feet, a high tide change, and a minor reef where the outgoing tide would bring food over the reef, with salmon expected to lie just in front or behind. An underwater boulder would provide a similar trout lie in a river. I unlimbered my 9-foot, 8-weight graphite fitted out with the front end of a 700-grain shooting head attached to the customary monofilament running line. Although it was raining, there was encouragement as no wind was blowing.

After making a wide circle with the boat, we motored in well uptide from the shoal, cut the motor and started to drift. I lobbed the 3½-inch olive-backed tube fly out to the edge of the current and let it sink with the line for a 25-second countdown. I was hung on the bottom in nothing flat. We worked our way back, and Bill retrieved the fly undamaged. I resharpened the hook. Another run to the head of the rip, and another drift. A third and fourth try

was made. Still nothing. I had changed to a countdown of 17 seconds to keep from getting hung up, but knew I was still in the fish zone.

About the fifth drift through, making the usual pronounced two-foot erratic retrieve, pausing occasionally to let it settle, I was within 20 feet of the boat when there was a rolling flash of silver and all hell broke loose. The salmon roared off into the backing, wallowing or jumping at the end of each run. Only barbless hooks are legal, so you always say a prayer when a good fish gets on the other end. I said one. Blackmouth fortunately run straight out without twisting and flailing around, and this one was no exception. When netted, it weighed seven pounds, and measured 26 inches. For a resident of Alaska or British Columbia, this isn't a avery large fish, but where the average feeder chinook is between three and six pounds, a seven-pounder in these waters looks like, and is, a trophy on a cast fly.

To make the day complete, we decided to fish for the 14- to 16-inch coho that were starting to show on the surface. As we joined our friends on the coho grounds, one of them asked if we'd done any good. I held up one finger, so they motored over to see. I had shoved the chinook under the bow seat of my 12-footer. Only a little of the fish stuck out. When they looked over the side and spotted the size of the tail, the comment: "Go to hell, Ferguson," was the sweetest music I'd ever heard.

Toward dusk, Bill and I landed several resident coho and headed for home — well satisfied fishermen to say the least. Using the right techniques had paid off in spades.

Bucktailing. Bucktailing is the art of trolling a bucktail fly of a size to imitate baitfish in the area. Whatever baitfish flies work in fly casting will also work for this method, although a larger, bushier model is often in order. This is not fly fishing under the I.G.F.A. rules, but it is still a lot of fun, and a way to locate fish when they are scattered. Originating in British Columbia close to 40 years ago, it is effective, especially for coho and pinks, but also does well on chinook when they're near the surface. The principle is to drag the fly on the surface 25 to 40 feet behind the boat in a zigzag fashion for maximum effectiveness. Tide rips and the kelp edges are favored spots. Speed should be two to four miles per hour so that the unweighted fly is just below the surface, creating a "V" wake, but not a rooster tail. The number one rule of thumb for coho in this situation is, "If you don't get a hit, go faster." The strike under these circumstances can be breathtaking. If a husky coho can be seen, making a "V" behind your fly, but won't take, try dropping it back quickly by stripping off line, or strip it in fast. Regular pulling on the line in one-foot jerks is tiring, but it will add immeasurably to your catch. Be ready for a hard strike.

Catch and Release

Many times salmon will need to be released after capture. This can be for a variety of reasons. Seasons may be closed on certain species. There may be minimum or maximum legal sizes, or the fly fisher may elect to fish solely for the pleasure of it, and not to put any in the box. Whatever the reason, it's important to practice release methods that will ensure a maximum survival rate. It is also essential that the fly fisher realize there is always some hooking mortality no matter how careful he is, so that if he intends to keep fish, he should retain those that are bleeding, have been hooked through an eye or have taken the fly in the gills or throat. He should do this rather than sorting out the biggest and brightest fish with which to awe family and friends. Attention to the following points will ensure more fish surviving to fight another day.

When salmon are smolting and during their entire saltwater existence, the scales become quite loose, and prone to falling off on contact. Even though they'll regenerate, any significant scale loss can cause mortality due to reverse osmosis, whereby too much salt is absorbed in the body of the fish through the unprotected skin. This situation is quite different from that of salmon in fresh water, where the scales are tight, as is also the case with trout found in inland waters. It is essential to recognize this special problem in handling and releasing saltwater salmon.

First, use a rod and a leader tippet that will allow you to land your fish promptly. This way you can release the fish before exhaustion limits its chances for survival.

Second, don't bring the fish in the boat or even touch it, if possible. This means leaving it in the water. A net, especially one with rigid plastic webbing, will not only remove lots of scales, but will damage the eyes. Instead, bring the salmon alongside your boat, reach over with a pair of needle-nose pliers, grasp the hook and turn it over, thereby releasing the fish. Even better is a device developed by the staff of the Washington Department of Fisheries. An ordinary teacup hanger is screwed into a piece of doweling which, incidentally, can be cut at a length equalling the prevailing minimum

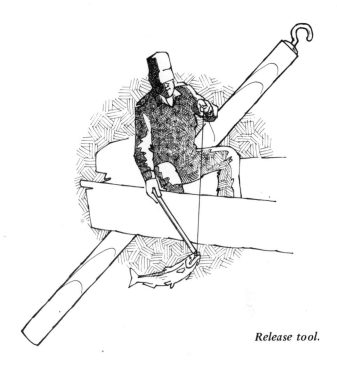

Release tool.

legal size. With the fish ready for release, merely loop the teacup hanger on the end of the dowel through the bend of the hook, lift up on the dowel, and at the same time pull down on the part of the leader leading to the fly line. With nothing to hold the hook in, the fish drops off immediately. Using barbless hooks (in Washington's Puget Sound, the only legal way to fish for salmon) makes this procedure very simple and fast.

Shore fishers in salt water should use the same techniques, taking care not to let the fish bang themselves on the rocks in shallow water.

Finally, if the salmon is so exhausted it cannot swim away in an upright and lively condition, hold it gently under the stomach away from the gills with one hand and by the wrist, just ahead of the tail with the other. Rock it back and forth until it is breathing normally, and swims vigorously out of your hands.

Stretching the supply of fish by reducing handling mortality is an increasingly important factor in maintaining our sport.

FRESHWATER ANGLING TECHNIQUES

I was fishing on Washington's Olympic Peninsula in August just before Labor Day of 1956 when I saw my first salmon come to a cast fly. It was on the Quillayute River not far below the mouth of the Sol Duc. The morning was drizzly and a gray overcast shrouded the conifer tops overhead. The river was clear and low as there hadn't been any substantial rains for a few days. There were at least a dozen nice sea-run cutthroat trout in the pool I was working and several large chinook salmon, probably stragglers of the main summer run. The sea-runs were my quarry and my tackle, a brand new 7-foot Phillipson fiberglass rod and a 6-weight line wound onto a small J.W. Young reel, was just right.

A No. 8 Thor aroused the interest of a cutthroat on the first cast and after a short, vigorous battle, I beached a fat 15-incher. I took two more cuts, then noticed the salmon beginning to move in an elongated formation from about mid-pool to the tailout. Without hardly considering the possibility of getting a strike, I stripped off some more line, cast and let the little Thor swing down a bit further. A bronze-flanked chinook of about 20 pounds casually

A typical pool on the Smith River in northern California. The Smith is noted for fall chinook salmon of exceptional size. LJ

grabbed the fly while making a turn toward the tail of the pool and was indifferent for a few seconds until it found out that something was impeding its progress — then the fun began!

For the next five minutes that salmon literally plowed the pool bottom into a sandy cloud, spooking every other fish out and giving my light outfit a monumental trial by fire. At just the moment when a giddy rush came over me that I might actually land this monster, it ripped off upstream, peeling out my fly line, 50-odd yards of backing and redlining the little Young before the leader snapped. The remainder of the day was spent stalking cutthroat but every time I spotted a salmon I would send a cast or two in its direction. While I did manage to take several more cuts, I could muster only casual interest from any of the chinook but it mattered little. The seed was planted and the throbbing strength of that first river salmon against my fly rod remains vivid to this day.

Despite the fact that the roots of fly fishing for Pacific salmon were established more than a hundred years ago and that a fresh run salmon of any size is a noble adversary when taken fairly with a fly rod, there is a lingering notion among a great many fly casters that taking these fish on a fly is a lowly pursuit and that the Pacific salmon is inferior to the steelhead or Atlantic salmon. In his fine volume, *The Well Tempered Angler*, the late Arnold Gingrich, a devoted fly fisherman of unexcelled skill, and founding father of *Esquire* magazine, had this to say regarding Pacific salmon, "And when I say salmon I include, of course, grilse and sea trout, sea-run browns, brooks or salters and rainbows and steelheads, but excluding Pacific salmon, which as far as this form of fishing (fly fishing) is concerned is something that comes in cans." Arnold Gingrich penned *The Well Tempered Angler* in 1959.

Even today with the tremendous increase in fly fishing publications there aren't very many anglers who are aware of the viability of this exciting and high quality fishery. The thinking persists by and large that Pacific salmon can only be taken with any hope for success by trolling the salt chuck or by using hardware or bait in fresh water. The fact is, however, that the fly fisher determined to learn a little about the techniques of the salmon fishing game is likely to do every bit as well as the skilled bait fisherman.

The Wet Fly Swing

In every type of salmon or steelhead fly fishing technique, there is some form of the basic downstream swing of the wet fly employed. This method of sweeping the line in an arc from the far side of a pool around until the fly hangs nearly straight below the angler's position is effective, with certain variations, on all salmonid forms. With Atlantic salmon or steelhead, the swing of the fly may be just under the surface or actually skittering on top with some fuss since these fish will rise actively at times. Pacific salmon are not nearly as prone to rise so the most effective wet fly presentation is deep with the pattern riding close to the bottom of the pool.

Whenever possible, depending on water volume and clarity, it is a good idea to first look for salmon in a pool. This can be accomplished by wearing a good pair of polaroids to cut the surface glare. There is comfort in knowing for certain that a pool has several salmon in it as chances of hooking one improve proportionately with the number of holding fish. When utilizing the wet fly swing, it is important to get the fly down quickly so it will have a long ride at the level where the salmon are lying, thus being presented to the greatest number of fish on every cast.

The initial cast should be made slightly downstream from straight across and be allowed to swing freely through the arc. By the time it has quartered downstream, the fly should be riding deep and the line drawing tight in the current. When the swing of the fly is ending, below the angler's position, it should be bumping and dragging along bottom. If the fly did not reach bottom, the next cast should also be downstream but mended to slow the drift, allowing it additional time to sink. If there is reason to believe that the fly is still not being presented deeply enough, ensuing casts should be sent straight across or even slightly upstream to increase sinking time during the line swing. Most anglers avoid a quartering upstream cast if at all possible since it allows the fly to drift with no line control for some distance before the slack tightens up. The take of a salmon can be very subtle at times, not unlike a trout picking up a drifting nymph, so any loss of line control can allow a fish time to mouth a fly for a few seconds and reject it without the angler knowing that there had been a strike at all.

When using the wet fly swing, we usually start with short casts and lengthen subsequent casts until we have the fly working at the comfortable limits of our casting abilities. For most of us this will be the 60- to 80-foot range. There aren't many fly casters who can maintain control of a longer cast than this and many highly successful anglers land salmon in enviable numbers without ever casting beyond 50 feet. When a section of a pool has been fished thoroughly and there is room to move, we need only take a step or two downstream (or upstream if such is the case) and repeat the process. A salmon pool can be covered completely and efficiently using the wet fly swing with only minor adjustments in cast placement and line mending to ensure that every inch of the pool has been probed.

The wet fly swing is the cornerstone for all our fishing techniques and the importance of learning to master it cannot be too strongly stated. Regardless of where our salmon angling adventures take us, there will not be many situations on any river when we can't present a fly to a salmon with the wet fly swing or a creative variation of it.

The Downstream Drift

Most easily accomplished from a drift boat or raft, the downstream drift can, on occasion, urge salmon into striking in spectacular fashion. It works very well on coho, chinook, sockeye, and chum salmon. Oregon-based guide, Denny Hannah, with whom I fish at least once annually and

Oregon fishing guide Denny Hannah prepares to revive a chinook salmon for release. Hannah feels that salmon should be released only if they respond well to revival efforts. Fish that are extremely weak or bleeding should be dispatched and added to the day's catch. LJ

more often if I have a chance, has become so confident of the downstream drift for fall chinook that he rarely lines the boat up on a salmon hole for any other presentation. The first salmon we hooked while fishing together fell for a downstream drift in a pool just above tidewater on the Sixes River in southern Oregon. While the battle terminated in favor of the chinook, which showed us a tail broad as a kitchen broom, Denny decided to line us up the same way on the next drop just to make sure that the hookup hadn't been the direct result of an overly generous measure of his renowned Irish luck.

"The salmon will be holding just at the butt of that deadhead log on the deep side of the pool, Les," Denny said. "Where do you want me to line up the boat?"

"About ten feet above the upper end of the log," I answered as I stripped several yards of line from the Hardy. "I want to make a short cast and shake out some slack so the fly drifts drag-free directly down through the fish."

As Denny positioned the boat, I honed the barb of a No. 4 Rusty Squirrel to a point sharp enough that it would catch when dragged across my thumbnail. The casting distance was no more than 30 feet and my first cast sailed a bit, smacking down right over the holding water on a tight line. The surface exploded in a shower of spray but the fly wasn't taken. I shortened the next cast and shook some slack out through the guides. The line drifted drag-free into the holding area, then suddenly just took off! I dropped the rod tip until I felt firm pressure, then drove home the hook with three hard stabs of the 8-weight boron rod. Our luck held — even improved — as our second salmon of the day, a fat, mint-bright 14-pounder, was brought to net.

Denny dropped the salmon into the fish box and said, "This downstream drift should really work well at the Honey Hole, up near the hatchery on the Elk River. If we hustle we can make it up there and put in for a short drift."

Less than an hour later we were moving into the Honey Hole, a big, green pool that pushes against a rock cliff, then tails off to the right into a long, fast chute. Denny lowered the anchor to hold us just above what he called, "the honey part of the hole." Before beginning to cast, I rigged up Denny's fly rod with a floating shooting head with a 10-foot sinking tip. He got the first cast laid out and had an immediate strike that yanked the rod tip into the water and snapped the leader tippet almost at the same instant.

Looking at me, Denny wiggled his red eyebrows and said, "Get your line in there, Les. These chinook are prime candidates for the downstream drift."

I worked several drifts of the fly down into the honey part of the hole, then feeling a light tug, tug, tug, I leaned into the rod and was fast to a good fish. It turned out to be a dark-headed but firm-fleshed 12-pounder. It was a happy drift the rest of the way to camp where we landed just after sundown and moments ahead of the first hard rain of the day.

The most important aspect of the downstream drift is that the srike, or take, of the fly is oftentimes easily detected. As the fly drifts by, a salmon will turn and grab it, then make a swing back into its holding position. This pickup of the fly and corresponding swing back into position is telegraphed to the angler either by a gentle tugging action or a decided tightening of the fly line. Care must be

taken at this moment to remain calm and not to pull the hook from the salmon's mouth by attempting to set it too quickly. A salmon will hold the fly for the time it takes to return to its holding station after the pickup. *It is vital to drop the rod tip and wait until the line has tightened enough to pull out most of the slack before reefing back to set the hook.*

Although it can be worked very easily from a boat, the downstream drift is also an excellent technique for the bank angler to use in certain situations. It is almost always a good method of fishing the deep, or slot side of a pool where a wet fly swing would take the fly out of productive water rather than through it for much of the drift. The downstream drift can also be used to advantage wherever the riffle at the head of a pool forms a buildup of gravel that can be negotiated without too much foolhardy wading and this will usually occur where the riffle dumps into an eddy that in turn feeds a deep rock- or sand-bottomed pool. From a position on the gravel bar, both the eddy and the adjoining pool can be worked very effectively with the downstream drift.

The downstream drift can be accomplished as described when we were fishing from Hannah's drift boat by casting short and releasing slack to be carried downstream by the current. It can also be performed with an "S" cast. The "S" cast is made by stopping the power stroke of the cast up short and wiggling the rod tip back and forth which drops the line onto the water in a series of serpentine bends.

The Downstream Cast and Retrieve

There are times when casting downstream and slowly inching the fly back through a pool will produce strikes when a standard swing or drift of the fly isn't working. It is also a method that can be used in conjunction with the downstream drift by letting the fly drop drag-free through the holding area and then retrieving it ultra slowly back through the same spot. The downstream cast and retrieve is pretty standard among anglers who line up across a good salmon pool in small skiffs so closely together that they can only work straight downstream and it is the best method of working an eddy that doesn't have enough current to move a fly along at all.

A day early in the fall chinook season found angling guide Todd Hannah and I enjoying fantastic autumn weather while drifting the Elk River through stands of Douglas fir, cedar and myrtle and basking in unseasonable sunshine but more than a little frustrated since we'd lost two fish and with the water extremely low and clear, not many fresh run salmon were moving in from the Pacific. We slid into a nice hole that was sufficiently deep even with the low water and decided to have a bite of lunch before trying our luck.

With sandwiches, fruit and coffee finished, Todd positioned the boat so that we could take maximum advantage of the deepest part of the pool. Twenty minutes of casting gave us a zero, then while I was aimlessly bringing a small, green Comet along the bottom with a slow retrieve, my rod tip slammed downward and a shiny, 20-inch jack chinook cartwheeled into the air and took off in a fast burst across the pool. Seconds later, Todd set the hook into another bright jack that fell for the crawling retrieve. During the next hour we caught and released several more jacks before relinquishing the spot to three anglers anchored upstream where the action was non-existent. At day's end, near the takeout, we boated a bright henfish of 17 pounds that had made it through the skinny tide pools. It also fell to a downstream cast and retrieve.

The downstream cast and retrieve is used very successfully by the fly casting groups who line the tide pools of salmon rivers from the Chetco in southern Oregon to the Eel in northern California. Since the skiffs are rarely anchored more than a few feet apart and reach from bank to bank, there is precious little room for a standard wet fly swing. Success for these anglers is most often attributed to a very practical application of the downstream cast and retrieve, or the downstream drift brought back with a slow retrieve. I sat on the bank of the Chetco River one sunny November afternoon and enjoyed watching a group from the Sacramento Fly Casters Club work a pool just above Highway One with impressive results.

Most of the anglers had the little eight-foot prams tricked out for maximum comfort, complete with padded seats, small ice chests and all the basic requirements a dedicated fly fisher might need during a session on the river. Using overhead casts to avoid driving a fly into a neighbor's anatomy, the anglers would send extremely long lines directly downstream using heavy, extra-fast sinking shooting heads, then wait a few minutes until they were certain that the fly

was resting on bottom before starting a slow retrieve alternated with dropping the fly back from time to time, a technique employed to keep it close to the bottom. When one of the casters hooked a fish — and several did during the time I was watching, he would hoist the anchor if need be and drift away from the others in order to have room to play the salmon out.

The bank angler can use the downstream cast and retrieve to advantage, especially on small to medium size streams. I often use this technique when working the holding pools on the Green River as it winds between the towns of Kent and Auburn, Washington. The pools host chinook starting in September with coho showing up about mid-October. One such pool, lying below an old sweeper log that has dug in solidly to the bottom, not only affords good fishing but when the water is low and clear before the first heavy seasonal rains have added volume and color to its flow, I can sometimes see the salmon move to my retrieved fly.

I prefer to wade nearly to midriver, provided the water is low enough when working this pool, taking station just above the sweeper log where the water tumbles over it, digging out a long emerald green cut. A moment of peering through my polaroids will nearly always ease my insecurities as I spot one, then another, and another salmon milling at the lower end of the pool. My cast is made straight downstream with several seconds allowed for the line to sink

Sacramento Fly Casters Club lined up just above tidewater on Oregon's Chetco River. They are casting straight downstream and retrieving flies back through the pool. LJ

before bringing the fly back slowly, in a crawling motion, through the salmon. Most strikes occur deep in the lower end of the pool, a sudden resistance telegraphed through the rod from a fish strong and unseen. Occasionally though, I am rewarded by the sight of a fine salmon moving out of the green depths to grab the offering in a classic, swinging strike.

Another situation where the downstream cast and retrieve can be applied is when fishing the deep side of a classic pool. Anglers making wet fly swings from the shallow side — and we are talking about other bank fishermen — are only able to present a fly one way. When fishing from the deep side, which is not usually considered to be the best

Guide David Tye shows a prime sockeye salmon taken from the river behind him. Polaroid glasses aid in cutting glare to locate salmon. — Jim Teeny photo

side for fly casting, it is possible to use the downstream cast and retrieve quite effectively with just a bit of modification. Since the current can be substantial in a deep side slot, it is sometimes impossible to get a fly down with anything but the fastest sinking line or lead core shooting head.

The variation on theme is to cast upstream, allowing the line to settle as it is swept downstream. When using this technique, I don't hesitate to shake out additional slack when the line passes my position to be certain that it hits bottom even though I risk hanging my line around some unseen tooth in doing so. Once the line is resting on the pool bed, I begin a very slow, twitching retrieve punctuated with long pauses to keep the fly riding deep as it moves through the salmon.

We probably don't use the downstream cast and retrieve often enough since we've accepted the idea — with some justification — that Pacific salmon will not pursue a fly. At times, though, they are quite willing to chase a pattern some distance to grab it, and to discover just when these times will happen we are well served by the downstream cast and retrieve.

The Interception Cast and Retrieve

When migrating upstream, salmon will often seek out quiet eddies, backwaters and deep sloughs in which to find respite from the main channel current. Most Pacific Coast streams have at least a few such places that can be counted on to hold salmon from time to time. When moving into these countercurrents and backwashes, perhaps because of the quiescence of the water, salmon will get into a mood of swimming about actively, often clearly visible just beneath the surface. It is very similar to the behavior we witness at times when salmon gather in the estuaries before pushing on into the tidal pools of natal rivers. When salmon demonstrate this action they are inclined to strike a fly pulled enticingly past their noses.

The toughest part of fishing over these productive slack water environs is in locating an adequate position from which to make a decent cast, as these sites are often banded thickly with tenacious rows of willow intermingled with tangles of berry vines and maybe even a smattering of devil's club. Pure hell on lightweight waders, the reward is often worth the effort one must make to gain a small clearing that affords room for even a modest backcast.

If the salmon aren't moving around, it is best to start with random casts and a crawling retrieve along the bottom. When the salmon begin to stir though, swimming just under the surface in singles or small pods and breaking water occasionally, it is time to change tactics. A floating or sinking tip line is most often called for in this situation. The stratagem is to watch for cruising fish, and upon spotting one or more to cast quickly ten feet or so in front of and beyond them, then rapidly strip the fly back across their line of travel. It can get dreadfully frustrating at times when one seemingly perfect cast after another is ignored. Then, suddenly, a salmon will swing out of a passing pod, grab the fly and turn to resume its position with the others. The turning motion of the salmon drags the hook into the corner of its jaw so the barb can be set solidly.

The basic casts and retrieves delineated here — or some variation of them — will work on any West Coast salmon

Fish on! — Bill Ludwig photo

stream from the Togiak in Alaska to the Trinity in California. To make them work it is important that we learn to handle our tackle and understand the intricacies of the streams we fish. Our purpose is to present a pattern to the salmon at the right depth, speed and angle. Executing these basic casts and retrieves competently is the first step.

A FLY LINE FOR EVERY SITUATION

Given the wide range of conditions we will face on almost every salmon stream we fish, our hopes of success will hinge not only on skill and a bit of luck but will be impacted by the selection of fly lines we have stoked our vest pockets with. There is always need for a floater and a sinking tip line (fast sinking type 4 or 5). An extra spool should also be set up for using shooting tapers or heads of which we need slow sinking (type 1) through extra fast sinking (type 4 or 5) and one of lead core for extreme situations. Only by having the right line selection on hand can we present a fly at the right depth, speed and angle to entice a salmon into striking. Additional items needed to fine tune our fishing in depth are twist-on sinkers and several short lengths (from one to three feet) of lead core looped at both ends for use as extensions for any of our other lines.

If there is a prevailing principle to apply in salmon fly fishing, it is, "work at it." The reason we carry a selection of fly lines and shooting heads is to reach the fish regardless of water depth or speed. Nevertheless, it is not uncommon to see an angler casting time after time for hours on end without ever putting his pattern in front of a fish simply because he is not experimenting to find the right combination of line and leader length to do the job. Admittedly, it is true that sitting down to rebuild a leader or change a reel spool or switch a shooting head can be a pain at times. If, however, the alternative is to be constantly swimming a fly through a barren level of water, I'll expend a little extra effort to play around with line combinations every time.

To minimize the hassle of line changes, especially late in the season when even gloved fingers become numb and rebel at knot tying, the true value of a loop system for connecting lines and leaders becomes evident. By using the Russ Peak Loop detailed in the equipment chapter for fly lines and a Surgeon's Loop for attaching leaders, there are only tippets and flies that need knot tying. Another advantage in using loops is that they facilitate line changes much more quickly than knot tying.

It is generally agreed that the most pleasant fishing is with a floating line since it casts and picks up easily. Anytime the breadth, depth and speed of a river is such that we can present a fly to a salmon with a floating line, it is definitely the one to use. Although floating lines are most efficiently plied on small streams, they can be worked to advantage on larger rivers in places, especially in the spring before snow melt has raised water levels or in early autumn when flows are low and clear prior to the rainy season.

There is practically no end of situations on West Coast rivers where a floating line with a 10-, 15- or 20-foot sinking tip can be used to advantage. We have probably not employed sinking tip lines as intelligently as we should in salmon angling since pushing a fly to the bottom of a pool is accomplished with greater certainty by using a full sinking line or fast sinking shooting head of 250 to 350 grains. There are times, though, when a sinking tip line of the right density can be used to swim a fly through a pool just over the bottom, allowing us to detect strikes much more readily than with a full sinking line or shooting head dragging through the same spot. In our obsession to get the fly swimming along the bottom we need to keep in mind that it is not necessary — or even desirable — to have the entire length of our sinking line plowing the detritus of the pool floor. The often light take of our fly by a salmon is much easier to detect when the offering is drifting freely just over the bottom than when it is dragging and sending many messages up through the rod, any one of which, garbled among the others, may be the strike of a good fish.

The introduction of super high floating lines with very fast sinking tips of 10 or 15 feet have given us an entirely new dimension in freshwater salmon angling. With these lines, called Ultra or Hi-Flote, depending on the company offering them, we can fish most small to medium rivers — particularly from a boat or raft — with a degree of efficiency we once thought restricted to shooting heads. During the fall chinook seasons of 1982 and 1983, I used these lines on the Elk, Sixes and Pistol rivers in southern Oregon and on the Kalama River in southwest Washington when the water level was moderate, and not only enjoyed easy casting but racked up an impressive score on salmon hooked. The floating sections of the new lines ride so lightly on top and the sinking sections get down at such a sharp angle that the fly drifts just over the bottom of a salmon pool as if suspended from a bobber, free of obstacles so that even the gentlest of strikes is vividly transmitted to the angler.

On larger rivers, or when rain has raised water levels enough that a sinking tip line will not do the job, some anglers go to a full sinking line but more often the change is to a shooting head system. Even though shooting heads have been around for a long time (Leon Martuch sent me one of the first experimental Scientific Anglers shooting tapers for testing in about 1955 as I recall), there is still some resistance among anglers to use them. The fact is that shooting heads are not very difficult to master and on big, swift or deep water, no other line type works quite as well.

An item that simplifies using a shooting head system is the shooting or stripping basket. Constructed of cloth or mesh and shaped like a small, rectangular dishpan, the basket is secured around the waist with a belt or elastic cord. In use it holds the monofilament or fine diameter shooting line that backs the shooting head to keep it from tangling around the angler's feet or catching in the rocks. Once the angler gets accustomed to using a basket, it becomes

Cam Sigler, fishing with Bruce Ferguson, connects with a stout May coho on a long, accurate cast. Ferguson has another salmon almost to the boat. LJ

easy to make long casts with just a single backcast of the head and a double haul to develop line speed.

Given the problems connected with using shooting heads (tangled running line primarily), there is not a handier nor more compact method for carrying a full complement of fly lines — from floating through all the sinking rates including lead core. When we consider the fact that many veteran West Coast fly anglers use not only standard shooting heads but hand-spliced hybrids of half floating and half sinking combinations, it becomes evident that the equivalent of a dozen or more fly lines can be easily toted in just a couple of plastic boxes.

Skill notwithstanding, our opportunity for a good salmon fishing experience lies in our capability to work a fly at the right depth in almost any situation. It is our selection of fly lines that gives us the mechanical aspect of this capability. Knowing that we have the right lines on hand goes a long way toward helping us stride to the river bank confident that we can put a fly in front of a salmon in any reasonable situation.

LEADERS

The primary consideration in selecting a salmon leader is that it be strong enough to hold whatever size salmon may be hooked. Of secondary importance is that it be able to do a passable job of turning the fly over even though delicate presentation is not a criterion. In fresh water, where a pool may commonly hold frisky little jacks on up to slab-sided adult fish, the breaking strength of a tippet should never be less than 10-pound test. If the salmon are running large or rowdy, tippet strength of 15- to 20-pound test is warranted. On rivers where the salmon are really giants, with fish over 50 pounds a distinct possibility, savvy anglers will not hesitate to jump to 30-pound test tippets to avoid breakoffs.

Water volume is another factor that must be taken into consideration in determining leader strength needed. A good size salmon might be handled pretty easily in a small, slow moving river even with a 10-pound test leader. The same salmon hooked in a big, swift stream like the Cowlitz could get into the heart of the current and break off a tippet of 20 pounds. By carrying several tapers in a compartmentalized wallet and a half dozen spools of tippet material, the fly fisher can be confident of coming up with the right leader for almost any situation.

Since keeping the fly in close proximity to the bottom is important, leader length is an issue with a short leader most often called for. Many anglers use leaders of only six to 18 inches with excellent results. I prefer a leader of three feet if the water is swift and a bit murky and one of four feet if slower, clearer water affords better visibility. When water conditions are very low and clear I have found that a floating or fast sinking tip fly line or shooting head and a tapered leader of six feet works very well. It should be noted though many veteran anglers swear by light leaders of 9 to 12 feet for hookups in low, clear water.

The simplest of short leaders — up to three feet — can be nothing more than a length of level monofilament of appropriate breaking strength. With leaders of even three feet, though, most anglers prefer to use one that is tapered to

keep it from collapsing on the forward cast and tangling the fly and fly line. I hand-tie my three- and four-foot leaders and purchase my six-footers off the shelf or from a catalog. Anglers preferring that all their leaders be hand-knotted tapers will find recommendations in the tackle chapter.

SALMON TRAITS IN FRESH WATER

Upon arriving in fresh water, salmon provide us with signals, such as jumping, rolling or milling in a pool. These signals, when correctly read, can be beneficial in determining our approach in presenting a fly to them. During fluctuating water levels, salmon can also be predictable in their movements upstream which allows us to calculate where we should be stationed from one day to the next for the best chance to intercept them.

Rolling and Jumping

The most important aspect of seeing salmon rolling or jumping in a pool is that we know they are present. They

Donna Teeny with a bright Alaska sockeye salmon that hit a Teeny Nymph. — David Tye photo

will at times show themselves in this manner anywhere from tidal pools to spawning gravel. If fish are jumping all over a pool, it almost always means that they are present in significant numbers. If they are showing in a localized spot in a pool, it is probable that a small pod of salmon is present and holding directly under the place where they are jumping or rolling. Whenever this behavior is occurring, the salmon are coming up off the bottom and settling back down with the others. The technique for this situation is any of the casts appropriate to the water conditions and pool configuration, keeping the fly deep as the salmon will rarely hit a fly when they are surfacing or turning back for the bottom.

Milling

When salmon are visibly milling in elongated patterns — and this can take place in a short space of 20 feet or for the full length of a pool 100 yards long — experienced fly anglers have learned that they will strike quite readily. The hitch is that they will only strike with any regularity as they turn and rarely on the straightaway. This gives the angler four places on the milling route where strikes are most apt to happen. Since the milling phenomenon often takes place in low, clear water, it is pretty easy to see the turning points along the route. Taking advantage of this activity requires accurate placement of the fly so that it forms a tangent with the turning arc of the salmon.

Since the salmon travel in an irregular formation of singles and pairs to pods of six or more interspersed along the route, the angler must put as many casts as possible across the turning radii of the fish during the milling action. This requires timing the speed of the salmon with the drift and angle of the fly. Often a quick line change must be made in order to bring the arcing fly together at the right depth with the turning point of the salmon. The strike of a salmon during a milling period is just taking the fly on the turn and continuing to swim along. When the line tightens, the hook should be set solidly.

The Individual

There are times when we'll happen upon a salmon that is holding away from the rest of the school. It is often tempting to try for such a fish, especially if it is exceptionally large, or because of the one-on-one feeling of the challenge. While working on an individual salmon can sometimes be successful, it is not generally as productive as showing the fly to several fish holding together. Not many among us, though, will ever pass up a chance to make a few casts in the direction of a big salmon holding alone, regardless of how long the odds may be for a hookup.

A qualifier to the individual fish situation must be noted in the case of very ripe salmon, especially males showing vivid coloration along their flanks, holding alone in the

This precocious "jack" chinook fell for a Green Machine pattern fished on a sinking tip line. Jack chinooks, while rarely exceeding three pounds, are aggressive strikers and put up a good battle. LJ

spawning riffles in the upper reaches of a river. These fish are highly vulnerable to flies entering their territory and will strike savagely. The opportunity to make several hook-ups in short order is vastly offset by the fact that these fish are very near spawning, drawing on the final remnants of their strength, and are better left alone.

Subsurface Activity

There are times when salmon that have been in the river awhile but are still holding in the lower to middle reaches will swim about actively just under the surface much as they do when moving into sloughs or back eddies. This zipping around in a holding pool invariably takes place at first light before the fish have been disturbed by angling pressure. If there is a time when the Pacific salmon angler can hope to experience anything close to a greased line technique so productive on steelhead and Atlantic salmon, this is it.

During another trip on the Elk River, Todd Hannah and I saw several chinook working just under the surface as we drifted into the Five Mile Hole. Todd quickly and quietly lowered the anchor while I honed the point on a green hackled Comet and stripped off several yards of sink tip line. I cast across and downstream. The current pulled the slack straight and the fly was riding about a foot under the surface. There was an enormous swirl at the fly and the Hardy went into instant overdrive as a powerful salmon feeling the hook headed for the Oregon Coast. The take was so strong that I didn't have a chance to set the hook and the sharply bowed rod suddenly snapped up straight as the line went slack. As a parting shot the chinook made a nose-to-tail arching leap, clearing the surface neatly and reentering with a plopping splash. It was bright as silver and big. The technique accounted for an equally bright salmon in the next pool downstream, but not nearly as large.

MOVEMENT BY TIDE AND WATER LEVEL FLUCTUATION

When working the lower reaches of a river, specifically the tidal pools and the first few lies above tidal influence, every bit as important as good tackle and a proper fly selection to the serious angler is a tide book of the local area. Fishing in tidal pools and lagoons is usually best when there has been a high tide at night, allowing schools of fish to move in from the salt water under the cover of darkness. Having moved through the rivermouth at night, they will be holding in the tidal pools at dawn awaiting the next rising tide before pushing further upstream. Fishing in the tidal pools will be productive until the next incoming flood raises pool levels sufficiently to allow the fish to continue upriver. When the salmon start moving upstream on the rising water, the bite will fall off quickly.

The high-tide-at-night rule applies accurately only during periods of low to normal flow and relates better to small rivers than larger ones. On large rivers there is often sufficient water volume and depth even at low tide to allow salmon to move through. The best fishing will still be during the low tide as there is a natural tendency for salmon to hold in the tidal pools of any river for a time before moving upstream.

When substantial rains hit West Coast rivers, the increased volume of water and turbidity allow salmon to enter tidal pools at any time of the day or night. When this happens, the pools and drifts above tidal influence will often be where the salmon stack up. If the rain is such that rivers are knocked out of fishing condition completely, the only recourse is to wait until the water drops back into shape and begin searching from midriver down toward the tidal pools.

PLAYING A SALMON

The angler who has been accustomed to playing trout and bass on fly tackle is going to find that life with an adult salmon on the other end of the line is a very different experience. A prime salmon, full of strength and knowing how to work the current to advantage, is a formidable adversary that harbors a tenacious lust for freedom. Some are landed and others are lost but if we pay attention to what we are doing, have reel tension adjustments properly set and have snugged up our knots carefully, we should bring to net a great many more than we lose. More than anything else in regard to mature fish, we need to display patience. Attempting to force a salmon too quickly to the net nearly always results in a breakoff. Even when playing jacks of 16 inches to five pounds, attempting to horse them in can cause a hook to tear out from the frantic gyrations of the fish getting a solid pull against the rod. A light hand on the tackle is the name of the game during the early stages of an encounter with any salmon.

It is important to keep a salmon working against the rod pressure during every possible moment of the battle. If allowed to sulk and not move around much, a big salmon can maintain resistance for a long, long time. Campfire lore is rich in stories of huge salmon that were played for five or six hours before breaking off. While Pacific salmon — chinook, coho and chum in particular — can reach herculean dimensions and possess extraordinary strength, it should never take several hours for the outcome of a contest to be decided.

When a stubborn salmon is sulking downstream from the angler's position and holding well out in the current, it can be next to impossible to make it budge upriver. If the terrain allows, the angler should attempt to gain a position downstream from the fish, all the while maintaining rod pressure. Most of the time the rod pressure coming from below will prod it into a run. Even if the fish doesn't respond with an upstream run, it will be working much harder to hold its position against the downstream rod pressure and tire more quickly. If it is not possible to get downstream from a sulking salmon, tapping on the rod handle with the palm of the hand will send vibrations down the line, agitating the fish into a run. As a last resort, when seemingly all else has failed and the salmon continues to sulk, throwing a few big rocks in its direction is a ploy that can be tried. A word or two of caution is advised regarding this strategy. First, a well-placed rock may panic the salmon into a reel screaming run that is difficult to manage, resulting in a breakoff rather than a slow, steady run that can be controlled. Finally, if the assigned thrower happens to place a chunk of streamside granite not simply near the fish but directly on the line or leader, response from the muscle-tight angler as his line goes limp is probably not going to be in the form of a smiling thank you.

Sometimes a salmon will offer very little fight when hooked and can be led easily almost to the net before turning to make a line-smoking run that gives the angler no choice but to wait for the appearance of the backing knot on his reel spool or to snub the fish down to snap the leader tippet. About the only chance of landing one of these torpedoes is to give chase up or down the bank, cranking in whatever line can be regained in an effort to keep the reel from being stripped. With an upstream fish, odds are pretty fair that it will stop at some point along the way while there is still backing on the reel. A downstream fish is a different story, using a combination of speed, strength and the river current in its bid for freedom. About the only chance to land a big salmon barreling downstream under a full head of steam is to be fishing from a boat or raft so it can be followed for as far as need be to wear it out.

Very large salmon, usually males, will commonly take off upstream when hooked. Coho and chum can pull a surprising length of line and backing out on an upstream run while a big chinook can very well strip a reel. Most often though, the upriver run is tiring and the fish will hold, fighting both the current from upstream and the rod pressure from downstream. If the angler is patient, it is only a matter of time before the salmon tires and begins to drift back toward the angler's position. Extremely robust fish will attempt the upstream run several times before giving out to be led over the net.

There is an old bugaboo about not allowing a fish to get any slack in the line in the belief that it can throw the hook more easily. This is true when using conventional tackle as the weight of a heavy sinker or spoon swinging back and forth will pull a hook loose or snap a leader. A fly though, weighs almost nothing and a salmon leaping and shaking its head in an effort to throw the hook should be given slack on each leap by dropping the rod tip and pointing it, arm extended, right at the fish. A salmon will hardly ever be able to dislodge the fly against the slack line.

Salmon are often hooked around down timber, logs and mazes of tree roots. Invariably, the fish will attempt to wind the line through the limbs and roots in an effort to get leverage enough to pull the barb out or break the leader. Trying to pull a salmon directly away from a snag will only succeed in the salmon pulling in the opposite direction straight toward it. Moving to another position to change the direction of the rod pressure will sometimes veer the fish away from the obstacle. If, however, the salmon is too big and strong to be controlled by this tactic, the only resort may be to feed out slack line, relieving the rod pressure. With nothing pulling at it, the salmon will quite often stop — or if it has already circled a snag, it may retrace its path, freeing the line. Once the slack line is again taken up, the contest can continue.

When water is low and clear, salmon will often only respond to small flies tied on hooks from size 8 through 12. Playing a salmon on a small fly, particularly one that is a wild, thrashing battler, requires patience, the lightest permissible drag pressure and a fair share of luck. For the most

This coho grabbed a fly and cleared the surface of Puget Sound by four feet. Even small feeder cohos are acrobatic fighters with great energy. LJ

In Puget Sound, Bruce Ferguson and Field and Stream camping editor, Steve Netherby, work on a fast moving school of coho salmon. LJ

part, my experience in landing salmon on small flies has been good, as it has been with other anglers I exchanged information with during the course of researching this chapter. Fish that are lost usually pull the hook loose when the narrow hook gap has not gained a substantial hold rather than breaking or straightening the wire.

During the final moments of playing a salmon, the angler is arm-weary and a bit tired and the salmon is circling and rolling on a short line, nearly worn out but still holding onto a tiny reserve of strength to use if there is a fleeting instant of error on the angler's part. The leader has been stretched until it has no elasticity and the hook has opened a hole in the salmon's jaw so that the barb is not set nearly as tightly as when the fray began. This is a critical time — when a great many trophy size salmon are lost.

Salmon up to about 15 pounds can be beached by leading them into the shallows, then backing up to the beach, rod high and line tight while the salmon kicks its way out of the water. Larger salmon can be landed in a similar manner if a fishing partner is ready to grab the wrist of the fish's tail, giving it an additional boost onto the gravel. A net is much preferred for large salmon. When a salmon is tired enough to lead, it should be brought to the net head first with the net handler holding the net angled into the water. When the salmon's head is well over the hoop, the angler releases rod pressure, allowing the fish to dive into the bag while the net handler at the same time raises the net to carefully secure the catch.

If a salmon is to be released, it should be kept cradled in the water while the hook is removed and its physical condition evaluated. Some salmon fight so hard and long that they are very near death upon netting and may not respond to revival techniques.

To revive a salmon for release, take it from the net and cradle it upright, facing the current, with one hand supporting its belly and the other grasping the wrist of the tail. Gently move the fish back and forth, forcing water through its gills to replenish its oxygen supply. If the salmon is going to recover, it will soon regain voluntary gill action and begin to breath on its own. Within minutes, a revived salmon will swim from the angler's grasp and scoot out of sight into deep water. If, after several minutes of revival effort, a salmon appears to have only a marginal chance to recover, it should be quickly dispatched, placed in the fish box and noted on the angler's punchcard.

FINAL THOUGHTS ON ANGLING TECHNIQUES

It would be easy to stretch a chapter on salmon angling — however laboriously — into a small volume. It doesn't seem necessary since most people reading this will have some knowledge of angling and by building on that knowledge with the information contained here, they will be pretty well prepared to counter most of the stunts a salmon can perform. When a salmon is hooked that brings a few new tricks to the contest, so much the better as it can only add another element of excitement to the sport. Salmon fishing with a fly is tough and thrilling and full of surprises. This is how it should remain. Heaven forbid that we ever turn salmon fly fishing into a perfect science.

7.

Fly Types and Patterns

THE ETERNAL QUESTION FOR THE FLY fisher always seems to be, "What fly shall I use?" We can make some sense out of it when we are trout fishing by matching the hatch or probing with a nymph or wet fly that imitates an aquatic life form. But a person stalking Pacific salmon with a fly must deal with an altogether different set of feeding responses — in fact, *three* different sets of feeding responses.

When the salmon are in salt water, they are active feeders. And there is actually a "cycle of the season" to the feed availability which makes "hatch matching" more of a reality. In salt water we can present a euphausid, a squid, or any number of herring, anchovy or candlefish (sand lance) patterns, depending on the general timing of the cycle, to represent something resembling daily salmon fare. But when the salmon move into the natal estuaries where the feeding urge is greatly diminished, and later when they seek out the river proper where sustenance feeding stops altogether, enticing them to strike becomes an entirely different game.

Salmon gathering at the river estuaries are fish in transition. They will often spend several days alternately pushing into the flow of fresh water and dropping back to the salt again before making that final trip upstream to the spawning beds. They may hit most anything when they go on the bite: a herring imitating pattern, a shrimp, or a sparsely tied bright attractor fly, but there's no discernible order. It's literally catch as catch can.

Once in fresh water for good, salmon will still go on the bite from time to time. These bite periods may correspond to atmospheric pressure changes or in some way relate to similar feeding times in salt water; of this we aren't certain. Another theory is that salmon in fresh water hit a fly out of anger or in defense of their territory. All we do know is that the flies salmon find appealing at these times range from imitator to attractor, from garishly bright to subtle in

hue, and from 4/0 bucktails to sparsely dressed patterns on No. 12 hooks.

While the right fly can be any pattern, more often than not it will be something tried and true. So it pays to carry a smorgasbord of proven producers. To supplement this selection of standards, it is wise to be alert for the mention of new patterns during streambank conversations and to always attempt to get a peek when a salmon is landed to check out the fly that did the job. Be prepared to trade flies with other anglers when out fishing and prowl tackle stores when on trips to ferret out local favorites. Reading outdoor publications on the subject of fly fishing is also helpful as there are usually a few articles each year devoted to fly fishing for salmon.

The foundation of a well-stocked salmon fly box is formed through an evolutionary process with certain flies giving way to new patterns and other dependable dressings eventually filling an entire row of clips. No matter how many flies we stuff into the vest, though, we should always reserve a little space for those patterns we happen upon that are unusual or different — patterns that just might work during one of those trips where all our best offerings fail to garner a hookup.

With that as an introduction, let's move now to an examination of the patterns that have already evolved — to that "smorgasbord of proven producers," as it were — for the three major stages of fly fishing for Pacific salmon. In this chapter we attempt to catalog the fly types and patterns used by the pioneering anglers who ply this sport from northern California to Alaska. But first a word on hooks.

HOOKS

Salt water is corrosive. In a day's fishing with ordinary bronze finish hooks you can almost see them rust away before your very eyes. Cadmium-plated (tinned), and nickel-plated hooks work fairly well but far and away the best for salt water is stainless steel. In fresh water, bronze or gold finish and black lacquered finish Atlantic salmon hooks work very nicely. An important consideration when selecting hooks for salmon flies is to be certain to choose ones that are constructed of strong wire. Salmon simply love light wire hooks since they straighten so easily.

Here are the hooks we have found most useful for our own fly tying:

Mustad 37140 or 37160. English bait hook. Nos. 2-14. Bronze finish. For shrimp patterns used in fresh water.
VMC 9800. Wide gap hook. Nos. 2-14. Available in nickel, perma-plate and perma-steel finishes, this is the same hook that VMC manufactured for Herters as a 707N. For shrimp patterns used in salt water.
Wright and McGill, Eagle Claw 1197. (N)nickel, (G)gold, (B)bronze. Nos. 2-8. A stout, 1X long hook used for shrimp, comet and hairwing patterns. Also favored by some anglers for optic patterns.
Mustad 34007. Ring eye. Stainless steel. Nos. 4/0-6. A short shank hook used for tandem hook streamers, extended body baitfish, shrimp and optic bucktails. A standard for any and all saltwater fishing.
Wright and McGill, Eagle Claw 66SS. Stainless steel. Nos. 5/0-6. An offset bend, ring eye hook. Model 66CA is cadmium-plated.
Wright and McGill, Eagle Claw 1206. Nickel-plated, Nos. 4/0-8. No. X long, turned down eye hook for baitfish imitations.
Mustad 92615. Nickel-plated, Nos. 5/0-6. A long shank, ring eye hook with an offset bend. The offset bend can be straightened but we often leave it to enhance the fluttery, "injured minnow" action of our baitfish imitations.
Mustad 92608. Stainless steel. Nos. 5/0-6. Stainless steel equivalent to the 92615. Excellent saltwater hook.
Mustad 9174. Bronze finish. Nos. 2-8. A 3X short, ring eye hook of extra strong wire. Used for tying roe or glow bug patterns.
Mustad 7957 BX. Bronze finish. Nos. 1-16. An extra strong hook often used for sparsely dressed, low water comets, spiders and bucktails.
VMC 9299. Bronze, nickel and perma-plate finish. Nos. 5/0-10. A roe bait hook for salmon and steelhead fishing. Used for wool body or roe imitations. 9399N is nickel-plated, barbless equivalent.
Mustad 36890. Black lacquered finish, loop eye. Nos. 5/0-12. The classic turned up eye (TUE) hook for traditional salmon and steelhead patterns.
Mustad 7970. Bronze finish, 5X strong. Nos. 1-10. A stout wire, heavy hook used for comets, optics and bucktails that must sink very quickly.

One caution about using stainless steel hooks. Although they do not corrode from use in salt water, neither do they disintegrate if they are broken off in the mouth of a salmon. So please — take extra care in playing your fish to prevent this from happening.

SALTWATER FLIES — THE FEEDING PERIOD

In Chapter II we recounted how the very first anglers to try for salmon in the salt used patterns dressed originally for Atlantic salmon. Gradually these classic dressings gave way to simple silver-bodied bucktails. It was not until 1936, when a group of Seattle-area fly fishermen led by Letcher Lambuth began to study what the fish actually fed upon in salt water, that any effort was given to systematic fly development.

Lambuth and his cohorts made a good start. Unfortunately, World War II intervened, and the sport never acquired a widespread following after that. Any further development was limited to isolated individuals who rarely if ever met anyone else who shared their interest. With so little opportunity to compare notes, it was every man for himself.

A great many patterns did evolve even so. We'll catalog these patterns according to the outline presented in Chapter IV, Salmon Feed.

Baitfish Imitations — The Herring

There have been a number of noteworthy efforts to imitate specific baitfish since Letcher Lambuth's pioneering experiments back in 1936. Lambuth viewed the actual baitfishes in a glass tank illuminated to simulate the upper five to ten feet of water. He reported the herring to have an opalescent quality that he could only capture with blended polar bear hair over a silver tinsel body. The colors too were different from what you'd see if you held the little baitfish in your hand. The herring as viewed in Lambuth's tank were bright green on the back shading to very pale green on the sides and belly, with a prominent gunmetal gray median line.

What you'd see in deeper water, or in water with different clarity or optical qualities, might be entirely different. But one prominent herring feature which you can see quite readily by viewing the fish in your hand is its full, chunky, heavily scaled body. Other baitfishes are more slender and the scales aren't anywhere near so prominent. Braided mylar piping does a fair-to-middling job of capturing the impression of scales, but to get the fullness of a proper herring body you must slip the piping over some kind of pre-shaped form. Irwin Thompson's Beer Belly fly exhibits this feature, as does Les Johnson's Herring fly. Larry Hicks, formerly of Tacoma, came up with another way of getting that full-bodied shape while at the same time achieving a flexible, wiggly action. His Hicks' Herring, first tied about 1966, is a tandem hooked pattern using three strands of the largest-diameter piping tied between the hooks for the body.

Even better than braided mylar piping for capturing the large-scale effect is that prismatic mylar tape now on the market in a variety of fish scale finishes. Just cut a couple of chunks out of a sheet of this material and stick them on the hook shank back to back and, *voila!* you have it — full body shape, big scales, and all. Jim Darden's prismatic Herring flies, intended for deep-feeding chinook, are examples of this type of fly.

BEER BELLY

Hook: 6 to 3/0, long shank. Tail: Light blue over pink bucktail. Body: The underbody is formed by bending a piece of aluminum beer can to shape and lashing/cementing it to the hook shank. Over this, slip a silver braided mylar sleeve. Secure the piping at head and tail. Wing: Light blue over pink bucktail.

Pattern by Irwin Thompson, Sebastopol, California. Said to be one of the best patterns along the northern California coast for taking deep-feeding chinook.

CHRISTMAS TREE

Hook: 6 to 2, ring eye. **Thread:** Red. **Head, Wing:** Mixed bunch of multicolor unravelled lamé or Flashabou — blue, red, green, silver, orange — tied in to protrude over the eye of the hook, then tied back to form a "bullet" head, with the remainder of the material extending back both over and under the hook shank for a wing.

Pattern by Russ Johnson, Seattle, Washington. An unlikely herring pattern, it is nevertheless successful when herring fry are present in the spring. It is also a good zooplankton fly.

DARDEN CHINOOK FLIES

Hook: 6 to 5/0, ring eye. **Tail:** Pattern 1 — Yellow over white hair. Pattern 2 — white hair with strands of pearl Flashabou. **Body:** Weighted at the fore end of the hook, then overwrapped with any suitable material. Strips of prismatic mylar tape cute to a full-bodied shape, but with "ears" fore and aft for tying to the hook shank, are secured back to back at the rear of the hook, then folded forward and secured after the wing is tied on. **Wing:** Bunches of FisHair tied along the hook shank. Pattern 1 — From rear to front, olive, lime green, and peacock green FisHair; topping of peacock herl optional. Pattern 2 — From rear to front, pale blue, blue, and dark blue Fishair. **Throat:** On pattern 2 only white hair with a bit of red in front.

These flies are reminiscent of Dave Whitlock's Prismatic Minnows. They differ in that Whitlock used marabou extensively while these flies feature FisHair and bucktail. Tied by Jim Darden, Bellingham, WA.

HICKS' HERRING

Hook: Tandem, two short bait hooks, No. 4, joined either by a length of monofilament or by the tied-down lashings of the body construction or both. **Thread:** White. **Body:** Three lengths of silver mylar piping stacked vertically and tied at one end to the trailer hook and at the other end to the front hook. **Wing:** Generous bunch of peacock herl. **Throat or belly:** White bucktail the same length as the wing. **Head:** Built up with tying thread and painted red with white eyes, black pupils.

Invented by Larry Hicks, formerly of Tacoma, Washington. The specimen in the color plate is an original that was in the possession of co-author Bruce Ferguson.

LAMBUTH HERRING

Hook: 6 to 3/0, long shank. **Body:** Flat silver tinsel. **Wing:** Three layers. Bottom, pale green mixed with white polar bear. Median line, gunmetal gray. Top, bright green topped with a few strands of olive.

Developed by Letcher Lambuth, Seattle, Washington in 1936. A standard Puget Sound area bucktail.

LES JOHNSON HERRING FLY

Hook: As above. **Thread:** White. **Tail:** Unraveled strands of silver mylar piping. **Body:** Silver mylar piping over an underbody built up to be deep in the shoulder. **Wing:** Olive yellow over white bucktail with pearl Flashabou tied in alongside. **Throat:** Orange hackle fibers.

A simple herring pattern by one of the co-authors.

LITTLE HERRING

Hook: 6, long shank. **Body:** Flat silver tinsel. **Wing:** Light blue over sparse white over green bucktail, topped with several strands of peacock herl. Grizzly hackles are tied on each side of the wing to depict the scaly effect of the real herring's body. **Head:** Black with white eyes, black pupils.

Pattern of Kirk Giloth, Lynnwood, Washington. A small streamer most useful in late June and July when the average size of the bait is small.

MARC BALES HERRING

Hook: 6 to 2, long shank. **Thread:** Red. **Body:** Red tying thread. **Wing:** Blue over white polar bear or synthetic topped with four to six strands of peacock herl. Keep all layers sparse.

Developed by Marc Bales, proprietor of Kaufmann's Streamborn Fly Shop in Bellevue, Washington.

POLAR HERRING

Hook: 4 to 2/0. **Thread:** White. **Body and tail:** Silver mylar piping tied down at the hook bend and unraveled for the tail. **Wing:** White over pink polar bear or FisHair, topped with a barred mallard flank feather, stem and all, trimmed to match the length of the hair. Entire wing is tied down at the hook bend to form a back. The wing should be fashioned so that the pink hair shows along the sides.

Invented by Jim Crawford, Kelowna, B. C. for fishing cohos in the Campbell River area. Barry Thornton, several times past president of the Steelhead Society of B. C., ties a pattern almost identical with this except it has a woodduck flank feather in the back and a black head. The fly in the color plate is Thornton's.

Baitfish Imitations — The Anchovy

"When you look down in the water and see the 'nickels and dimes' fluttering around, you know you're on top of a school of anchovies," said former charter boat skipper Dave Allen, and he ought to know. In a sense, he relied on them for his livelihood for many years when he operated out of Westport, Washington. The salmon also see those nickels and dimes. That is very likely what triggers their feeding instinct.

An important characteristic like this should not be overlooked in developing a successful imitation, but what causes it? Well, if you look closely at a real anchovy, you see a slender little baitfish *with an unusually big mouth and large, perfectly smooth gillplates.* When it opens its mouth to feed or simply to force water through its gills, those gillplates catch and reflect the light like so many nickels and dimes fluttering through the water.

One way to capture this effect in an artificial is to cut out sections of heavy grade smooth mylar film and mount them as shoulders on the fly. The heavier the film the more durable the gills. We try to tie these so that they flare away from the fly, much like the pectoral fins on a sculpin imitation. We always add a fluff of bulky red yarn behind each one to help hold them out, and also to create the effect of opened gills. This fly works, but it's only one idea. There's plenty of room for pattern development here.

ANCHOVY

Hook: No. 4, regular length. **Body:** Flat silver tinsel. **Wing:** Black over white bucktail topped with strands of peacock herl. Make the wing about three times the hook length.

A Jim Green pattern fashioned originally for albacore off the California coast. This fly is made with a little harness of leader material tied on at the bend of the hook to keep the wing from wrapping under.

ANCHOVY STREAMER

Hook: Very short shank ring eye, up to 1/0. **Thread:** White. **Body:** None. **Wing:** From bottom up, a layer of white bucktail, several strands of silver mylar, green bucktail, blue bucktail, and peacock herl. **Head:** Built up of tying thread and painted green over blue over white. Yellow eyes, black pupils.

A California pattern sent in by Dennis P. Lee, Eureka, California.

HUMBOLDT BAY ANCHOVY

Hook: 1/0 ring eye, regular shank length. **Tail:** Gray squirrel hair stuck in the end of a length of silver mylar piping and tied in place. **Body:** Extended body made by threading the mylar tubing over the hook and jabbing the point through about halfway along the length. **Wing:** Blue over green over white polar bear, bucktail or synthetic.

Another northern California pattern, this one fashioned in the manner of the East Coast Snake series developed many years ago by angling editor Frank Woolner.

JANSSEN STRIPER FLY

Hook: Up to 5/0, regular shank. **Thread:** White. **Body:** Flat silver tinsel. **Wing:** Green over blue over white bucktail. **Throat:** White bucktail the length of the wing. **Head:** Built up of tying thread, then painted green over blue over white. Also paint on yellow eyes with black pupils.

Developed by Hal Janssen for striped bass, not salmon, but nevertheless used successfully for the latter. The green-blue-white or more typically blue-green-white color combo is widely used to depict the anchovy.

TROTTER'S ANCHOVY

Hook: Tandem, short shank offset bend, size 6 for the trailer, size 4 or 2 up front. Construct the fly on the front hook. **Thread:** White. **Wing:** From bottom up, several long strands of silver mylar unraveled from piping; layers of white, green and blue bucktail or FisHair; peacock herl topping. Keep all layers sparse. **Throat:** Long white bucktail or FisHair, also sparse. **Gills:** Tufts of large red or fluorescent red yarn, one on each side of the hook shank. **Gill Covers:** Nickel-size pieces of silver mylar film tied on top of the gills. **Head:** White with yellow eyes, black pupils.

An experimental fly developed to capture the bright, reflective gillplates of the actual anchovy. Leave the hook bend offset so the fly will wobble and flutter on the retrieve.

Baitfish Imitations – The Pilchard or Sardine

These baitfish were formerly plentiful along the northwest coast, but have not been seen in significant numbers since the mid-40's. They are considered a good source of food for chinook and coho when present, but fly tiers of this region have not bothered to develop specific dressings. As described earlier, pilchards are slender with dark metallic blue or green backs shading to silver on the sides and bellies. Many of the fly patterns listed in the other baitfish categories would suffice as well as pilchard dressings.

Baitfish Imitations – Candlefish and Sand Lance Patterns

Both the eulachon, a species of smelt, and the Pacific sand lance or needlefish are commonly called candlefish in the Pacific Northwest, so we have listed patterns for both baitfishes in this category. However, we believe that many of the bucktail-type streamers with "candlefish" in their names, like the Lambuth Candlefish and the Alaskan Candlefish, were intended to imitate the eulachon. The sand lance or needlefish, *Ammodytes hexapterus*, is eel-like in appearance and swimming motion. The Roselyn Sand Lance pattern listed below is intended to capture that effect.

ALASKA CANDLEFISH

Hook: 6 to 3/0, long shank. **Body:** Flat silver tinsel. **Wing:** Three layers. Bottom, white bucktail, polar bear or synthetic. Middle, olive. Top, light blue with a few pink and purple hairs mixed in.

Based on a pattern published by Ernest Schwiebert in the 1978 Daiwa Fishing Annual.

CANDLEFISH

Hook: 6 to 2, long shank. **Body:** Embossed silver tinsel or mylar piping. **Wing:** Green over white polar bear or bucktail with strands of pearl Flashabou or silver lamé tied alongside.

The origin of this fly is unknown. It is, however, very effective for coho and blackmouth when the "yearling" baitfish are around. Try both the Flashabou and lamé variations. These materials produce quite different effects in the water.

DARDEN CANDLEFISH

Hook: 6 to 5/0 ring eye. **Tail:** Long, slender white FisHair with strands of lime green Flashabou tied alongside. **Body:** Weighted at the fore end; overwrapped with thread as the wing is tied in. Long, slender strips of silver prismatic tape are placed on each side after the wing is constructed in a manner similar to the construction of the Darden Herring fly. **Wing:** Long, sparse bunches of FisHair tied in along the hook shank. Pattern 1 from rear to front, alternate bunches of fluorescent chartreuse and lime green, with a bit of peacock blue at the front. Also, about halfway up, catch in a few strands of lime green Flashabou. Pattern 2 from rear to front, alternate bunches of fluorescent chartreuse and peacock blue with a bit of royal blue at the front. **Throat:** On pattern 2 only, short tuft of red FisHair. **Eyes:** Doll eyes glued on at the front of the prismatic strips.

These are companion flies to Jim Darden's Herring patterns. These too are intended for deep fishing but are tied with the more slender profile of the candlefish.

LAMBUTH CANDLEFISH

Hook: 6 to 3/0, long shank. **Body:** Flat silver tinsel. **Wing:** Three layers. Bottom, mixed pale blue and pale green polar bear or synthetic. Median line, carmine red. Top, mixed French blue and a bit of green.

Developed by Letcher Lambuth, Seattle, in 1936. A standard Puget Sound area bucktail.

LEFTY'S DECEIVER

Hook: Up to 3/0, ring eye. **Tail:** Six long saddle hackles, three on each side, tied to flare out. Add several strands of 1/32-in. silver mylar on each side. **Body:** Silver mylar tinsel. **Wing:** One generous bunch of bucktail tied to be evenly distributed around the hook shank. Tie another bunch in on top to establish the baitfish silhouette and to help the fly ride upright. This last bunch can be a different color to depict the back of the baitfish. Peacock or ostrich herl can also be added for topping.

A now-classic saltwater fly by Lefty Kreh. The pattern variations are myriad. Shown in the color plate is a specimen tied in the Lambuth Candlefish color scheme. Many materials can be used to build up the basic silhouette, such as bucktail, neck hackle, or marabou. You want a long, slender tail, then heavier at the shoulder and head. In the water these flies slim down to rakish baitfish-like proportions with the fullness at the shoulder where it belongs.

HURN'S CANDLEFISH

Hook: 6 to 3/0, long shank. **Tail:** White polar bear. **Body:** Oval silver tinsel. **Wing:** Green over white over red polar bear. Hurn applies the colors with felt pens. Top the wing with a few strands of peacock herl.

Pattern submitted by David Hurn, Victoria, B. C. Hurn also ties this fly upside down for "weedlessness" when fishing in kelp or in the debris you'd find associated with a well-defined rip line.

MIHEVE CANDLEFISH

Hook: As above; can also be tied tandem using two size 6 regular shank hooks. **Tip:** Red thread. **Body:** Copper piping or tinsel. **Wing:** From the bottom, blue bucktail, a few strands of red bucktail, green bucktail, and peacock herl. Sometimes a few thin strands of blue and green Flashabou are added and a few strands of crinkled silver mylar along the sides. **Throat:** White bucktail as long as the wing. **Head:** Black with white eyes, black pupils.

Pattern by Greg Miheve, formerly of Tacoma, Washington.

ROSELYN SAND LANCE

Hook: 1/0 or 2/0. Can be tied tandem using a pair of short shank size 6 or 4 hooks. **Thread:** Brown. **Body:** Fine gold mylar piping. **Wing:** Three very sparse layers. Bottom, white. Middle, VERY sparse red. Top, black. Use bear hair or FisHair. **Throat:** White hair or FisHair as long as the wing. **Cheek:** Jungle cock or a substitute, or paint white eyes with black pupils.

An Alaskan needlefish pattern by Hank Pennington. If tied tandem, thread the mylar piping between hooks and tie the wing and throat down at the bend of the rear hook.

Baitfish — General Patterns

In addition to the specific baitfish imitations noted above, there are many fish-getting patterns that defy classification. We have lumped them all in here.

As you will undoubtedly conclude when you peruse this section, the hairwing streamer has always been the hands-down favorite type of general baitfish imitation in the Pacific Northwest. Polar bear hair supplanted bucktail back in the middle thirties, and it remained the material of choice until just recently when it became so hard to get. Goat hair is an acceptable natural substitute, but even better is the synthetic material known as FisHair. The northeastern style of featherwing streamer has never been popular here, although Roderick Haig-Brown did tie a couple of patterns that combine hair and feathers in the wing.

Marabou, a material that breathes and pulses in the water, is represented in the pattern list by E. H. (Polly) Rosborough's Silver Garland Streamer. This was an early marabou pattern that also marked the introduction of tinsel chenille. The fly was not originally intended for saltwater fishing, but it could be tied in many color combinations and one of these — shown in the color plate — proved deadly in the salt chuck, particularly for silvers.

Much has been written the last few years about the Matuka, a fixed-wing style of streamer from New Zealand. The advantage of the Matuka is that the wing and body stay together as one unit when the fly is twitched through the water. The traditional American streamer flares and hinges apart with every pause in the retrieve. While this "breathing" action does attract fish, no true baitfish behaves this way and neither does the Matuka. Reports from all over the country say that in side-by-side tests the Matuka outfishes the standard American streamer. Even so, nothing much has been done with this style of streamer for saltwater salmon angling. This remains an area open for experimentation.

Perhaps because corrosion-resistant streamer hooks have not always been available in a full range of sizes, saltwater fly tiers have never adhered particularly strongly to the North American tradition of tying streamers on long-shank hooks. More often than not they modified the style of the fly so as to use whatever hook was available in a saltwater-resistant finish. If they wanted a longer body, they might let some mylar piping trail back as in the Humboldt Bay Anchovy pattern listed above. Or they might employ a trailer hook. The latter always struck us as the preferable choice, simply because Pacific salmon can be notorious for striking short. They grab a mouthful of the fly's long, sweeping wing, but miss the barb altogether — unless there's a tandem hook trailing back there. If you do take the tandem hook route, be careful not to use too big a set of hooks or your flies will be too large to be cast with anything other than one of those 15-foot, two-handed monster rods used on some English Atlantic salmon rivers. But if you keep your hooks small, say no larger than a short-shank size 4 up front and a size 6 trailer, your flies should cast perfectly well.

ACKERLUND HUMPY FLY

Hook: Size 4, regular shank. **Body:** Silver mylar tinsel or piping. **Wing:** Pink over white polar bear, FisHair or bucktail, twice the length of the body. **Head:** Black with silver bead chain eyes lashed on.

A pattern attributed to Bill Ackerlund, deadly during the summer pink salmon runs. The "humpies" run in Washington waters only every other year, in the odd-numbered years. This same fly tied with green hair instead of pink is good for coho.

AL'S SALMON STREAMER

Hook: Tandem, size 4 up front (tie the fly on this hook), size 6 trailer. **Body:** Oval silver tinsel. **Wing:** White over yellow over orange (white on top) bucktail with badger hackles tied alongside. **Shoulders:** About nickel-size rounded pieces of cut-out silver mylar film. **Head:** Painted blue.

Pattern by the late Alvin Trotter, a professional fly tier from McKinleyville, California, for the Trinidad area of the California coast. An attractor pattern for either casting or trolling; it is often fashioned as a tube fly.

BILL NELSON SALMON STREAMER

Hook: Up to 5/0 regular shank ring eye. The hook shank is left bare. **Wing:** Three patterns: green over white bucktail with a few strands of red for a median line; also blue over white and purple over white, both with the red median line. Alongside the top layer of bucktail tie several thin strands of unbraided mylar from a piece of piping.

Submitted by Bill Nelson, April Point Lodge, B. C. These three-to four-inch bucktails are used for the fall fishing. The green is used in the early morning on sunny days until the sun reaches about 30 degrees. The blue is used also on sunny days, from about 11:00 a.m. to 3:00 p.m. The purple is a cloudy day fly, and is also used anytime the sun passes 30 degrees. The green fly seems to be more effective than the others on days when you have to go deep.

CAMERON BAITFISH

Hook: Up to 2/0 regular shank ring eye. **Tail:** Long hair in any color combination. The Coronation pattern, blue over red over white, is shown in the color plate. **Body:** Silver mylar piping. **Wing:** None.

Submitted by Charles R. Cameron, Chuck's Sport Shop, Seaview, Washington. Distinctive in having the wing where the tail should go, reminiscent of the Comet flies of California.

COHO BLUE

Hook: 6 to 3/0, long shank. **Tail:** Light blue hackle tip. **Body:** Flat silver tinsel. **Wing:** Light blue over white polar bear or substitute, with one light blue and one badger hackle tied on each side.

A Roderick Haig-Brown pattern published in *The Western Angler*, 1939.

COHO GOLDEN

Hook: As above. **Tail:** Orange polar bear or substitute. **Body:** Silver tinsel. **Wing:** Olive over white polar bear or substitute with feathers from the base of a jungle cock "eye" neck tied alongside. Substitute well-marked ginger furnace or a deep golden badger for the latter feathers. **Topping:** Golden pheasant crest.

Another Roderick Haig-Brown pattern from *The Western Angler*, 1939.

DIEKER'S TANDEM BUCKTAIL

Hook: Tandem, size 4 up front and size 6 trailer. **Thread:** White. **Wing:** A bunch of silver mylar strands followed by blue bucktail extending just past the end of the trailer hook. Top with strands of peacock herl. **Throat:** White bucktail the length of the wing. **Head:** White.

Mike Dieker fishes out of Pacific City, Oregon, where they launch their boats into the open ocean right through the surf. He uses this tandem-hook fly with a Hi-D or lead-core line, fishing right in close to the onshore rocks. Sounds a bit risky, but Mike claims to have had fish hit within 20 feet of the rocks, as though they were waiting for stunned baitfish that had been dashed against the rocks by the waves.

DISCOVERY OPTIC, PATTERNS 1 AND 2

Hook: 2/0, 3XL. **Body:** Flat silver tinsel ribbed with oval silver tinsel. **Wing:** Pattern 1 — Bottom, white polar bear or substitute. Top — Light blue polar bear or substitute mixed with light green crimped nylon. Pattern 2 — Bottom, white polar bear or substitute. Top — orange polar bear or substitute mixed with yellow crimped nylon. **Head:** Build up to a large optic style with tying thread. Paint white with black eyes, yellow pupils.

DISCOVERY OPTIC, PATTERN 3

Hook: As above. **Body:** Flat gold tinsel ribbed with oval gold. **Wing:** Bottom, yellow polar bear or substitute. Top, scarlet polar bear or substitute mixed with red crimped nylon. **Head:** As above.

The Discovery Optics were developed by A. J. McClane for fishing in the Campbell River, B. C. area. McClane fished the April Point area before the present resort, which, by the way, caters to fly fishermen, was built. He filmed his fishing exploits in the nearby waters for one of the government tourist agencies. Copies of that film were still available for viewing, last time we checked, from *Field & Stream* magazine.

FRANK'S STREAMER

Hook: Up to 1/0, ring eye Siwash or O'Shaughnessy. **Tail:** Gray squirrel hair stuck in the end of a piece of silver mylar piping and bound down with white thread. **Body:** Silver mylar piping. Insert the hook about halfway up the piece containing the tail, so that the back half of the piece becomes an extended body. **Wing:** White polar bear or substitute topped with strands of peacock herl. **Head:** Black with white eyes, black pupils.

Submitted by Frank Lawrence, El Sobrante, California, but probably based on the Snake series referred to earlier.

FERGUSON'S GREEN AND SILVER

Hook: 8 to 1/0, long shank. **Tail:** Sparse white polar bear or substitute. **Body:** Silver oval tinsel with a shoulder of large fluorescent green chenille. **Wing:** Sparse white polar bear or substitute.

Dave Hurn, Sooke, B.C., fishes a modification of the Joe Brooks Blonde series in the Strait of Georgia. Bruce Ferguson combined elements of Hurn's fly with a California shad fly to create this pattern which has to date proven effective in Puget Sound, the Queen Charlotte Islands, and even in fresh water. Ferguson says that if he had to confine himself to one fly only, this would be it, provided he could have it in the full range of hook sizes. He notes it is particularly good in the spring when the zooplankton are swarming.

FERGUSON'S MARABOU

Hook: 6 to 3/0. **Thread:** White. **Tail:** Unraveled silver mylar piping. **Body:** Silver mylar piping. **Wing:** Bunch of fibers from a white marabou feather topped with crinkled strands unraveled from silver lamé fabric, then a bunch of peacock herls over all.

Another Bruce Ferguson pattern used in Puget Sound for salmon when they go over to baitfish in midsummer.

GILOTH SALMON STREAMER

Hook: Up to 3/0, short shank ring eye. **Butt:** Built up with red thread which is used to tie down the butt-end of the body. **Body:** Silver mylar piping. **Wing:** Light blue over green over white bucktail. **Head:** Build up large with thread. Paint white with yellow eyes, red pupils.

Submitted by Kirk Giloth, Lynnwood, Washington.

HUMBOLDT BAY SALMON FLY

Hook: 2 to 2/0, long shank. **Tail:** Green over white bucktail with silver mylar piping frayed out to half the length of the hair. **Body:** Silver mylar piping. **Wing:** Green over yellow over white bucktail. **Shoulder:** Strips of wide flat silver mylar about two-thirds the length of the body.

Submitted by Mike Foster of Mike's Fly Shoppe, Miranda, California. Said to be one of the standards in the Humboldt Bay area.

HUMPY FLY, MALE

Hook: 6, 3XL. **Tail:** Red hackle fibers. **Body:** Flat silver tinsel. **Throat:** Black hackle fibers. **Wing:** Black marabou feather tips back to back, topped with peacock herl. **Head:** Red thread or painted red.

Pattern by Bill Nelson, April Point Resort, B. C. A small, simple marabou used when the humpback salmon are on the scene. The male humpies seem to be particularly attracted to this black fly.

HUMPY FLY, FEMALE

Hook, Tail, Body: All as above. **Throat:** White hackle fibers. **Wing:** White marabou tips topped with peacock herl. **Head:** White.

Companion fly to the pattern above. For some reason the female humpies respond to the white fly the best.

INJURED BAITFISH

Hook: 6 to 3/0, long shank ring eye. **Thread:** White. **Tail:** Unraveled silver mylar piping with a bundle of white marabou fibers tied on top. Also allow the material used for the back of the fly to extend back so it can be tied down and become part of the tail. **Body:** Section of quill shaft from peacock, goose, or other large feather cemented to the hook shank and bound down with thread. Slip over this a sleeve of silver (or gold) mylar piping. **Rib:** Clear monofilament which will be used to bind down the back materials. **Back:** A bunch of bright green synthetic hair topped with strands of peacock herl. These are tied down over the back with the monofilament ribbing. **Head:** Painted red with yellow eyes, black pupils.

When a baitfish is wounded or disoriented by the slashing attack of marauding salmon it flutters about, sending out signals that it is in distress. Cruising salmon seeking out the cripples isolated by their tactics home in one these vibrations. Charles E. Brooks, author of *The Trout and the Stream, Larger Trout for the Western Fly Fisherman*, and other books, devised a floating streamer made with a goose quill body for analogous situations in fresh water.

Whygin Argus did likewise to come up with his Quill-Bodied Mylar Minnow, a pattern featured in *The Fly Tyer's Almanac*, by Robert Boyle and Dave Whitlock. Pat Trotter's Injured Baitfish is fashioned along the same lines. Being hollow, this fly fishes on the surface, or just under it if you use a sinking line. You can wiggle and twitch it as pathetically as you like. With a sinking line, its buoyancy will cause it to drift up with each pause, then flutter down with every pull, just like a real injured baitfish. Another successful color combination for this fly is the blood-red scheme used in the Discovery Optic Pattern 3. Many others could be used as well. The nice thing about this pattern is that it is general and adaptable to change.

JULY FLY

Hook: 6 or 4, regular shank turned down eye. Leave the hook shank bare. **Wing:** Green over white bucktail with a few strands of red for a median line. Tie strands of unraveled silver mylar and a few strands of pearl Flashabou alongside. Top the wing with peacock herl.

Another fly from Bill Nelson, April Point, B. C., this one for the late June and July fishing when the baitfish are running small.

LAMÉ STREAMER

Hook: 6 to 3/0, long shank. **Body:** Silver mylar piping. **Wing:** Any combination of colors. The Coronation pattern, blue over red over white, is shown in the color plate. Mix polar bear or FisHair with strands unraveled from mylar lamé fabric. The key to its success is the crinkly nature of the mylar resulting from the weaving process.

Conceived by Frank Sailors of Lodi, California, in the mid-'60's, when mylar lamé was first marketed. The specimen in the color plate is an original tied by his late brother, Bob, of Gig Harbor, Washington, that was in the possession of co-author, Bruce Ferguson.

NORTH STAR

Wing: Green polar bear or bucktail over white polar or buck, with red polar or buck on either side. Hair should be 3-4 inches long. **Thread:** Heavy tying thread painted with a metallic green paint.

The pattern is tied on a formed heavy gauge wire to accomodate a sliding hook set-up.

PARR

Hook: 6 or 4, regular shank down eye. **Tail:** Gray squirrel hair. **Body:** Silver mylar piping painted green on the sides and blue on the back. **Head:** Black with painted-on white eyes.

Submitted by Frank Lawrence, El Sobrante, California. While not a streamer, this fly is another excellent representation of the small baitfish available to the salmon in late June and July.

PINK CISCO

Hook: 6 to 3/0, long shank. **Tail:** Frayed out end of braided mylar piping. **Body:** Silver mylar piping. **Wing:** Pink over white bucktail topped with six strands of peacock herl. **Shoulder:** Jungle cock or substitute (optional). **Throat:** White bucktail. **Head:** Build up with black thread; paint on yellow eyes, black pupils.

YELLOW CISCO

Hook: Tail, Body, Head: As above. **Wing:** Yellow over white bucktail topped with peacock herl. **Shoulder:** As above. **Throat:** Yellow bucktail.

The Pink and Yellow Ciscoes are freshwater flies from the Lake Iliamna district of Alaska that proved quite effective in the salt.

SALMON KILLER

Hook: 6 to 3/0, long shank. **Tail:** Lavender over blue bucktail. **Body:** Oval silver tinsel. **Hackle:** Blue. **Wing:** Black over lavender bucktail. **Head:** Build up large with thread; paint gold with white eyes, red pupils dotted with black.

Conceived by Irwin Thompson, Sebastapol, California, and used in San Pedro Bay and elsewhere along the California coast. The lavender-black-blue combination is said to be particularly attractive to silver salmon in that area.

SALMON TREAT

Hook: As above. **Tail:** Unraveled silver mylar piping, about 3/4 to one inch long. **Body:** Silver mylar piping. **Hackle:** Mixed hot orange and white. **Wing:** Pattern 1 - purple over bright green over white FisHair topped with 12 to 15 strands of peacock herl. Pattern 2 - hot orange over yellow over white FisHair topped with peacock herl. Pattern 3 - bright or lime green over yellow over white FisHair topped with peacock herl. On the wings of all patterns make each layer of hair just slightly longer than the layer beneath.

Patterns developed by Errol Champion, formerly of Seattle and now residing in Juneau, Alaska, for southeastern Alaska waters. The color plate specimen shown was tied by Errol Champion.

SANDSTROM BAITFISH

Hook: As above. **Body:** Silver tinsel or diamond braid. **Wing:** Unraveled lime-green lamé over white polar bear or FisHair. **Head:** Lime-green thread with a collar of red thread at the base of the wing.

A "tried and true" fly in south Puget Sound by Garry Sandstrom, owner of The Morning Hatch in Tacoma, Washington.

SILVER GARLAND STREAMER

Hook: As above. **Body:** Silver tinsel chenille. **Wing:** Pair of whole white marabou feathers back to back, topped with strands of royal blue over light blue ostrich herls. **Shoulder:** Jungle cock or substitute (optional).

Conceived by E. H. (Polly) Rosborough. The specimen in the color plate has the marabou portion of the wing tied Matuka style.

SILVER MINNOW

Hook: As above. **Body:** Silver tinsel. **Wing:** White bucktail or polar bear topped with a generous bunch of peacock herl. **Throat:**

Red hackle fibers. **Head:** Split brass bead painted red with yellow eyes, red pupils.

Developed by the late Don Harger of Eugene, Oregon, for B. C. waters.

STROUD'S HUMDINGER TROLLING FLY

Hook: Tandem, size 2 or 4 up front with size 4 or 6 in the rear. **Body:** Tied on the front hook, fluorescent green chenille. **Wing:** Long white polar bear, bucktail, or FisHair with pairs of long white hackle feathers tied alongside; four to six strands of unraveled lamé tied alongside the hackles. **Throat:** Long but sparse white polar bear, bucktail, or FisHair.

Originated by Carl Stroud. Bruce Ferguson calls this fly his "season extender" because it works so well for him in that late-May-through-August period when the fish are difficult to hook with any consistency with other patterns and methods.

TWINKLEFISH

Hook: 6 to 1/0, regular shank turned down or ring eye. **Body:** Silver mylar piping. **Gill:** A turn or two of fluorescent red yarn just at the front of the body. **Wing:** Fluorescent bucktail in pink, green or yellow, with strips of the iridescent rainbow-hued mylar used on squid lures tied along each side. **Head:** Peacock herl.

Invented by co-author Les Johnson.

WHITLOCK MARABOU MATUKA MINNOW

Hook: 6 to 5/0, ring eye. **Thread:** White. **Body:** Weighting optional. Orlon dubbing, chenille, or silver tinsel chenille with fine stainless wire or silver tinsel for the rib. **Wing:** Two marabou feathers tied Matuka fashion with silver mylar strips caught in under the rib. Top with peacock herl. **Gills:** Red dubbing. **Cheeks:** Barred mallard breast or flank feathers. **Eyes:** Painted on the cheek feathers with fluorescent yellow paint; black pupils.

A Dave Whitlock pattern tied in two colors, white and fluorescent yellow. The latter is used quite often for deep fishing.

TUBE FLIES. Another approach Pacific Coast anglers have been experimenting with the last few seasons is the tube fly. These patterns are, as the name implies, tied on hollow plastic tubes of one sort or another so that they can be strung on a leader with a hook attached. The ends of the tubing are usually softened in a flame and pressed against a hard surface to make little raised collars to keep thread and materials from sliding off the ends. Mylar tube bodies are tied off fore and aft to prevent the mylar from unraveling. Most any of the patterns in this chapter could be tied as tube flies but the six that appear in the color plate are good representations that have turned in good results:

PATTERN 1

Body, Tail, Throat, Head: All as above. **Wing:** Peacock herl over bright green FisHair over light blue FisHair with strands of silver mylar alongside.

A Neah Bay pattern submitted by Dave Wands. This one is said to be especially good for silvers.

PATTERN 2

Thread: Olive. **Body and Tail:** As above. **Wing:** Olive FisHair or bucktail. **Throat:** Long white FisHair or bucktail with a tuft of red yarn in front. **Head:** Olive with white eyes, black pupils.

PATTERN 3

Before tying this fly, soften the plastic tube in warm water and bend into a gentle curve about three-quarters of an inch behind the head. This causes the finished fly to flutter slightly in the water on the retrieve. The fly is made only of a length of silver mylar piping slipped over the curved tube and bound down fore and aft, with a little of the protruding tail unraveled. The sides and back are painted with marking pens, dark green on the top, bright green

GENERAL BAITFISH

PLATE 1

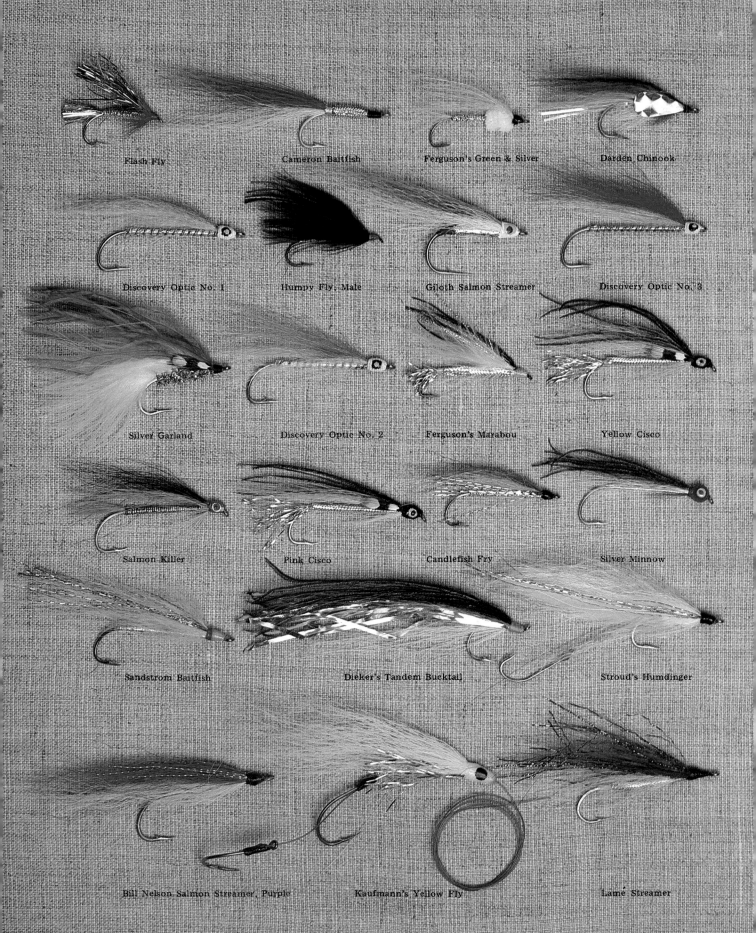

Flash Fly   Cameron Baitfish   Ferguson's Green & Silver   Darden Chinook

Discovery Optic No. 1   Humpy Fly, Male   Giloth Salmon Streamer   Discovery Optic No. 3

Silver Garland   Discovery Optic No. 2   Ferguson's Marabou   Yellow Cisco

Salmon Killer   Pink Cisco   Candlefish Fry   Silver Minnow

Sandstrom Baitfish   Dieker's Tandem Bucktail   Stroud's Humdinger

Bill Nelson Salmon Streamer, Purple   Kaufmann's Yellow Fly   Lamé Streamer

PLATE 1

GENERAL BAITFISH

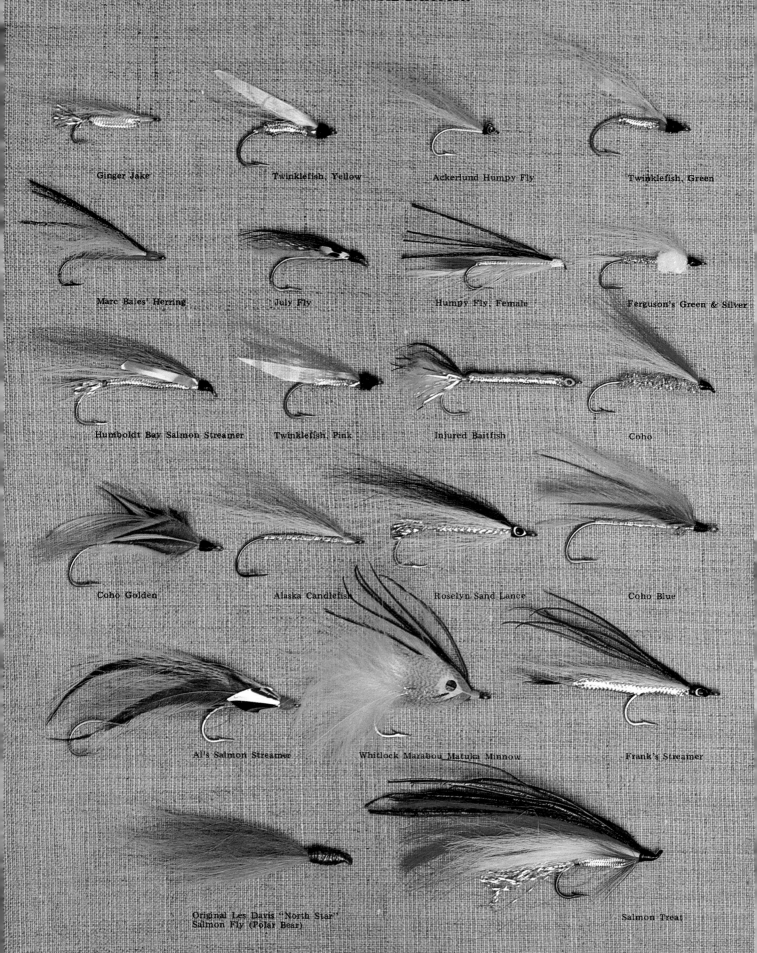

Ginger Jake

Twinklefish, Yellow

Ackerlund Humpy Fly

Twinklefish, Green

Marc Bales' Herring

July Fly

Humpy Fly, Female

Ferguson's Green & Silver

Humboldt Bay Salmon Streamer

Twinklefish, Pink

Injured Baitfish

Coho

Coho Golden

Alaska Candlefish

Roselyn Sand Lance

Coho Blue

Al's Salmon Streamer

Whitlock Marabou Matuka Minnow

Frank's Streamer

Original Les Davis "North Star"
Salmon Fly (Polar Bear)

Salmon Treat

PLATE II

TUBE FLIES

PLATE III

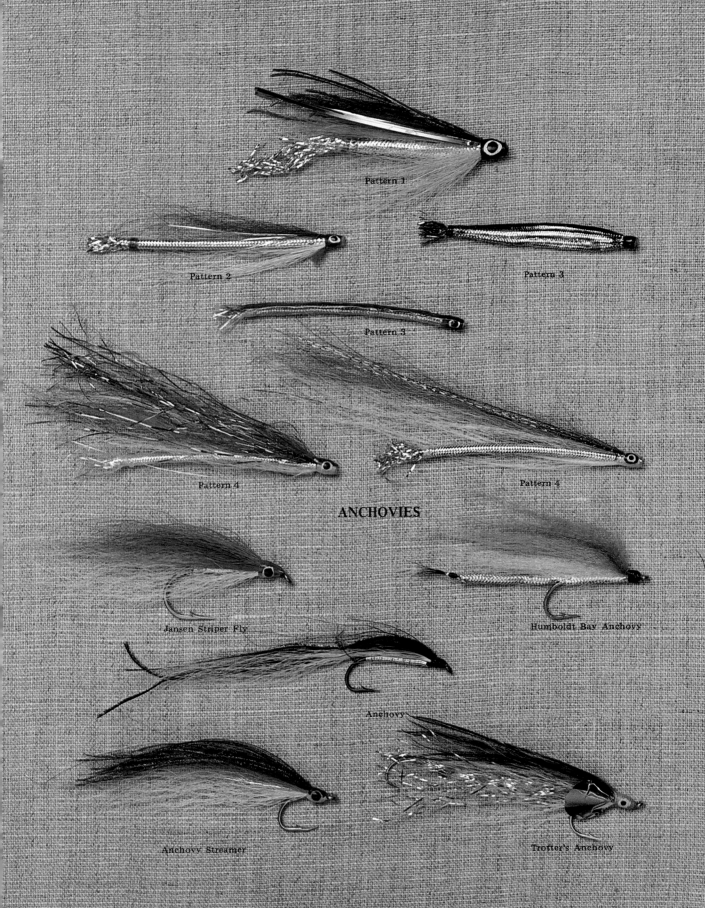

Pattern 1

Pattern 2

Pattern 3

Pattern 3

Pattern 4

Pattern 4

ANCHOVIES

Jansen Striper Fly

Humboldt Bay Anchovy

Anchovy

Anchovy Streamer

Trotter's Anchovy

PLATE III

WAITING PERIOD

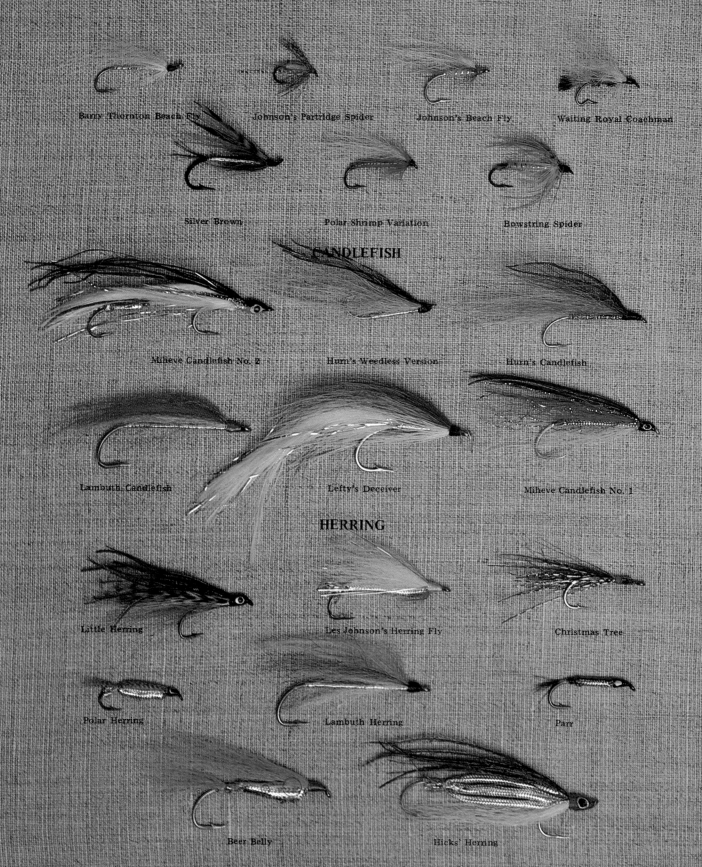

Barry Thornton Beach Fly   Johnson's Partridge Spider   Johnson's Beach Fly   Waiting Royal Coachman

Silver Brown   Polar Shrimp Variation   Bowstring Spider

CANDLEFISH

Miheve Candlefish No. 2   Hurn's Weedless Version   Hurn's Candlefish

Lambuth Candlefish   Lefty's Deceiver   Miheve Candlefish No. 1

HERRING

Little Herring   Les Johnson's Herring Fly   Christmas Tree

Polar Herring   Lambuth Herring   Parr

Beer Belly   Hicks' Herring

PLATE IV

SQUID

Loligo II

Sea Arrow Squid

ZOOPLANKTON

Low Water Shrimp No. 1

Pink Feed

Martin Sea Shrimp

Flashabou Euphausid

Walkinshaw Euphausid

Low Water Shrimp No. 2

King's Shrimp

Hale's Pinky

Pink Shrimp

Burnt Orange Amphipod

Green Weenie

Johnston Special Shrimp

Orange Shrimp

Horner Silver Shrimp No. 1

Ferguson's Amphipod

Green Amphipod

Fredrickson's Olive Amphipod

Sparkle Shrimp No. 1

Sparkle Shrimp No. 2

Horner Silver Shrimp No. 2

PLATE V

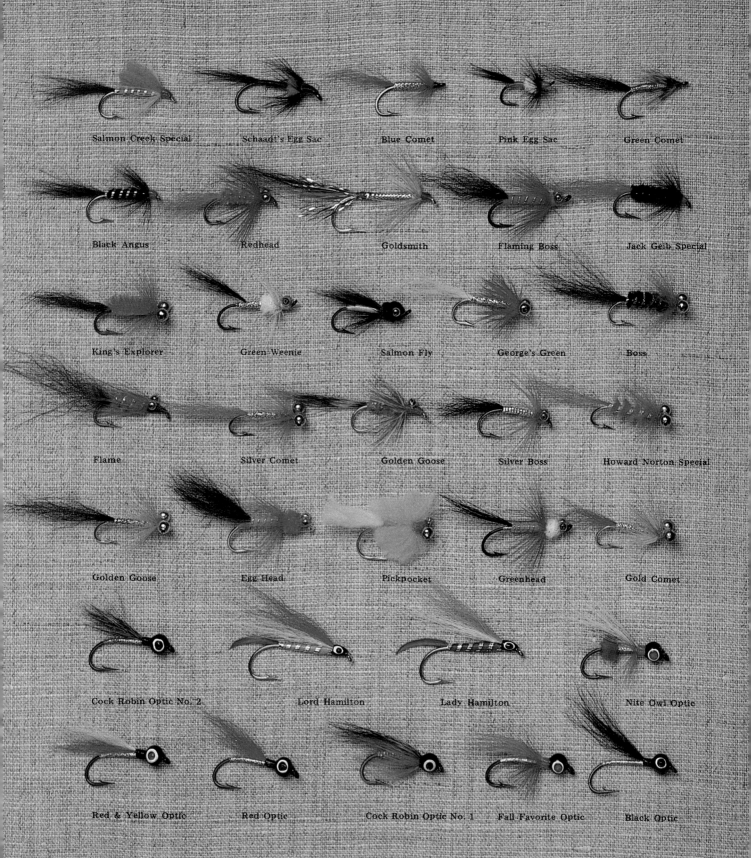

Salmon Creek Special	Schaadt's Egg Sac	Blue Comet	Pink Egg Sac	Green Comet
Black Angus	Redhead	Goldsmith	Flaming Boss	Jack Geib Special
King's Explorer	Green Weenie	Salmon Fly	George's Green	Boss
Flame	Silver Comet	Golden Goose	Silver Boss	Howard Norton Special
Golden Goose	Egg Head	Pickpocket	Greenhead	Gold Comet
Cock Robin Optic No. 2	Lord Hamilton	Lady Hamilton		Nite Owl Optic
Red & Yellow Optic	Red Optic	Cock Robin Optic No. 1	Fall Favorite Optic	Black Optic

PLATE VI

Lakefork Orange Paper Mill Green Machine No. 1 Glo-Bug Teeny Nymph, Black Teeny Nymph, Brown

W/O Trinity BBL Idaho Sunset Chief Fat Dog Walker Shrimp

Green Machine No. 2 The Dredge Black & Blue Polar Shrimp Green Machine No. 3

Denali Green & Black Burlap Atherton Squirrel Tail Outrageous

Brad's Brat Gray Squirrel Tail Gloria's Green Skirt Pink Death Flame Shrimp

Lavender Lady Two Egg Sperm Fly, Orange Idaho Sunset Two Egg Sperm Fly, Pink Purple Comet

Bristol Bay Matuka Winter's Hope Aztec Dungeness Silver

PLATE VII

Mel and Bert Nelson of Kitsap Bait Sales, Port Orchard, Washington, pulling a beach seine while collecting baitfish specimens for photographs used in this chapter, under special license from the Washington Department of Fisheries. BMF.

Particular pains have been taken by the authors to provide photographs of many of the principal salmon feed items while they were alive and, therefore, showing true life coloring. It was found that specimens would change hues rapidly upon or even approaching death. We hope that this extra attention to color detail will prove useful to the fly tiers among our readers.

Baitfish 1-7
Squid 8
Zooplankton 9-15

Northern Anchovy
Engraulis mordax
Bill Ludwig, photo

Northern Anchovy (Undulating)
Engraulis mordax
Bill Ludwig, photo

Pacific Herring
Clupea Harengus Pallasi
Bill Ludwig, photo

Pacific Sardine
Sardinops sagax
Calif. Fish & Game Dept., photo

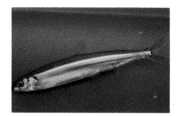

Surf Smelt
Hypomesus pretiosus
Bruce Ferguson, photo

Pacific Sand Lance
Ammodytes hexapterus
Bruce Ferguson, photo

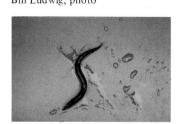

Pacific Sand Lance (Undulating)
Ammodytes hexapterus
Bruce Ferguson, photo

Squid
Loligo
Bill Ludwig, photo

Shrimp
Pasiphaea pacifica
David Roetcisoender, photo

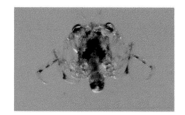

Crab Larvae
Unknown
Lee Hendrickson, photo

Krill (Euphausid)
Euphausia sp.
Lee Hendrickson, photo

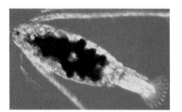

Copepod
Diaptomus sp.
Lee Hendrickson, photo

Amphipod
Unknown
Lee Hendrickson, photo

Barnacle Larvae
Unknown
Lee Hendrickson, photo

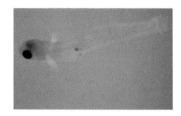

Prickly Sculpin Larvae
Unknown
Lee Hendrickson, photo

next, and lime-green on the sides. A red "throat" is also added with a marking pen. Then the entire fly is given a coat of epoxy.

PATTERN 4

Thread: White. **Body and Tail:** Silver mylar piping. **Wing:** FisHair or bucktail in various colors over white with strands of silver mylar or pearl flashabou alongside. **Throat:** White FisHair or bucktail. **Head:** Black with white eyes, black pupils.

This pattern and Patterns 2 and 3 were developed by Brian Steel of Tacoma, Washington. They are very effective in Puget Sound for coho and chinook, especially when tied sparse.

YELLOW FLY

Hook: Tandem, size 4 or 2 up front with size 6 in the rear. Tie the fly on the front hook. **Wing:** Fluorescent yellow over sparse white bucktail. **Throat:** Generous bunch of silver mylar from unraveled piping or lamé. **Head:** Large, painted fluorescent yellow with black eyes.

My adaptation of a trolling streamer by Stan Kaufman of Lynnwood, Washington. I wanted to scale the fly down somewhat for casting without losing length. The specimen in the color plate is Kaufman's original trolling bucktail. This fly gained its fame in the waters off Possession Point at the south end of Whidbey Island. Kaufman always said that when fished deep, the fly lost just enough chroma to emulate the herring and candlefish colors when seen at the same depths.

Squid Patterns — *Loligo Opalescens*

The squid is another salmon feed around which there has been but little experimentation. When Pat Trotter did the research for his article, "Salmon in the Salt," which appeared in the season opener, 1976 issue of *Fly Fisherman* magazine, he developed one pattern for the *Loligo opalescens*, the type of squid commonly found in Puget Sound. Another style of squid fly, used by saltwater fly anglers in the warmer currents off the coast of southern California, is called the Sea Arrow Squid. The original version was developed by Dan Blanton and Bob Edgely. A variation called the Tutti-Fruity Squid was created by Harry F. Kime.

SEA ARROW SQUID

Hook: 3/0 ring eye. **Thread:** White. **Tail:** Ten white neck hackles 2½ inches long, tied to flare in all directions. Two 4½-inch white hackles, one on each side, serve as tentacles. Add a few strands of purple bucktail on each side as blood veins. **Cheeks:** White marabou. **Eyes:** Glass eyes, flat amber or black, 8-mm. **Body:** Large white chenille. **Fin:** Tie in four, one-inch strands of acrylic yarn. Comb these out, soak with lacquer, and spread the strands so as to radiate out around the hook eye. Trim to an arrowhead shape.

This is the now-standard saltwater pattern developed by West Coast anglers Dan Blanton and Bob Edgley. The specimen in the color plate was submitted by Jim Johnson of Port Orchard, Washington.

TUTTI-FRUITY SQUID

Hook: As above. **Thread:** White or fluorescent red or orange. **Tail:** Bunch of white marabou along with four very long white saddle hackles. Tie in a few strands of fluorescent pink or cerise bucktail and/or marabou as blood veins on each side. **Body:** White chenille. **Eyes:** Painted on at the back of the body, white with black pupils. **Back:** White yarn which is colored with a fluorescent orange felt pen. **Fin:** Fashion as in the Sea Arrow Squid above. **Coloring:** When the fly is completed, dot it all over with small dots from fluorescent yellow, orange and cerise marking pens.

A Harry F. Kime variation of the Sea Arrow Squid. Originally tied to be eight inches long for use in teasing billfish into a strike.

LOLIGO II

Hook: 4, 3XL. **Thread:** White. **Tail:** Two long white marabou plumes as tentacles along with a thick bunch of mixed pale pink, pale blue, and white hackle fibers. **Eyes:** About a quarter of the way up the hook shank, tie in a pair of bead chains painted white or amber with black pupils. **Body:** Yarn dubbing made of two parts white and one part each of pale pink and pale blue. **Hackle:** Palmer the front part of the body with four hackles, two white and one each pale pink and pale blue. Trim the fibers off on top and bottom to produce a flat shape.

This is the Pat Trotter version of the baby squid.

Zooplankton — Shrimp Larvae

Zooplankton flies depict the array of smaller creatures that salmon eat in salt water. We have chosen to list these flies by category: shrimp larvae, euphausids, amphipods, etc. But remember, many of these patterns are interchangeable. A euphausid imitation may do equally well during an amphipod swarm and vice versa. There are also some important categories of zooplankton for which we have no patterns. The crab larvae, the copepods, and the barnacle larvae are examples of zooplankton salmon feed that are small and hard to imitate. To date nobody has attempted to develop any specific patterns.

JOHNSTON SPECIAL SHRIMP

Hook: 8 to 4, ring eye. **Tail:** Polar bear or calf tail dyed light fluorescent pink. **Body:** Fluorescent pink chenille palmered over with true orange hackle and ribbed with one-quarter inch gold scalite. **Back:** Pull the butts of the hair used for the tail forward and secure at the head. **Feelers:** Spread out the butts of the back hairs and trim to shape.

A shellback-style shrimp fly by Jim Johnston of the Washington Game Department.

ORANGE SHRIMP

Hook: 12 to 4, English bait hook. **Thread:** Fluorescent true orange. **Tail:** Orange bucktail. **Body:** Orange chenille. After the back is formed, rib with heavy fluorescent true orange monocord-type tying thread. **Hackle:** Hot orange palmered over body. **Back:** Hot orange bucktail secured to the hook shank before the body is formed, then, after the body and hackle are wound, brought forward over the back and secured at the head. **Head and Eyes:** Heavy fluorescent true orange monocord with black dots painted on.

Another shellback-style shrimp fly by Mike Foster, Miranda, California. He also likes this fly with a brown bucktail back, and an all-pink version with pink and orange hackles. Frank Lawrence's Orange Shrimp, also shown in the color plate, is similar except the back and feelers are barred gray mallard flank fibers.

PINK FEED

Hook: 12 to 6, English bait hook. **Thread:** White. **Tail:** Wisps of dyed hackle (dying instructions below). **Body:** Dubbing mixture, picked out along the bottom to depict legs after the fly is completed. Simulate the reddish veins in the shrimp with fluorescent red-orange thread. Bring one strand forward over the back and tie it down at the front. Then rib the fly with a second strand. **Shellback (optional):** Clear polyethylene strip pulled forward and tied down. **Rib:** Fine-diameter clear monofilament, placed so as to over-rib the vein rib. **Hackle:** Wrapped at the head and clipped off on top and sides. **Feelers:** Wisps of dyed hackle.

This is a particularly successful style of shrimp which Pat Trotter developed in 1976. The pattern has evolved considerably since then, with new materials and altered colors to get a better match with the krill we have collected from our local waters. To tie the present version, we dye our own hackles and body dubbing. It's the only way we've found to get just the shades we want. They dye bath consists of 1/4 teaspoon each of fluorescent pink and fluorescent orange dye in one pint of water. Formerly we used Herter's radiant color dyes, which called for sulphuric acid in the bath but we always substituted vinegar. This kept the dyes from developing full color intensity, which is just what we wanted. The idea was to keep the colors *pale*. We started with white feathers and left them in the dye bath only a couple of minutes. We also threw in a length of white polypro yarn — the sparkling, translucent kind sold under the trade name Poly X Wing. This stuff you could boil seemingly forever and it would take up only the merest hint of the color, which again, was just what we wanted. This of course became the body dubbing.

PINK SHRIMP

Hook: 4, 6, or 8. Thread: Pink or white. Tail: Pink bucktail tied in at hook bend. Leave butts extending forward for the shellback. Body: Silver tinsel or pink chenille ribbed with silver tinsel. Hackle: Pink, can be tied either palmer style or at the front only. Shellback: The butts of the pink bucktail brought forward and tied down.

This pattern is imported from the Florida bonefish flats. There are many variations.

Zooplankton — Euphausid Patterns

FLASHABOU EUPHAUSID

Hook: 10 to 4, regular shank. Thread: White or black. Tail, Body and Thorat: Pearl Flashabou tied in a bunch, leaving a short tail, then wrapped forward to form the body. Tie the ends off under the hook shank for a throat.

True euphausids lack the usual shrimp-like shape in the water. This Gary Strodtz pattern is excellent in the spring when the coho are line feeding and very selective.

WALKINSHAW EUPHAUSID

Hook: 4, 6, 8, long shank. Cream-colored sparkle yarn. Throat: White or cream polar bear, very sparse.

Pattern by Walt Walkinshaw of Seattle, Washington. Very effective in south Puget Sound in February when the euphausids are the principal feed.

Zooplankton — Amphipod Patterns

Strictly speaking, amphipods are the tiny scud-like creatures that inhabit the coastal waters. They come in a variety of hues: pastel pink, orange, green, violet, rust, and olive. Most of the shrimp spawn flies listed earlier will work in this category, as well as the specific patterns listed below.

BURNT ORANGE AMPHIPOD

Hook: 6 or 8, either regular shank or English bait hook. Body and Legs: Burnt orange-dyed seal fur dubbing picked out a bit, especially on the underside.

Pattern by Tom Fredrickson, Olympia, Washington. Also tied in gray and olive colors. The burnt orange pattern depicts the most common pelagic amphipod in south Puget Sound. The gray and olive patterns imitate amphipods that hang around the kelp beds.

FERGUSON'S AMPHIPOD

Hook: size 6 English bait hook. Thread: White. Tail: Tip of a pale ginger hackle, about one-half inch long. Body: Fluorescent pale pinkish-orange chenille. Hackle: Remainder of the hackle feather used for the tail, tied palmer style over the body. Clip the fibers on the top and sides so that just the bottom fibers are left protruding for the legs.

This is the simple bread-and-butter pattern that served Bruce Ferguson so well during the many early years when he was pioneering the development of fly fishing techniques for the resident silver salmon in south Puget Sound.

GREEN AMPHIPOD

Hook: 4, 6 or 8 regular shank or English bait hook. Thread: Tan. Tail: Deer body hair tied in well around the hook bend to get a definite droop. The butts of the hair will form the back. Body: Fluorescent green chenille. Hackle: Blue dun tied palmer. Back: Deer body hair. Rib: Tan thread over body and back.

This fly, by Lloyd Morrell of Tacoma, Washington, works amazingly well when the salmon are feeding on amphipods (euphausids, too) despite its gaudy fluorescent garb. The same pattern in salmon-pink or fluorescent white chenille also does well. Tied in either a regular shank version or on an English bait hook. The English bait hook sample was tied by Bruce Ferguson. The offset English bait hook provides a more erratic action on the retrieve.

"GREEN WEANIE"

Hook: 6 or 8, TULE. Tail: Red hackle fibers. Body: Fluorescent green chenille ribbed with silver tinsel. Hackle: Sparse white. Wing: Sparse white polar bear or bucktail.

There must be dozens of flies called "Green Weanie." We'll see another one later on in the section on flies for fresh water. This particular one was developed by Jerry Wiese, Al Saas, and Earl Averill, all members of the Puget Sound Flyfishers of Tacoma, Washington. It is good in the winter and early spring for zooplankton-feeding coho. It is also a good fall "waiting period" fly. The key to its effectiveness, according to its creators, is to *keep it sparse*.

HALE'S PINKY

Hook: 10 to 6, regular shank. Thread: White. Body: Mottled pink and white medium chenille. Throat: Long white polar bear, bucktail or calf tail. Head: White with silver bead chain eyes lashed on.

A pattern by Carl Stroud for use on south Puget Sound in May and June when the coho are very selectively feeding on zooplankton. A good choice when the salmon are on crab spawn. The name of this pattern derives from Hale's Passage, a popular angling locale for resident silvers in Puget Sound.

SALTWATER FLIES — THE WAITING PERIOD

There comes a time, just prior to actually ascending into fresh water, when the salmon stop their active feeding and gather close to the mouths of their spawning streams. They concentrate along the beaches and in the estuaries. They are not yet committing themselves to an actual spawning run at this point; they are just waiting for the propitious moment. The length of this waiting period varies. It ends when the fall rains finally bring on the freshets that draw the fish into the rivers for good. It is a prime time to find the fish concentrated, but hooking them consistently is something else again!

Since the fish are no longer feeding, the attractor type of fly associated more with freshwater fishing seems to work best. The "Green Weanie" pattern listed above is a good waiting period fly and is in fact typical of the style used effectively during this most difficult time for the fly fisherman. Listed below are some other good patterns that have proven themselves during the waiting period.

BARRY THORNTON BEACH FLY

Hook: 6, 8, long shank. Body: Silver tinsel. Hackle: Green, red, purple, or black. Wing: White polar bear or substitute tied very sparse.

Barry Thornton of Vancouver, B. C., uses a variety of flies for coho beach fly fishing. He has found that any of the color variations listed above are effective, as are such Canadian standards as the Ginger Jake (see below) and Coronation, just as long as they are kept sparse. Thornton also sent us a particularly effective specimen quite similar to the Polar Shrimp except the body is made from a strip of fluorescent plastic he cut from his daughter's old raincoat.

BOWSTRING SPIDER

Hook: 10 to 6, 2X or 3X long. Body: Fluorescent red-orange monofilament used in fashioning bow strings tied over flat silver tinsel. Soften the monofilament in hot water before use to give a tighter, closer wrap. Orange floss or mylar could be substituted. Hackle: Yellow, with a wood duck or dyed mallard flank feather doubled and wrapped on just in front.

A pattern derived from Al Knudson's famous sea-run cutthroat and steelhead fly by Earl Averill of Tacoma, Washington. An excellent fly during the fall waiting period, it also works for spring coho when they are feeding on zooplankton.

GINGER JAKE

Hook: 6 or 8, long shank. Tail: Frayed out end of mylar piping used for the body. Body: Silver mylar piping. Wing: Orange over white. Use bucktail, polar bear, or FisHair and tie very sparse.

JOHNSON'S BEACH FLY

Hook: 6 or 8, long shank. Thread: Fluorescent orange. Tag: Fine gold tinsel. Body: Very slender fluorescent orange yarn. Fine gold tinsel rib (optional). Hackle: Sparse badger. Wing: White calf tail or arctic fox tail, very sparse.

Pattern by co-author Les Johnson.

POLAR SHRIMP

Hook: As above. Tail: Fluorescent hot orange/red hackle fibers. Body: Fluorescent hot orange/red yarn. Hackle: Fluorescent hot orange/red. Wing: White bucktail, polar bear, arctic fox, or synthetic. Tie the wing just a bit longer than normal and VERY sparse. Use only about a quarter of the material you'd normally use in a wing.

This fly, originated by the late Clarence Shoff in 1936, and an old standard Pacific Northwest steelhead pattern, is one of the best of the so-called "beach flies." A fluorescent green version is also good.

WAITING ROYAL COACHMAN

Hook: 4, 6, 8, regular shank. Tail: Golden pheasant tippet fibers. Body: Peacock herl fore and aft with a band of red floss in the middle. Hackle: White, sparse. Wing: White polar bear or bucktail, also quite sparse and at least twice the length of the hook shank.

An Al Allard adaptation of the standard Royal Coachman. Mr. Allard is one of the originals, if such a thing can be said, when it comes to fly fishing the waiting period for salmon.

FRESHWATER FLIES

We pointed out in preceding chapters that success on salmon in the rivers depends on getting deep. Roderick Haig-Brown described how salmon, upon first entering fresh water, seek out the deepest runs — deeper even than you'd associate with a typical winter steelhead lie. Only gradually do the salmon work their way into steelhead-type water. To reach such tentative, deep-holding fish, look for flies with a sparsely dressed, built-in compactness for a quick, deep sink. We will show you several styles of flies that have evolved over the years to have these ingredients. Couple them with a modern fast sinking fly line or shooting head and you have the key to hooking big salmon on fly tackle in fresh water.

ATHERTON SQUIRREL TAIL

Hook: 2/0 to 6. Tag: Flat silver tinsel. Tail: Golden pheasant tippet fibers. Butt: Fluorescent yellow or chartreuse floss or fine yarn. Body: Slender black dubbing ribbed with fine oval silver tinsel. Throat: Brown hackle fibers. Wing: Red squirrel tail hair.

Originally an Atlantic salmon pattern, this fly is used extensively in the Great Lakes region and has been transplanted to the Pacific Coast.

AZTEC

Hook: 2/0 to 6. Thread: Red. Tail: Long strands of acrylic yarn, combed out. Body: Oval silver tinsel. Wing: Strands of acrylic yarn are looped onto the hook shank with tying thread. Then the body tinsel is wound carefully between the acrylic strands. The strands are combed out and trimmed to shape.

The folks at Bristol Bay Lodge, Alaska, provided us two patterns of the Aztec fly, both commercially produced by Aztec Anglers, Los Gatos, California. One is an all-purple pattern. The other has a three-part tail consisting of blue over olive over white coupled with an all blue wing.

B. B. L.

Hook: As above. Thread: White. Body: Silver polyglitter tinsel. Wing: Purple over red bucktail, no longer than the body. Throat: Bright blue-green bucktail, also body length. Head: White thread.

Another of the Bristol Bay Lodge patterns, this one for freshwater coho.

BLACK ANGUS

Hook: As above. Thread: Orange. Tail: Black bucktail, Comet length optional. Body: Black wool ribbed with flat silver tinsel. Hackle: Black. Head: Orange.

Pattern by Irwin Thompson, Sebastopol, California.

BLACK AND BLUE MARABOU

Hook: 2, 4, 6, extra strong. Can be weighted with lead wire. Tail: Black marabou, comet style, hook shank length or longer. Body: Oval silver tinsel. Thorax: Blue chenille, two turns. Hackle: Black, two to three turns. Thread: Blue monocord.

Submitted by Bob Guard of The Caddis Fly Angling Shoppe, Eugene, Oregon. Used effectively on all Oregon and northern California coastal streams for coho and chinook salmon.

BOSS

Hook: As above. Tail: Black bucktail tied Comet style. Body: Black chenille or yarn ribbed with silver tinsel. Hackle: Hot orange or red, fluorescent colors optional, long and flowing. Eyes: Silver bead chains (optional).

A Russian River, California, steelhead pattern adapted for salmon fishing. I am told that the Boss fly was not originally tied as a Comet style fly, but the tail gradually lengthened until now it is more common to see it Comet style than not. There is actually a whole series of Boss flies in different colors. Darrell F. Arnold submitted the specimen of Silver Boss shown in the color plate.

BRAD'S BRAT

Hook: 2/0 to smaller, 4 a good average. Tip: Gold tinsel. Tail: Orange and white bucktail hairs mixed. Body: Back half orange yarn, front half red yarn. Rib with gold tinsel. Hackle: Brown. Wing: Top one-third orange bucktail, bottom two-thirds, white bucktail.

A longtime standard Northwest steelhead pattern by the late Enos Bradner, Seattle, Washington. Particularly good for silvers that have just entered a pool and are milling around in circles. Fish with a fast, jerky retrieve.

BRISTOL BAY MATUKA

Hook: 4/0 to 6, heavy Atlantic salmon style. Thread: Fluorescent orange. Body: Form a base with yellow CSE nylon and overwrap with CSE gold mylar braid. The rib, which holds down the Matuka wing, is gold-dyed, 25-pound-test Cortland Cobra flat monofilament. Wing: Two fluorescent orange or yellow hackles inside of two red hackles. Gills: Bunches of fluorescent orange or red marabou fluff tied on each side of the wing in the shoulder position. Hackle: Fluorescent orange.

Don Hathaway is a commercial fly tier from Lake Fork, Idaho. He originally tied this fly for the Salmon River, Idaho, chinook run. He sent a few to John and Maggie Garry for their lodge at Bristol Bay, hence the name.

BURLAP

Hook: 2/0 to 6. **Thread:** Yellow. **Tail:** Red squirrel tail hair. **Body:** Light brown strands from an old burlap bag, or any rough yarn of about the same color. **Hackle:** Cree or grizzly. **Wing:** Red squirrel tail hair. **Head:** Yellow.

A Bristol Bay Lodge version of the old standard steelhead fly.

CHIEF FAT DOG

Hook: As above. **Tail:** Unraveled strands of silver polyglitter tinsel. **Body:** Silver polyglitter. **Wing:** Under, strands of unraveled silver polyglitter about half the body length. Over, purple bucktail the length of the body. **Throat:** Hot orange bucktail, body length.

Boy, would I like to know the origin of this name! Another pattern from Bristol Bay Lodge, said to be good for freshwater coho.

COHO

Hook: Size 2, long shank. **Body:** Silver tinsel chenille or, as an option, leave the hook bare. **Wing:** Various colors of bucktail or FisHair. Red over white is a standard combo.

Excellent in Alaska's Russian River and nearby streams, not so much for coho, as the name might imply, but for sockeye (called red salmon in Alaska).

COMET, GOLD

Hook: 2/0 to 12, goldplated hook optional, lead wire weighting also optional. **Thread:** Yellow or orange. **Tail:** Very long orange bucktail, bear hair, or other suitable hair. I'm told by fly tiers familiar with the Comet's origin that to be a true Comet the tail should be at least three times the body length, and it should be tied with a wrap of body material behind it to hold it up and out. **Body:** Gold tinsel, either flat or oval, or gold mylar piping. **Hackle:** Mixed yellow and orange. **Eyes:** Pair of gold bead chains (optional, but helps to weight the fly).

COMET, SILVER

Hook: Sizes as above, nickelplated hook optional. **Thread:** White. **Tail:** Orange bucktail or bear hair tied as above. **Body:** Silver tinsel or mylar piping. **Hackle:** Orange. **Eyes:** Silver bead chain optional.

The Comets, with their long, flowing tails, are mainstays for freshwater salmon angling. There are many colors, including an Orange Comet which differs from the Silver only in the use of fluorescent orange or flame-colored hackle and tail instead of plain orange. There is a Blue Comet (also called Blue Death) with a blue hackle and tail, and a Green Comet which features a green tinsel body, grizzly or black hackle, and black hair for the tail.

DENALI

Hook: Size 2, Mustad 36715 is recommended. **Tail:** Red hackle fibers. **Body:** 24-gauge copper wire. **Hackle:** Yellow tied as a throat. **Wing:** Three layers of bucktail, Silver Doctor blue on top and bottom with orange in the middle.

An Alaskan sockeye salmon pattern by Dr. Tom Elliott, Wasilla, Alaska.

THE DREDGE

Hook: 2 or 4, heavy Atlantic salmon type, weighted with several wraps of .025 lead wire wrapped well forward on the hook shank. The fly is tied "low water" style and should be about a size 8 in bulk. **Butt:** Red or hot orange fluorescent chenille. **Body:** Flat silver tinsel. **Wing:** Red or hot orange fluorescent yarn clipped to be no longer than the front of the butt.

Another severely compact, fast sinking winter steelhead fly that should be ideal for salmon in streams, this one by Mark Bachmann. The Pink Frammus and Green Frammus steelhead patterns are similar and should be equally useful for salmon.

DUNGENESS SILVER

Hook: 1 to 2/0, heavy Atlantic salmon type. **Body:** Rear half, fluorescent orange yarn. Front half, fluorescent yellow yarn. Rib entire body with flat silver tinsel. **Wing:** Fluorescent yellow over fluorescent orange marabou.

A pattern by James Garrett, Sequim, Washington. He says it works particularly well for coho in heavier water.

EGG HEAD

Hook: 8 to 2/0. **Thread:** Fluorescent red-orange. **Tip:** Fluorescent red-orange thread. **Tail:** Black bucktail tied Comet style. **Body:** Fluorescent true orange yarn ribbed with oval gold tinsel. **Hackle:** Orange. **Head:** Fluorescent red-orange chenille with bead chain eyes tied on ahead.

A good-anywhere pattern that originated in the northern California or southern Oregon area.

EGG SAC

Hook: As above. **Tail:** Black bucktail, Comet style. **Body:** Rear two-thirds, thin black floss or yarn. Front third, large hump of fluorescent red-orange chenille. **Hackle:** Black.

A pattern attributed to various of the anglers comprising the "Smith River fraternity," such as Bill Schaadt or Grant King. There is an all-black version (including the egg sac hump) and a Pink Egg Sac which features a fluorescent red-orange body with fluorescent pink egg sac.

FALL FAVORITE OPTIC

Hook: Size 2, Mustad 7970. **Body:** Flat, oval, or embossed silver tinsel. **Hackle:** Red. **Wing:** Orange bucktail. **Head:** Quarter-inch brass bead clamped on and painted black with white eyes, red irises.

The Optics are another group of winter steelhead flies that produce well on salmon. Optics were invented by C. Jim Pray back in the 1940s. Pray tied the originals on extra-stout size 1 hooks that were 5X short. That gave a fly about the equivalent of a No. 6 in bulk. They would cast with relative ease, despite being quite heavy for their size, and they would sink like rocks. The hooks Pray used aren't available anymore, but you can achieve the same effect just about with the No. 2 Mustad 7970. The original Pray Optic series included the Black, Red, Red-and-Yellow, and Cock Robin Optics. Lloyd Silvius invented two other excellent Optics about the same time: the Nite Owl Optic and the Fall Favorite Optic listed here. By the way, the Fall Favorite is a pretty good salmon pattern with or without the optic head.

FLAME SHRIMP

Hook: 2/0 to 6, heavy Atlantic salmon type. **Tail:** Fluorescent hot orange hackle fibers. **Body:** Fluorescent true orange chenille ribbed with medium gold embossed tinsel. **Hackle:** Fluorescent hot orange. **Wing:** White calf or polar bear hair.

Pattern by James Garrett, Sequim, Washington.

FLAMING BOSS/FLAME

Hook: 2/0 to 12, lead wire weighting optional. **Tail:** Black bucktail, Comet style. **Body:** Fluorescent flame chenille ribbed with silver tinsel. **Hackle:** Fluorescent orange. **Eyes:** Silver bead chain optional.

This is a variation of the Boss fly developed by Grant King, Guerneyville, California. Sometimes this pattern is called simply Flame.

FLASH FLY

Hook: 2/0 to 6, standard shank, extra strong. **Tail:** Silver Flashabou. **Body:** Silver Flashabou, wrapped like wool or chenille. **Wing:** Purple Flashabou under (1/4) silver Flashabou over (3/4). **Hackle:** Red, in front of wing as a collar. **Thread:** Red.

Recommended for Alaska silver salmon in the fall by Mike Michalak, The Fly Shop, Redding, California.

GEORGE'S GREEN

Hook: 4, 6, 8. **Thread:** Black. **Tail:** Black hackle fibers. **Body:** Fluorescent green floss. **Hackle:** Black. **Wing:** Black kip, bear, or squirrel hair. **Head:** Black chenille with silver bead chain eyes tied on ahead.

This is one of several recent northern California-southern Oregon patterns in the green theme.

GLORIA'S GREEN SKIRT

Hook: 2/0 to 6, heavy Atlantic salmon type. **Butt:** Fluorescent green chenille wound to form an egg shape. **Hackle:** Fluorescent yellow tied just ahead of the green butt. **Shoulder:** Fluorescent hot orange or flame chenille wound to form an egg shape.

Pattern by James Garrett, Sequim, Washington, for the Dungeness River. The Gloria in the fly's name is Mrs. Garrett. The fly is said to be especially good for chum salmon.

GLO BUG

Hook: 2-6, extra strong, extra short, ring eye. **Tail:** None. **Body:** Tie 3 to 5 strands of Glo Bug yarn in center of hook shank with a small amount of alternate color on top to form eye. Pull thread around middle of yarn stack several times, then make additional turns next to shank, parachute style. Pull yarn straight up and trim in semicircle with scissors. Result is egg-shaped ball of yarn with small spot for eye. A handy pattern to roll past a salmon in clear water.

GOLDEN GOOSE

Hook: 2/0 to 12, lead wire weighting optional. **Tail:** Black or dark brown bucktail or bear hair tied Comet style. **Body:** Flat or oval gold tinsel or gold mylar piping. **Hackle:** Yellow and red wound together. **Eyes:** Gold bead chain optional.

This pattern is credited to pioneering Smith River angler Bill Schaadt.

GOLDSMITH

Hook: 2 to 10, Eagle Claw 1197G, lead wire weighting optional. **Tying Thread:** Red. **Tail:** Black over hot orange bucktail, Comet style. **Body:** Gold mylar piping with a bit of the back end frayed out to form part of the tail. **Hackle:** Mixed yellow and hot orange. **Eyes:** Gold bead chain (optional).

A Smith River/Chetco River pattern attributed to Ed Given. The Silversmith pattern (not shown) is a companion fly tied on a nickel-plated hook and with silver mylar piping and silver bead chain substituted for the gold. Otherwise the patterns are the same.

GRAY SQUIRREL TAIL

Hook: 2/0 to 10. **Tail:** Gray squirrel tail hair. **Body:** Silver tinsel. **Wing:** Gray squirrel tail hair.

A very simple but highly effective pattern for sockeye and silvers. Darrell F. Arnold of Novato, California, submitted the specimen in the color plate.

GREEN AND BLACK MARABOU

Hook: 2, 4, 6, extra strong. Can be weighted with lead wire. **Tail:** Green marabou, comet style, hook shank length or longer. **Body:** Fluorescent green Amnesia monofilament. **Thorax:** Black chenille, two turns. **Hackle:** Fluorescent green, 2 to 3 turns. **Thread:** Green monocord.

A Bob Guard pattern used alternately with the Black and Blue Marabou.

GREEN HEAD

Hook: 4, 6, 8. **Thread:** Fluorescent green. **Tip:** Fluorescent green thread. **Tail:** Black kip, bear, or squirrel hair tied Comet style. **Body:** Fluorescent red-orange yarn or floss ribbed with small oval gold tinsel. **Hackle:** Bright orange. **Head:** Large fluorescent green chenille with gold bead chain eyes tied on ahead.

Pattern created by Californian Rex Collingsworth about 1980 as a green modification of the Egg Head pattern (see above).

GREEN MACHINE 1-2-3

Hook: 4 to 10. **Thread:** Black or brown. **Tail:** Black, gray, or brown bucktail or other hair tied Comet style. **Body:** Fluorescent green chenille or floss. Ribbing with gold or silver oval tinsel is optional. **Hackle:** Grizzly, black or brown. Either match or contrast with the tail (your choice).

Pattern attributed to Al Perryman of California; said to be very successful on Oregon's Chetco River for big kings.

GREEN WEANIE

Hook: 4, 6, 8. **Tail:** Black kip, bear, or squirrel hair tied Comet style. **Body:** Back half, silver tinsel. Front half, fluorescent green chenille. **Hackle:** Bright green. **Head:** Black with silver bead chain eyes.

I promised you another Green Weanie pattern earlier, and here it is! This one was originally a shad fly, but was adapted to fishing for freshwater silver salmon. A variation by Tom Ugrin of Fort Bragg, California, calls for the hump of fluorescent green chenille to be tied at the butt of the fly rather than at the front.

HORNER SHRIMP

Hook: 2 to 6, lead wire weight optional. **Tail:** Brown bucktail with the butts left long to form a shellback. **Body:** Silver tinsel over a white floss core. **Hackle:** Pale olive tied palmer style. Blue dun and grizzly are sometimes also used. **Back:** Butts of the brown bucktail pulled down over the body.

A now classic pattern developed by Jack Horner of San Francisco. First used on the Eel River for steelhead in 1938, the Horner Shrimp has become one of the standard fly types for river salmon. Shrimp flies are especially effective for jacks, those small, sexually precocious first-year males that always seem to be present in a run of larger salmon.

HOWARD NORTON SPECIAL

Hook: 2/0 to 12, lead wire weighting optional. **Thread:** White. **Tail:** Fluorescent orange bucktail or polar bear, Comet style. **Body:** Fluorescent flame chenille ribbed with silver tinsel. **Hackle:** Fluorescent orange. **Eyes:** Silver bead chain.

This is essentially a chenille-bodied version of the Orange Comet referred to above in the remarks under Comet, Silver.

IDAHO SUNSET

Hook: 2/0 to 2, heavy Atlantic salmon type. **Thread:** Fluorescent orange. **Body:** Form a base of fluorescent orange thread or floss, overwrap with red mylar tinsel, and rib with silver tinsel. **Throat:** Fluorescent red marabou fluff or hackle fibers. **Wing:** Fluorescent orange bucktail or marabou no longer than the end of the body. **Collar Hackle:** Just a turn or two of a fluorescent yellow marabou feather ahead of the wing (this is optional).

A Don Hathaway pattern for the Salmon River, Idaho district.

JACK GEIB SPECIAL

Hook: 2/0 to 12. **Tail:** Fluorescent red or orange hair, or flame colored yarn, tied Comet style. **Body:** Black chenille. **Hackle:** Black.

Another pattern by a Smith River pioneer.

JOHNSON'S PARTRIDGE SPIDER

Hook: 10, standard or 1X short shank, extra strong. **Tail:** Wisps of partridge hackle, 1½ times hook shank length, sparse. **Body:** Danville's fluorescent yarn, orange, green, red or yellow. **Hackle:** Partridge hackle, two to three turns, spider style. **Thread:** Danville's fluorescent orange.

Originated for sea-run cutthroat in clear water. Has proven to be effective in very clear water on long fine leader for salmon, particularly coho. A twitching retrieve that activates the partridge hackle works best.

KING'S EXPLORER

Hook: As above. **Tail:** Black buck or bear hair, Comet style. **Body:** Silver tinsel with fluorescent red or orange chenille strands tied down over the back. **Hackle:** Fluorescent orange. **Eyes:** Silver bead chain.

There is a series of these flies in different colors. Created by Grant King, yet another of the Smith River pioneers.

KING'S SHRIMP

Hook: 2 to 6. **Tail:** Orange bucktail, fairly long. Leave the butts intact to form a shellback. **Body:** Silver tinsel. **Hackle:** Orange tied palmer style. **Back:** Pull the butts of the tail hairs down over the back and tie off.

A Grant King variation of the basic Horner Shrimp. The use of fluorescent colors in this pattern is optional.

LADY HAMILTON

Hook: 6 to 3/0. **Tail:** Red goose primary strip. **Body:** Red floss ribbed with embossed silver tinsel. The floss is wound in several layers back and forth to build up a good taper, cementing heavily between layers. **Wing:** Orange over white bucktail. **Head:** Built up with tying thread; white eyes with black pupils painted on.

LORD HAMILTON

Hook: As above. **Tail:** Red goose primary strip. **Body:** Yellow floss ribbed with embossed silver tinsel. Construct the body as above. **Wing:** Red over white bucktail. **Head:** As in Lady Hamilton pattern.

The Lord and Lady Hamilton patterns were conceived by pioneering Washington steelheader, Ralph Wahl. They were designed for severe compactness and a very fast sink rate.

LAKEFORK ORANGE

Hook: 2/0 to 2. **Tag:** Copper tinsel. **Tail:** Yellow hackle fibers or golden pheasant crest. **Body:** Orange yarn or dubbing ribbed with copper tinsel. **Throat:** Fluorescent red marabou. **Wing:** Dark brown bucktail topped with golden pheasant crest.

A Don Hathaway pattern for the Salmon River, Idaho, district.

LAVENDER LADY

Hook: 2/0 to 6. **Thread:** White. **Tail:** Lavender-dyed bucktail over white bucktail, tied Comet style. **Body:** Silver polyglitter. **Hackle:** Mixed white and purple, heavily hackled. **Head:** White thread.

A Comet style fly used in Alaska for silver salmon, submitted by the folks at Bristol Bay Lodge.

LOW WATER SHRIMP 1-2

Hook: 6-8, extra strong. Can be weighted with lead wire. **Tail and shellback:** Natural brown deer hair. **Body:** Oval silver tinsel or variegated red and gray chenille. **Hackle:** Grizzly or fluorescent orange on tinsel body. Grizzly on red and gray variegated chenille body. **Thread:** Orange.

Traditional shrimp pattern with slight variations used by Bob Guard during low water periods on coastal streams.

MARTIN SEA SHRIMP

Hook: 10 to 12 English bait hook. **Thread:** Orange. **Tail:** Hackle fibers dyed pale pink. **Body:** Dyed synthetic dubbing with a polyethylene strip tied down over the back and ribbed with orange mylar tinsel. Pick out the dubbing along the underside for legs. **Eyes:** 25-pound-test Maxima leader material melted to little balls. **Feelers:** Dyed hackle fibers, pale pink.

Originated by Darrel Martin of Tacoma, Washington.

NITE OWL OPTIC

Hook: Size 2 Mustad 7970. **Tail:** Yellow hackle fibers. **Butt:** Red chenille. **Body:** Oval silver tinsel. **Hackle:** Orange. **Wing:** White bucktail. **Head:** Quarter-inch brass bead painted black with white eyes, red pupils. See remarks under Fall Favorite Optic.

OUTRAGEOUS

Hook: First seen tied on a long shank limerick hook. Substitute an Eagle Claw 1197G or 1197B, your choice of sizes. **Thread:** Red or hot orange. **Tail:** Orange hackle fibers. **Body:** Peacock herl ribbed with gold tinsel. **Hackle:** Purple and yellow mixed. **Wing:** Peacock blue bucktail.

Les Johnson explained how he came upon the Outrageous as follows:

"One morning on the Chetco River nice chinooks were rolling everywhere in front of the ten or so of us spaced along the gravel, but they steadfastly refused every pattern we cast to them. Finally, a woman hooked and skillfully landed the first fish of the day. I walked over for a better look at the salmon as did several others. It was a prime fish of about 25 pounds and embedded in its jaw was a fly that was completely new to me. 'What's your pattern called?' I asked. 'I don't know,' she answered. 'I picked it up in Coos Bay.'

Removing the fly from the salmon's jaw, she stroked back the wing, then broke into a wide grin. 'It is funny looking,' she said, 'but when the salmon aren't hitting my regular patterns I feed them something outrageous. It often prompts a strike, and this fly *is* outrageous!' I nodded, congratulated her and headed back toward my spot, casually rummaging through my fly boxes for something really funny looking."

PAPER MILL

Hook: Size 6, nickelplated. **Thread:** Red. **Tail:** Bunch of hot orange fluorescent bucktail tied at about a 45-degree angle to the horizontal and clipped very short. **Body:** Silver mylar piping bound down at head and tail with the red tying thread. **Wing:** Same as tail, clipped to just shy of body length.

Pattern by Frank Lawrence, El Sobrante, California. Named for Papermill Creek at the foot of Tomales Bay.

PICKPOCKET

Hook: 2/0 - 2 short shank salmon bait fishing hook. **Tail:** Wisp of white yarn, twice hook shank length, picked out. **Body:** Built up with tying thread. **Wing:** Glo-Bug yarn, any good salmon color, one piece above and another below the hook shank, trimmed very short. **Head:** Monocord or a thread to match wing color. **Bead Chain Eyes:** Tie to inside of shank so hook will tend to ride barb up during drift. (See example in color plate.)

A fast-sinking pattern used by Les Johnson. Designed to probe small pockets in fast moving winter steelhead streams but has made the transition to salmon nicely. The hook-point-up drift of the fly makes for sure hooking even on a light strike. Effective on spring and summer chinook in Washington rivers.

PINK DEATH

Hook: 2/0 to 6, heavy Atlantic salmon type. **Tip:** Medium embossed gold tinsel. **Body:** Black angora ribbed with medium embossed gold tinsel. **Wing:** White polar bear or substitute just slightly longer than the bend of the hook.

Pattern by James Garrett, Sequim, Washington. The name derives from the fly's effectiveness on pink salmon in off-color water.

PRAY'S OPTICS (Black, Red, Red and Yellow, Cock Robin)

Hook: Size 2, Mustad 7970. **Body:** Oval tinsel (gold for the Black and Cock Robin Optics, silver for the Red and Red and Yellow). **Wing:** Black bucktail for the Black Optic, red bucktail for the Red Optic, yellow over red bucktail for the Red and Yellow Optic, and gray squirrel tail for the Cock Robin Optic. **Hackle:** Cock Robin Optic only, orange. **Head:** Split brass bead painted black, white eyes with black pupils (red pupils on the Red and Yellow Optic).

These are compact, fast sinking flies originally designed for winter steelhead by C. Jim Pray. As indicated, there are four flies in the series: Black, Red, Red and Yellow (sometimes called the Eel River Optic) and Cock Robin Optic.

PURPLE COMET

Hook: 2/0 to 6. **Tail:** Purple bucktail tied Comet style. **Body:** Silver polyglitter. **Hackle:** Purple.

Alaska silver salmon pattern. The fly in the color plate has a very short tail. It seems that the further north you go, the shorter the Comet style tail becomes!

REDHEAD

Hook: 1 to 12. **Thread:** Red or orange. **Tail:** Fluorescent orange bucktail tied Comet style. **Body:** Fluorescent orange chenille ribbed with silver tinsel. **Hackle:** Fluorescent red. **Eyes:** Silver bead chain.

The specimen in the color plate was tied by Darrell F. Arnold, Novato, California. He says the fly was created by the late Burney Butler of Santa Rosa.

RUSTY SQUIRREL

Hook: 2 to 10, goldplated. **Thread:** Orange. **Tip:** Oval gold tinsel. **Tail:** Dyed black squirrel tail tied Comet style. **Body:** Oval gold tinsel. Hackle: Orange. Head: One or two turns of fluorescent orange chenille with gold bead chain eyes tied on ahead.

Pattern by Jim Victorine, Loomis, California, also called the Rusty Nail. Created in 1974 originally for steelhead, but proved successful for silvers and chinook in northern California. The Silver Rusty Squirrel (shown in the color plate) is the same except tied on a silver hook with a silver body and silver bead chain eyes.

SALMON CREEK SPECIAL

Hook: 2/0 to 6. Thread: Fluorescent red. Tail: Black squirrel tail, Comet style optional. Body: Fluorescent hot orange floss built up to a good taper, ribbed with flat narrow silver tinsel. Wing: Fluorescent orange yarn topped with fluorescent white hackle fibers. Hackle: Fluorescent yellow ahead of the wing. Head: Fluorescent red thread.

Pattern by Irwin Thompson, Sebastopol, California.

SALMON FLY

Hook: 2/0 to 6, nickel-plated hook optional. Thread: White. Tail: Fluorescent white bucktail, Comet style. Body: Embossed silver tinsel. Hackle: Fluorescent red. Eyes: Silver bead chain.

SILVER BROWN

Hook: 2/0 to 6. Tail: Short wisps from reddish breast feather of golden pheasant. Body: Flat silver tinsel. Hackle: Either fiery brown hen or reddish feather from golden pheasant breast. Wing: Small bunch of orange polar bear, bucktail, or calf hair with strips of golden pheasant tail on either side.

A classic pattern by the late Roderick Haig-Brown.

SPARKLE SHRIMP 1-2

Hook: 4 to 8, Atlantic salmon type. Thread: Orange. Tail: Pearl Flashabou, extension of back. Body: Fluorescent salmon-pink chenille. Shellback: Pearl Flashabou. Hackle: Grizzly dyed hot orange. Head: Orange thread.

There are a number of variations of this Mike Foster pattern, distinctive in that they feature Flashabou as the tail and shellback. Fluorescent lime-green chenille body with hackle of the same color, and fluorescent hot orange chenille body with fluorescent lime-green hackle are also good.

TEENY NYMPH

Hook: 10 to 2; sizes 6, 4 and 2 most useful for salmon. Body: Dyed or natural fibers from a cock ringneck pheasant tail tied in butts first and wrapped up the hook shank. On the larger sizes, say 4 and 2, a two-segmented body can be fashioned with one bunch of fibers wrapped on the aft half of the hook and a second bunch wrapped on the front half. Throat: The tips of the fibers used to wrap the body are tied back under the hook. Wing: Optional, but nearly always included on the size 2 flies, another bunch of pheasant tail fibers tied in as a regular wing.

This is a patented pattern by Jim Teeny, Portland, Oregon, that exemplifies how a subdued fly can work well on river salmon. Although the fly does come in a variety of colors, Jim Teeny himself says that black has been the best color for chinook, with antique gold, hot pink, and flame orange being backup colors he goes to when there is no action on the black. For silvers he adds insect green and blue dun to his list of colors. Jim also suggests changing back and forth among the sizes, since at times one size will outfish the others. This pattern has a batch of *Field & Stream* contest winners to its credit.

TWO EGG SPERM FLY

Hook: 2/0 to smaller, heavy Atlantic salmon type. Body: Butt and shoulder are humps of fluorescent red, orange, or pink chenille separated by a band of silver tinsel or sometimes fluorescent green floss. Throat: Red hackle fibers. Wing: White marabou fibers.

A midwestern pattern developed for the transplanted chinook and coho in the Great Lakes. It has now proven itself on the Pacific Coast and Don Hathaway, the Lakefork, Idaho, fly tier, says that in size 2/0 it is the number one producer in the Salmon River drainage.

W/O TRINITY

Hook: 2/0 to 6, heavy Atlantic salmon type. Tip: Gold tinsel. Tail: Orange mallard primary feather section. Body: Three balls of fluorescent true orange chenille separated by wraps of gold tinsel. Hackle: Fluorescent orange. Wing: White calf or polar bear.

This and the R/O Trinity are patterns by James Garrett of Sequim, Washington. The R/O Trinity is tied the same except it uses red and fluorescent red materials rather than orange. Both flies are good for coho, pinks, and chum.

WALKER SHRIMP

Hook: 2/0 to 12. Thread: Orange. Tail: Orange bucktail, bear, or calf tail, fairly long. Body: Oval silver tinsel tied in two sections with a small orange hackle wrapped between. Hackle: Orange.

Darrell F. Arnold sent in this pattern with a note saying it originated with a man who lives near Walker Creek, California. An all-black version in which black yarn replaces the silver tinsel is also used.

WINTER'S HOPE

Hook: 1/0 to larger, Atlantic salmon style. Body: Flat silver tinsel. Hackle: Aft, two turns of turquoise blue. Fore, two turns of purple. Wing: Under, yellow calf or bucktail. Over, orange calf or bucktail. Top with a few strands of olive calf or bucktail.

A Bill McMillan pattern out of the Camas, Washington area. This gigantic fly was originally developed for winter steelhead using McMillan's floating line, heavy deep-sinking fly technique. It also proved to be very good for silver salmon using the same technique.

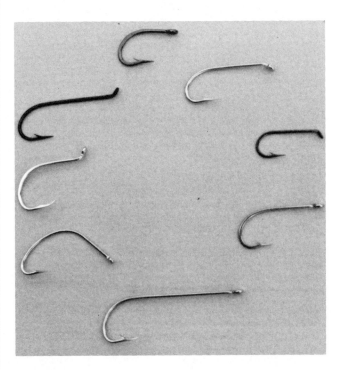

From the top, clockwise: Mustad 9174, Wright and McGill, Eagle Claw 1197N, Mustad 7957 BX, Mustad 34007, Mustad 92608, VMC 9800, VMC 9399N, Mustad 36890. Dan Berglund photo

8.

Tackle

IT IS DOUBTFUL THAT ANY OTHER TYPE OF fishing equipment possesses the mystique and prestige attached to fly tackle. Whether we envision the khaki-clad angler standing in the bow of a skiff being poled across a sun-painted tarpon flat, fly rod in hand, or someone waist-deep in a swift, western river casting a fly to chinook salmon, the fact that fly tackle is being used gives the activity special interest — even to those who do not use it. In this chapter we take an important step in bringing fly tackle into proper perspective by talking about what is available on the market, how all the parts fit together and which combinations are required for the fishing conditions found on West Coast salmon waters.

The contemporary Pacific Coast fly caster is offered an array of rods, reels, lines and various other paraphernalia that would have astounded even the most ardent and affluent angler of the 1920s. The early salmon fly fisherman relied strictly on long cane rods and floating silk lines which restricted his capability to seek salmon much below the uppermost few feet of a stream or bay. In contrast, the equipment available today allows the fly caster to go after salmon in deep, freshwater pools, estuaries and even 40 feet down in the swift rip tides of bays, inlets or the ocean proper.

In establishing our tackle requirements, there are a few factors that will hold true whether we are fishing fresh or salt water, coho or chinook salmon. Because fishing tackle tends to be subjected to some pretty severe treatment — whether from the environment, the fish, or the hand of the owner — durability is a primary concern. Since the angler may be driving a weight forward line or heavy shooting head all day — often into the teeth of a wind — light weight is a factor, but not to the point of critically sacrificing strength. Finally, attention to quality on everything from reel seats to guide wrappings, to drag systems to line splices, is non-

negotiable for the serious angler. A casual attitude to any one of these areas can often be identified as the cause of losing a particularly acrobatic, strong-minded salmon. You won't go wrong in your shopping if you keep these criteria in mind: Durability. Light weight. Quality.

Recent years have seen fly fishing technology advancing at such a rapid pace that almost anything written on the subject can be out of date by the time it hits print. We are bombarded unmercifully by new rods, reels, fly lines and auspicious accessory items intended to improve our angling success and lighten our wallets. A simple rule here is to keep an eye peeled for new developments that will genuinely add to the scope of your equipment. Do not, however, be overly influenced by cosmetic changes in equipment — such as fly line colors — since such things are usually more important to hyping sales than improving function.

THE FLY REEL

For much of the fly fishing we are privileged to enjoy — especially in ponds and streams where our quarry will be crappie, perch or trout of less than a pound — the fly reel is used as a storage spool for 30 yards of tapered line and perhaps a modest length of braided backing. It will generally be a single-action with an on/off clicker but no adjustable drag, or a handy spring-loaded automatic that will zip up loose line in a wink. While this caliber of reel will serve admirably for years if used as intended, it should not be counted on to make the transition to salmon fishing where sturdy construction, large line capacity and a dependable drag system is needed to deal with extremely energetic fish ranging from three to 50 pounds.

It may be a regional distinction but we on the Pacific Coast are rich with horror stories involving fly reels, usually recounted over campfires or after evening meals in the dining houses of hamlets near great rivers. These dramatizations invariably begin with the hooking of a monstrous chinook salmon, its hellbent run for freedom and the screaming windout of a reel culminating in a veritable explosion of screws, springs and rachets flying like shrapnel while the hapless angler grimaces, awaiting the gunshot snap of parting leader that announces the battle's end. Based on true experiences, always hilarious in retrospect and suitably articulated only after generous throatfuls of cool pilsner or a good bottle of pinot noir, such stories are vital to the building and perpetuation of western salmon angling lore.

The disintegration of a reel under stress can be, more often than not, traced to the fact that it was pushed well beyond the limitations of the originator's design. During some 30 years of fly fishing with much of the time spent going after big, strong fish, though I've heard my fair share of sad stories regarding fly reels, I can only recall a few occasions when any of my reels have caused me problems. Once, on a cold and wet November morning while chasing a broad-shouldered chum salmon down a rocky stretch of the Nisqually River, I slipped on a wet boulder, landing with a helluva thud against the unyielding surface. Getting up, I rubbed my backside gingerly as the chum tried to take off again, nearly yanking the rod from my hand. I

looked to see that the reel had also hit the rock, bending the spool solidly against the frame so that it wouldn't turn at all. Feeling the tight line, the chum roared through the surface in a spectacular leap that tore the hook loose. As I limped back to the car, all thoughts of changing reels and trying again were painfully pushed from my mind.

Aside from the Nisqually incident, which could hardly be blamed on the reel, I've had a couple of screws fly out of a Medalist while playing a rough and tumble coho in a coastal creek and watched the spool of a rim control Daiwa disengage from the spindle and fly overboard while playing a nice salmon from the deck of a Westport, Washington charter boat. I have since paid closer attention to the screws on my Medalist and have experienced no further problems with the reel which is now approaching its sixteenth year of heavy duty use. The Daiwa never again malfunctioned during several years of use — right up until its untimely expiration beneath the rear tire of a 4 x 4 pickup truck at a Hoh River fishing camp.

It is inappropriate to discourse further on fly reel problems and significantly more important to remember that the vast majority operate extremely well year after year while withstanding merciless stress from large, freedom-

Anglers who concentrate on big chinook salmon sometimes prefer a reel with a stout, adjustable disc drag rather than one with a click check or palming rim. The two shown (left to right) are a FinNor No. 3 and Martin MG-8, and feature adjustable disc drag systems. — Dan Berglund photo

bent salmon. As long as we shop prudently for a reel of good reputation and heavy duty design – and give it routine maintenance – there is every reason to believe that it will one day be passed along to an upcoming youngster to provide years of additional service.

Much has been written about using a balanced fishing outfit and while the process of tackle balancing has become quite simple – thanks to the efforts of manufacturers in developing certain standards for rods, reels and lines – we still find people struggling to coax a decent cast from a hopeless mismatch of components. In learning to put an outfit together it is not enough to just wind up with a rod, reel and line with which to thrash the surface of any handy body of water to a froth. We must know the type and size of fly or flies we will be using which will dictate the line needed to carry the fly over a given distance to the fish which will, in turn, determine the rod required to cast the line. This chapter will address the selection of a balanced outfit.

During our research of fishing tackle we were on the water for literally thousands of hours of hard casting while trying a great many rods, reels and lines. Some of this equipment was purchased off the shelf and some was provided by various manufacturers for the purpose of testing. When a manufacturer's name is specifically mentioned it will be because we had access to the equipment and can attest to its features firsthand. Any equivalent item of tackle will obviously do a particular job equally well.

While rods, reels and lines are certainly the nuts and bolts of salmon fly casting, they are not the only items that need to be looked at. To that end, this chapter will cover knots and splices, bags and boxes, clothing, sunglasses, binoculars and even touch lightly on boats and motors.

Selecting a Fly Reel

The first sort to make in selecting a fly reel is to look only at single action (one-to-one retrieve ratio) or multiplying (usually about a two- or three-to-one retrieve ratio) reels. As of this writing there are no automatic fly reels on the market designed to withstand the rigors of salmon fishing. If a particular reel catches your eye, look it over carefully, making certain that it has a good spool-to-frame fit and turns smoothly with a minimum of wobble or vibration. These tolerances should be close enough to ensure that the fly line cannot jump through from spool to frame to foul things up during the playing of a good fish. Reels on the upper end of the price curve will often have ball bearings in the spool for a nearly friction-free operation, admittedly a nice feature. There is no reason, though, to shy away from models designed with bushings as they will function nicely for many seasons with reasonable care and are often considerably less expensive.

What type of drag your salmon reel should have is a question capable of igniting no end of diverse responses. The incomparable Lee Wulff once landed a big billfish on a segment of *The American Sportsman* television series using a large capacity reel that had only a non-adjustable click type drag. Lee could, no doubt, land any salmon using a similar reel but then he cannot be labeled your average angler. By contrast, it is not completely uncommon to see an angler

trudging the banks of a Montana trout stream, his rod sporting a saltwater reel with an adjustable disc drag that would stop a tarpon, let alone an unsuspecting trout. As with most examples of extremes, the reality of things lies somewhere in between.

For most of the salmon fishing we enjoy on the West Coast, either in fresh or salt water, a reel with a good adjustable shoe type drag (example, Pflueger Medalist) or a combination adjustable click and palming spool (examples, Orvis CFO, Hardy Marquis) will be totally suitable. This category of reel allows control of a frisky two-pound coho in salt water without diminishing the battle on up to an adult ten-pounder or a 20-pound chinook provided the angler displays some patience on the larger fish.

When pursuing really big chinook, primarily in fresh water – and here we are directing our attention to critters that can easily weigh from 30 to more than 60 pounds in streams of note – there is some justification for a reel with a heavy duty, disc type drag. For wearing down big, incredibly strong fish in a confined, snag-laced pool, the disc drag fly reel (examples, Fin-Nor, Seamaster, Fenwick, Martin) is, in the view of a small corps of veteran West Coast anglers, the answer. The major complaint against the disc drag reel by the majority of Pacific salmon casters is that it will be heavier than a reel having less substantial innards, thus being more tiring to use during a day of hard casting.

being the combined total of a full fly line in 8 to 10 weight and braided dacron backing – keep in mind that it is better to have too much line than too little. Played lightly, even a two- or three-pound coho salmon can get into your backing line on a hard run and a mature ocean-run fish can rip off 75 yards or more in nothing flat. About 100 yards of 18- or 20-pound test backing line should be considered minimum with 150 to 200 yards being even better. Much more than 200 yards of backing becomes excessive for if a big salmon gets that much line away from you chances are it will be woven around a couple of kelp rafts in salt water or crocheted through the branches of a sunken log at the far end of a freshwater pool. In either case, the outcome invariably favors the salmon.

Since a salmon reel is probably going to see at least some action in salt water, corrosion resistance is a factor to consider. While shopping, never assume that a reel will tolerate extensive saltwater use just because it may be an expensive, top-of-the-line model. Many superb reels – especially those of English origin – are not intended for exposure to the salt. Reels suitable for use in salt water are constructed of stainless steel, heavily anodized aluminum, may incorporate some space-age materials like graphite or ABS and will more than likely be given a saltwater designation by the manufacturer. Any reputable fly tackle dealer will be able to advise you which of the reels he carries can be used in the salt. If you are shopping a large department store or discount house where the clerks aren't always familiar with fly fishing equipment, refer to the information provided by the reel manufacturer. Almost any reel can take an occasional saltwater excursion provided it is carefully washed and oiled afterward but if salt water is going to offer the large part of your fly fishing, you'll be best served by a reel built for the job.

Care of a reel over time will usually be more of an issue in how well it holds up than will design or construction

A selection of fly reels in a range of prices that have all seen duty and worked very well for Pacific salmon. Back row: Hardy Model Perfect 3-5/8", Scientific Anglers System 9 (now distributed as Hardy Marquis), Marryatt and Pflueger Medalist Model 1495½. Front row: Martin Model MG-8, Scientific Anglers Model 789 and FinNor Tycoon (an old wedding cake model no longer in production). — Dan Berglund photo

weakness, given that your selection is intended for rigorous use. Buy a lightly constructed reel either to save on weight or money and likely as not you've purchased problems. Go for the best you can afford with the features required for salmon fishing, care for it lovingly and you'll probably have it around for a good many years of trouble-free service.

The following companies either manufacture, or have fly reels manufactured to their specifications. All enjoy respected reputations in the industry and can be counted on to offer excellent products designed to provide years of service. This list does not represent all of the companies producing quality fly reels but does show a good cross section of what is available when making a selection. No effort has been made to indicate specific prices as they fluctuate considerably and are subject to change without notice.

Cortland. Cortland, New York.

Cortland offers two series of fly reels, a deluxe LTD Graphite and the Crown. Both are made in three sizes. The LTD has an adjustable drag and rim control feature while the Crown has a fixed click drag and rim control. A new, extra stout, large capacity model with an adjustable drag

has been introduced in the Crown line and designed the "S/S/S" for salmon/steelhead/saltwater.

Models for salmon fishing: LTD (large), Crown 3-5/8", Crown S/S/S.

Fenwick/Woodstream. Box 729. Westminster, California 92638.

Recently introduced are Fenwick's "World Class" fly reels in four sizes, Class 2, 4, 6 and 8. The Class 2 is a trout reel with a two-way adjustable click drag. The Class 4 (direct drive), Class 6 (anti-reverse) and Class 8 (anti-reverse) have metal-to-metal adjustable disc drags. The Class 4 and 6 will hold 200 yards of backing under a WF9 line while the Class 8 will take 370 yards of backing under a WF13. All models were machined from aluminum bar stock and carry a lifetime warranty for the original owner.

Models for salmon fishing: Class 4 and 6.

Harrich International. Industrial Rowe. Gardner, Massachusetts 01440.

Harrich International is the exclusive agent for Hardy of England. Not much ballyhoo is required for this legendary line of fly reels. The Model Perfect has been around since

1891 and the more recent Lightweight series has been adapted by contemporary trouters everywhere. The new Marquis series is a reintroduction of the Scientific Anglers/ 3M System reels. All Hardy reels are elegantly understated and solidly constructed.

Models for salmon fishing: Model Perfect 3-5/8", St. Aiden, St. George, St. John, Zenith, Husky, Marquis 9, Salmon 1, Salmon 2 and Ocean Prince.

Martin Reel Company. Mohawk, New York.

An old, respected name in automatics, Martin took on the heavy duty, single action and multiplying action market in earnest in the mid-1970s. They now offer a competitively priced line of reels incorporating smooth, stout, adjustable disc drag systems usually found in significantly more expensive winches. My prototype Model 71 has seen exclusive use in salt water since 1976 and shows only minimal signs of corrosion in places where well-deserved deep cleanings were skimmed over all too often. Handsome design, rugged construction and light weight make the Martin reel attractive to the budget-minded angler.

Models for salmon fishing: MG-7.5, MG-8, MG-9 and MG-10.

The Orvis Company. Manchester, Vermont 05254.

There are enough reels in the Orvis catalog to perk the interest of the most cavalier angler. Orvis has been offering fine fly tackle for more years than most of us can remember. Always their reels have been elegant and functional. Through the years Orvis has allowed no grass to grow underfoot in identifying the angler's needs and meeting these needs with the right stuff. There is never a question of quality with any reel purchased from Orvis, including the wide range of saltwater models that have been added to the line over the past few seasons.

Models for salmon fishing: CFO-V, CFO-VI, Battenkill Mark V, Madison V, Saltwater CFO, SSS7/8 and SSS9/10.

Ross Reels. 6325 Miners Creek Rd., Etna, California 96027.

Designed and manufactured from solid aluminum bar stock by Ross Hauck, Ross reels have a black anodized finish and feature a no-burnout adjustable drag. All models have good line capacity to reel weight and are guaranteed for life to the original owner. Thoroughly tested on salmon, steelhead and saltwater gamefish.

Models for salmon fishing: RR3, RR3½, S1, S2 and S3.

Scientific Anglers/3M. 3M Center. St. Paul, Minnesota 55144.

Back in the reel business after discontinuing their System line, Scientific Anglers now offers two economy priced, freshwater reels, the System 456 and 789. Both are single action, have a rim control feature and an adjustable click drag. The 456 is for line weights 4, 5 and 6 while the larger 789 is for line weights 7, 8 and 9. The spool is perforated and counterbalanced and the finish is gray baked enamel. Rugged, good looking reels for the bargain seeking angler.

Models for salmon fishing: 789.

Shakespeare Fishing Tackle. P. O. Drawer S. Columbia, South Carolina 29260.

The Pflueger Medalist is now owned and manufactured by Shakespeare and continues to roll on as one of the most popular fly line holders ever. My own Medalist, a model 1495½, has been with me in front line duty or as a backup since 1965 and has seen action from northern British Columbia to California. During this time it has been reliable in landing a great many salmon with only a few instances of unacceptable behavior.

Models for salmon fishing: 1495, 1495½ and 1498.

Tycoon-Finor. 29 Essex St. Maynard, New Jersey 07607.

The Fin-nor built a reputation on the Florida flats but is at home in any situation where big, strong fish are the quarry. Machined from solid aluminum bar stock and available in either direct drive or anti-reverse models, the Fin-nor with a disc drag system and distinctive gold anodized finish, is a reel made to last a lifetime.

Models for salmon fishing: Model No. 2 and 3.

Val-Craft, Inc. Dept. FF. 67 N. Worchester St. Chartley, Maine 02712.

Valentine reels are offered in two models, an anti-reverse and a single action direct drive. The anti-reverse model incorporates a planetary gear system so that when a fish runs off line, the side plate of the spool remains stationary while only the winding knob rotates. Valentines are well designed, strong, have a disc type drag and are anodized for use in salt water.

Models for salmon fishing: 350, 400.

THE FLY ROD

The majority of fly rods used for salmon angling, on the Pacific Coast side of the country, at least, are constructed of fiberglass, graphite or boron. There are still some cane rods artfully crafted by a handful of devoted manufacturers that are salmon tools of the most exquisite nature — completely suitable for use in salt water — but not many are seen being waved over the local streams and estuaries. This may be, perhaps, because after giving pause to the asking price, a prospective buyer has opted to use the money as a substantial down payment on a new Volvo. There are, however, well designed and detailed rods in fiberglass, graphite and boron to allow all among us to make a functional selection for salmon angling without seriously disrupting the family budget.

The fly rod rolled along for some 75 years in its split bamboo form — with tubular steel efforts slipped in from time to time — and it wasn't until the late 1940s, after World War II, that a major change was effected in fishing rod composition with the introduction of fiberglass. By the early 1950s, many among us had succumbed to the enticements of fiberglass rods and were happily winging flies over our favorite lakes and streams with these marvelous rods that wouldn't take a set even if they were left leaning against a tree overnight. I was delighted with fiberglass and figured that I would likely as not fish for the rest of my life with only a couple or three to serve all my needs.

The ability of fiberglass to stand up to almost no end of hard use with only the slightest signs of wear (with the exception of slamming the rod in a car door which would wear it out instantly), did not escape the notice of Shakespeare, Harnell, Heddon, Conlon and other rod manufacturers of the day. They too observed that the angling public could get along nicely with a small selection of fiberglass rods — a fact that would not bode well for the profit sheets or be well received at the annual shareholder meetings.

It wasn't long before we were virtually overwhelmed on every advertising front by rods with linear and spiral fibers, ultra-light rods, long rods, short rods and then — fast taper rods. With "Fast Taper" they had hit me dead center with a new design that would transform even the most bumbling of our numbers into a veritable Arnold Gingrich. As one who has always lived with the hope that technology could make up for genetic shortcomings, I went for the fast taper theory in no small way. By the time I decided that fast taper rods (described by A. J. McClane in a *Field & Stream* article as "rods with a profile like the Eiffel Tower") were not necessarily the answer to my prayers, we were into the classic action rod which was none other than a reincarnation of the ones I had shoved to the back of my closet to make room for the fast taper battery. In retrospect, I can see that I did more than my share in contributing to the research and development of fiberglass rods — and don't regret it a bit.

Graphite is the first rod material since fiberglass to impact the market significantly, partly I suppose because we were ready for something new after twenty-odd years but more importantly is the fact that graphite promised lighter weight and a faster recovery cycle than fiberglass, hence longer casts with less effort. On the Pacific Coast, where distance casting is a way of life, a rod that will load rapidly and push a fly 80 feet to intercept a feeding coho cannot be easily dismissed and a graphite rod will do this. Furthermore, the slender profile and light weight of a graphite rod allows an angler to shoot long casts all day without becoming a candidate for chiropractic realignment. For those of us who reflect on our days as "young lions" with a twinge of nostalgia, this feature alone makes the additional cost of graphite over fiberglass a flaming bargain.

Following closely on the heels of graphite, boron is the most recent space-age material to be wrapped around rod mandrels. Considerably more expensive than graphite (which is in turn more expensive than fiberglass) boron has not received quite the same open-arms acceptance. The fact that boron does not represent a quantum leap ahead of graphite is probably one factor in this regard. The other

Tackle for saltwater fly fishing. A proper rod, reel with floating or sinking tip line and an extra spool for a shooting head selection provide the cornerstone. A plastic box of fly patterns, extra tippet material and a compact pair of binoculars (for spotting feeding birds or surface activity) rounds out the equipment. It really doesn't take a lot of gear to get started. — Dan Berglund photo

may be that most of us were still paying down our VISA balances attributable to graphite when boron hit the market. In any event, boron has a bit slimmer profile than graphite and offers the same good action, especially in longer length rods.

To bring this scenario full circle, it should be remembered that while graphite and boron have been subjected to most of the recent hoopla, fiberglass technology has not been sitting idly by gathering dust. Fiberglass has continued to

The fly rod used in saltwater angling needs a fast action to put a fly on the fish with a minimum of back casting. The rods shown, all graphite, did an excellent job. Left to right: Orvis 9½' for line 8, Sage 9½' for line 8, Fenwick 9' for line 8 and Scott 9½' for line 8. — Dan Berglund photo

improve over the years and the new "super" fiberglass, called Fenglass, S-Glass, etc., depending on the manufacturer, is, simply stated, great stuff. Considerably lighter and stronger than what we first used so many years ago, the fiberglass rods of today are excellent casting tools.

Much has been chronicled about the relative merits, material formulas, construction details and casting dynamics of today's fly rods. Even so, the question of which rod to buy can be a confusing one for the new angler. Since this chapter is not intended to dig deeply into the technical intricacies of fly rods but rather to help the prospective angler choose one with a minimum of error, we asked Jim Green, chief rod designer and vice president of Fenwick/ Woodstream to encapsulate the essentials of choosing a new fly rod. Jim, a former world fly casting champion who has taken more than a few salmon — Pacific and Atlantic — on fly tackle, responded with the following:

For all my fishing I prefer a rod no shorter than 9 feet. Actually, I would choose a 10½ footer but unfortunately they are a bit unwielding and can be difficult to handle when bringing a fish to net while fishing from a boat. It is certainly easier for me to cast a 9-foot rod than a shorter one and it is definitely my choice for boat fishing.

For saltwalter angling I like a rod that is not too slow in action. I want the rod to respond quickly, especially when lifting the line off the water. The action should be such that I will get enough line speed to get the fly out to the fish quickly, a very important factor when casting into the teeth of a wind.

There are many good fiberglass rods on the market. I see no reason why a beginner should not try one first. I think it is necessary to find out if you really enjoy fishing before investing in a lot of gear. If it turns out that fishing is for you, it would be appropriate to start thinking about a rod of graphite or boron.

The primary difference between fiberglass and graphite is weight. While fishing for salmon you are executing a great many casts during the day. If your rod is too heavy it can be very tiring. A glass rod may be the right power and action — and cast quite well — but may prove to be too tiring to continue with for any length of time.

A boron rod will be about the same weight as graphite but have a smaller diameter. Because it is smaller in diameter it is even easier to cast into headwinds or through side winds. The line speed attainable with boron is very helpful in straightening the line and leader for placement in the proper position.

Price, of course, is a strong factor. It more or less has to be up to the indivdual on how much to invest in a fly rod. And the quality and workmanship cannot be overlooked. Wraps should be smooth and well sealed, the reel seat should lock the reel tightly, hardware must be of top quality and a good cork handle is a must.

Rod actions vary so much that it will be very difficult for a beginner to choose the one that is best for his or her fishing needs. One suggestion here is to choose a rod made by a known company that has been in the business for some time. You can almost always be sure that a rod that has been on the market for a long time will have a good action. A rod with good action — even if it isn't going to be exactly what you will ultimately need for your fishing —

will make casting easy and a pleasure and that is what we are trying for when fishing.

I hope this information proves useful.

The Pacific salmon angler has two distinct needs in fly rods. The first is for a rod that casts a 7 or 8 weight line. The second is a bit stouter rod for casting lines in the 9 to 10 weight range. In fiberglass these rods should be 8 to 9 feet long. Shorter rods in glass tend to be clubby while longer ones get a bit soft, or slow in action. Rods of graphite or boron, with more inherent stiffness than fiberglass, will usually be from 9 to 10½ feet long. For whatever type of rod is chosen, it is wise for the angler to purchase the longest practical rod, especially when some wading is involved where the extra length becomes a definite plus in keeping backcasts above the shoreline willows or beach rocks.

The 7/8 weight rod is a pretty standard item among fly casters since it is generally the one used for bass bugging and nymph fishing with heavily loaded patterns. As well, it is the standard for most summer-run steelheaders and is often referred to on the East Coast as a light salmon rod. This rod is close to ideal for casting to line feeding immature coho salmon in the one- to three-pound class while having backbone enough to wrestle mature October coho in fairly open estuaries. The 7/8 weight rod is light enough to cast all day long, allows a good fight from a young salmon and can be counted on to punch a cast into a fair breeze when need be.

The heavier rod for 9/10 weight lines is used primarily for offshore salmon fishing where big bucktail patterns are the order of the day and for freshwater angling for big chinook in deep pools using heavy, sinking shooting head lines and flies generally slugged with lead wire. In years past, rods for 9 and 10 weight lines were blamed for severe cases of tendonitis as they were pretty tough to deal with at the end of a long day's casting. The advent of graphite and boron has really proven to be a boon at this heaviest end of the fly rod scale in that they offer the power needed at considerably less weight, hence a casting style that is much easier on the arm. The 9/10 weight rod is a must when fishing Pacific coastal streams for fall chinook that can tip the scales at 50 pounds or more.

When selecting a new fly rod, remember that there is no substitute in the selection process for casting a line with it. Simply wiggling the tip back and forth in the store really doesn't bring out the casting properties of a fly rod. In better fly shops several rods are usually strung and ready for the purpose of test casting. Staff members in such shops are, in most cases, excellent fly fishermen who encourage some test casting in a nearby parking lot and offer the right amount of advice to assist the prospective buyer in picking out the correct fly rod. Keep in mind, however, that the rod you are looking for is not required to provide gentle presentation but to get a fly out to where the fish are quickly and with authority. Some rods with rather slow, classic actions cast beautifully under ideal conditions and will fairly kiss the water surface with the fly but be nearly useless in the often windy, choppy situations we realistically find ourselves in much of the time during salmon fishing.

The manufacturers of fly rods do a pretty good job of coming up with a finished product that fits the average person's hand size. Now if we all had that average hand everything would be just great. In truth, however, probably none of us has an average size hand. Most fly rod handles utilize a standard, half-wells, fishtail or full-wells shape with a certain amount of variation. The standard and fishtail do a good job of keeping the hand from sliding forward during vigorous casting while some feel that the wells style handles are more comfortable. Whatever style works best for you is the one to choose. Just keep in mind that a grip too small in diameter can eventually cause the hand to cramp while one that is too large in diameter does not allow a firm grip which can (and has) allow a rain-slickened rod to be wrenched from the angler's hand by a hard striking salmon.

In hardware — reel seats and guides — look for corrosion-resistant finishes such as stainless steel, heavy chroming or anodizing. Stripper guides should be large enough diameter to gather the shooting line during a long cast. On most high quality rods, stripper guides will be zinc oxide which is very durable and gentle on fly lines.

Whether a rod has an up or down locking reel seat is pretty much a matter of preference and a short, detachable or fixed butt extension is usually only needed when the fish get into the 20-pound class and up. In rod weights from 9 through 12, most manufacturers have a model or two available with butt extensions of two to five inches in length.

There is always the chance that the rod you want does not exist on the rack. Whatever the reason, when this situation arises there is the option of either making your own, which many anglers do quite skillfully as a hobby, or to seek out a professional custom rod builder. R. J. (Randy) Ruwe, of Edmonds, Washington, a rod crafter of national reputation, offered his observations on the subject. As we sat in his shop, sipping coffee and examining rods in various stages of completion, he commented that "the average person isn't likely to duplicate the quality of a factory rod right away, but with practice he can match, and in some cases exceed, the quality of certain factory-assembled rods. If a person does not want to build his own rod, he should check around to find a rod maker who has researched rod design, rod components and understands the dynamics of casting." Randy practices what he preaches in this regard, having acted as an advisor for several rod making firms, component manufacturers as well as being involved in the development of an excellent rod finish currently on the market.

Randy further commented that "In filling out an order for a custom rod I find out about the person's casting style and the type of fishing it will be used for. This helps me determine the proper blank and fittings." He also checks the customer's hand size and will turn the grip to the diameter and shape to fit exactly for comfortable casting. In reel seats alone Randy can put together more than one-thousand combinations. Says Randy, "Some guys want function and durability while others want nickel silver fittings and exotic wood spacers that can elevate the cost of a rod accordingly. When you consider that a fancy butt wrap can cost a hundred dollars, it isn't difficult to see that a custome rod can become a significant investment."

In closing, Randy said with admirable candor, "When an angler buys a top-quality, factory-made rod he can expect

Custom rod maker Randy Ruwe of Edmonds, Washington, wrapping a saltwater fly rod at his workshop bench. LJ

it to perform efficiently for years of enjoyable fishing because it will be a very good fly rod." He then smiled and said, "But when he goes the extra distance to have a rod custom made, he should darned well expect it to be not only esthetically pleasing but to become an extension of his casting arm."

To name every rod manufacturer currently supplying the marketplace with fly rods suitable for Pacific salmon fishing would nearly require an individual chapter. The following companies offer rods with which the authors are thoroughly familiar, having tested several production models or worked with custom-made prototypes in actual fishing situations in salt and fresh water.

Fenwick/Woodstream. Box 729. Westminster, California 92638.

Hard to miss with a complete line of fiberglass, graphite and boron rods designed by Jim Green and tested thoroughly, both in the factory and under rugged angling conditions. Several rods sport the fast action required when casting on open water for moving salmon. Budget priced graphite also available under the label Blackhawk. Catalog available.

J. Kennedy Fisher, Inc. P. O. Box 3147. Carson City, Nevada 89702.

A family-owned business designing and building fishing rods since 1922, J. Kennedy Fisher offers a wide range of

fly rods in fiberglass, graphite and graphite/boron composite. Available as factory finished rods, kits or blanks for the do-it-yourselfer and custom rod maker. A variety of lengths from 8' 6" to 10' 6" in two-piece and 9' to 10' in multipiece rods for appropriate line weights gives the salmon angler an excellent choice. Catalog available.

Orvis. Manchester, Vermont 05254.

Once famous for fine impregnated bamboo rods from the lightest slivers of cane to heavyweight sticks capable of taming the wildest of saltwater species (they still offer a limited selection of superb cane rods), Orvis now features a complete range of graphite and graphite/boron composite rods. There are rods of interest to the salmon angler in 7 through 10 line weights and lengths from 8' 6" to a two-handed Spey rod of 15'. Catalog available.

Rodon. 123 Sylvan Avenue. Newark, New Jersey 07104.

Though not commonly seen in western tackle shops, Rodon rods in boron/graphite composite are made in several models well-suited to West Coast salmon angling. Rodon also offers a complete line of rod components. Catalog available.

Sage. 9630 N. E. Lafayette St. Bainbridge Island, Washington 98110.

Sage builds an extensive line of superbly finished rods

designed by Don Green. With rods available in fiberglass and graphite, Sage has recently announced a new "Reserve Power" series and several models in material they are calling Graphite II. The new rod series features the faster action needed for casting aggressively over open water. In addition to finished rods, Sage sells kits and blanks. Several multi-piece models offered. Catalog available.

Scott Powr-Ply. 765 Clementina St. San Francisco, California 94103.

A high quality, low volume company offering graphite rods in blanks, kits and finished rods. The options available in factory-finished Scott rods actually puts them in a near-custom category with a variety of fittings, reel seats and handle shapes to order. Rods for 7 through 10 weight lines in lengths from 9' to 10' in two-piece models plus a nice selection of multi-piece rods of interest to the salmon angler. Catalog available.

Wright-McGill. Denver, Colorado 80216.

Wide selection of moderately priced rods in fiberglass and graphite. Good choice for the budget conscious shopper. Catalog available.

THE FLY LINE

Probably no single item has done more to improve the lot of fly casters during the past 30 years or so than fly line technology. Throughout the first half of the twentieth century we used either inexpensive enameled lines or quality lines of woven silk. The enameled lines — often purchased at a local grocery store or sporting goods shop for something under a dollar — had a finish that would crack easily and wear away with only minimal use. Silk lines were — and still are — marvelous to cast but required loving care and had to be dressed with Mucilin several times during a day of fishing to keep them afloat.

Then, after the end of World War II, a new material, nylon, became available to fly line makers. It was tried as a coating over a woven, hollow core but the problem of stretch very quickly put it out of favor with fly casters. In 1949, polyvinylchloride (PVC) was developed and proved to be a very satisfactory coating for fly lines. The methodology of coating a woven hollow core was still used, however, so while the PVC line proved to be an improvement, it would still take in water and when the core filled, the line would sink.

It was 1952 when a practical method of laying the nylon over a solid cure, then curing it, was perfected. This achievement impacted the fly line industry tremendously, since it allowed the taper and weight of a fly line to be put into the coating, not over a shaped hollow core. The result was a very durable fly line that could be produced at relatively low cost. The real advantage though, was that by controlling the specific gravity of the nylon coating, manufacturers could offer the fly casting public lines that would float all day without dressing and readily sink without soaking up water. We were starting a new era in fly fishing.

What has transpired since the first successful solid core fly line was developed is nothing short of awesome. There have been so many modifications and improvements in

floating qualities and sinking rates that we now have easy-to-cast lines that suit almost any situation. Floating lines ride high in the surface film and pick up easily even in the heaviest weights — and by selecting the proper sinking line for a particular water condition we can submerge a fly to any reasonable depth in search of salmon.

At first glance the selection of a fly line may appear to be quite confusing with all the various types stacked on tackle shop shelves. Take heart in that the code letters on each package, L5F, WF7F/S, ST-10, etc., though seemingly very mysterious, are actually pretty straightforward and easily understood. The first letter, or letters, of a fly line designation indicate the line taper, the number following is the line weight and the final letter represents the line function (floating, sinking, etc.).

Fly line tapers are designated Level (L), Double Taper (DT), Weight Forward (WF) and Shooting Taper (ST). Line weight is measured in grains based on the first 30 feet and given a number from 1 through 15. The most commonly used weights are from 4 through 12, the smaller the number, the lighter the line.

EXAMPLE
WF – 8 – F

Weight Forward   Weight   Function (floating)

Matching a line to a fly rod is accomplished by use of the numbering system which has been applied to all fly tackle by the American Fishing Tackle Manufacturing Association (AFTMA). For instance, a fly rod designated for a line weight of 6 will handle any 6 weight line regardless of manufacturer, taper or density.

The many diverse situations we face in salmon fly fishing dictate the type of line we'll need. There are four basic designs (tapers) in fly lines. Each has a specific place in fly fishing.

Level (L)

This line is level from end to end and is not particularly suitable for either gentle presentation or distance casting. A level line is inexpensive and often the first line purchased for the young, beginning angler. Veteran salmon and steelhead fishermen sometimes use level lines cut to desired lengths and bonded to other lines in designing highly specialized shooting heads.

Double Taper (DT)

Designed for gentle presentation, the double taper line has a level center section tapering to a fine point on each end. Often the choice of trout anglers, the double taper has limited application in salmon angling.

Weight Forward (WF)

The weight forward has a short, front taper, most of the line weight in the first 30 feet and quickly tapering down to a long, fine running line. Often called a rocket, or torpedo taper, the weight forward loads a rod very efficiently and drives bulky flies nicely, even into a wind. A favorite of Pacific salmon anglers for fresh and salt water.

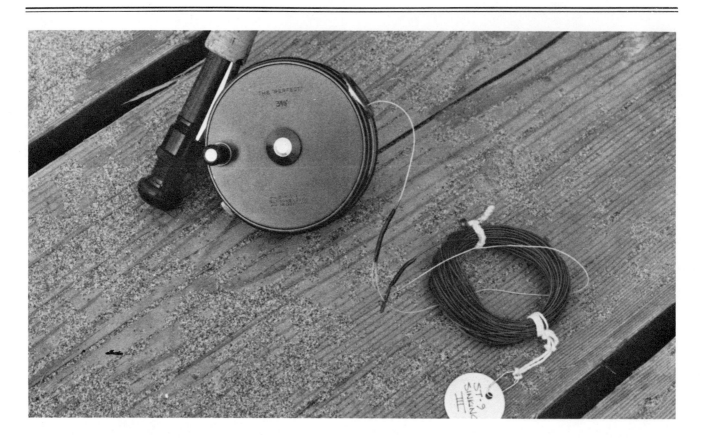

When using shooting heads, utilizing a large loop in the running line on the reel allows for easy changing of heads. Note how the large loop slips over the coiled head. — Dan Berglund photo.

Shooting Taper (ST)

Just 30 feet long, the shooting taper is actually similar to the front end of a weight forward line. Attached to either a light running fly line or monofilament, the shooting taper can be cast great distances, thus making it very handy when fishing wide, coastal rivers.

The following table details fly line standards as set by the American Fishing Tackle Manufacturing Association.

Fly Line Standards, Symbols & Types

No.	Weight[1]	Weights Range[2]	Symbols
1	60	54 - 66	L — Level
2	80	74 - 86	DT — Double Taper
3	100	94 - 106	WF — Weight Forward
4	120	114 - 126	ST — Single Taper
5	140	134 - 146	(Shooting Taper)
6	160	152 - 168	
7	185	177 - 193	Fly Line Types
8	210	202 - 218	
9	240	230 - 250	F — Floating
10	280	270 - 290	S — Sinking
11	330	318 - 342	I — Intermediate
12	380	368 - 392	(Float or Sink)

[1] *In grains (437.5 grains equal one ounce) based on first 30 feet of line exclusive of any taper or tip.*

[2] *Manufacturing tolerances.*

Our line requirements for salmon angling are really no different than those of trout fishermen or steelheaders in that we will — depending upon prevailing conditions — be using floating, sinking tip, full sinking lines and shooting tapers to reach the fish. With only four basic lines needed, it should be relatively simple, and it is, but of critical importance to success is having the right line on hand when certain conditions are present. Salmon go on the bite suddenly and can provide exhilarating action until they go off the bite which can be just as suddenly with the elapsed time of activity being anywhere from ten minutes to an hour or more. To have a fly line that is either not getting your fly down to the fish, or is quickly taking the fly down past the fish can turn a great bite into a personal nightmare.

There are times when a floating line combined with a leader of nine feet is a very efficient combination for working the fly from the surface film to a depth of perhaps six feet. This is the rig to have ready when offshore coho are slashing through the riptides driving vast schools of panicked baitfish to the surface, a phenomenon that is not uncommon during the late summer in Washington's Strait of Juan de Fuca or around Vancouver Island in British Columbia. Similarly, in the springtime the protected waters of Puget Sound are alive with euphausids running just under the surface, perfect targets for the small, feeder coho salmon, their dorsal fins visible above the surface, plowing through the tiny, shrimp-like morsels in a feeding frenzy. A floating line and amphipod pattern can result in euphoric action with upwards of a dozen salmon hooked in a short time. In estuaries or tidal pools of small, shallow streams, a floating line can be used to advantage on holding salmon that have essentially stopped feeding but are still healthy, bright and aggressive.

When salmon are working just a bit deeper, even though they still may be showing on the surface, or in larger streams where the pools are up to ten feet in depth, a sinking tip line is called for. The most popular of these will have either a 10- or 20-foot tip of the extra-fast sinking type. In salt-water situations, the sinking tip is cast to one side or the other of a sighted fish, then allowed to sink from a few seconds to several seconds before commencing a retrieve. In fresh water a sinking tip line combined with a weighted fly can be worked downstream into the depths of a pool, the floating section allowing a measure of control by line mending. Of all the sinking fly lines, the sinking tip is far and away the easiest to use, a point of no small significance during a long day of casting.

When pushing the fly down 40 feet or more to locate salmon hanging along the wall of a saltwater dropoff or deep holding slot, a high density, full sinking line is the order of the day. Washington and British Columbia fly rodders use the full sinking line to ride large, herring imitating buck-tails down to the deep feeding lanes of chinook salmon. In large tidal pools the full sinking line is cast downstream, usu-ally with the angler positioned in a skiff near the top of the pool, and allowed to sink flat to the bottom before bringing the fly back in a slow, crawling retrieve through the salmon. Not the most enjoyable line to cast, especially in the heavier weights needed to handle bulky baitfish patterns, the full

Some anglers use only shooting heads for all their fishing. This selection can be carried handily in a vest pocket and will cover all situations from floating line and sinking tip through all the various sinking speeds. — Dan Berglund

sinking fly line is, nonetheless, a valuable tool for the serious angler.

The shooting taper, which can be a floater or any of the available sinking rates, is most often used for casting a fly across wide streams or combing the depths of the deepest salmon pools. Backed with a good running line or mono-filament, the shooting taper (also called shooting head) in the hands of an expert can be routinely cast more than a 100 feet to hit the furthest lies in the stream. In salt water the shooting taper, like the full sinking line, is a deep water device. Many anglers prefer a shooting taper to a full sink-ing line for taking a fly down to the deepest and swiftest feeding lanes of chinook and coho salmon either in a fast sinking or lead core configuration. Considered tough to work with by some people, there is one distinct advantage to the shooting taper in that several of the 30-foot heads can be easily carried in a vest pocket or tackle bag and quickly changed to meet prevailing conditions.

Fly lines are available in seven types from floating through the fastest rated sinkers. Most manufacturers offer double taper and weight forward lines in both floating and sinking types, with perhaps a sink tip listed as a specialty item for salmon or nymph fishing. Depending on the manu-facturer, the many lines types are given designations to denote the particular floating or sinking characteristics of each intended to give a prospective buyer at least a glimmer-ing idea of what angling situation the line will be best suited to.

Most of us who have, through the years, been swept up in the mechanics of taking salmon (or steelhead) from late summer through spring on flies have also become mindful of how fast we must sometimes push a pattern down into a deep pool or heavy flow to manage even an abbreviated pre-sentation in front of a fish. During my formative years as a Pacific Coast fly caster in the 1950s, I spent a lot of time kneeling in front of a filled bathtub timing the drops of every conceivable line, ranging from water-soaked silk floaters to the then new sinking lines to lead core. Fortunately, this activity is no longer necessary since some manufacturers at least are listing the sinking rates for all their line designations.

The manufacturers offering the widest selection of fly lines and the most comprehensive information about each line are Cortland, Orvis and Scientific Anglers/3M. Beyond these three, the falloff in choices is pretty severe. When examining the listed sinking rate of any line type, bear in mind that a rate of "1.25 - 1.75 inches per second," as an example, has been determined under ideal, controlled con-ditions. It is also important to remember that the sinking rate of any fly line will be slower in salt water due to the increased buoyancy over fresh water. Additionally, sinking rate encompasses all line weights within a designation which means that a WF7 Hi-D will sink slower than a WF9 Hi-D. Ultimately, there is still no substitute for trying various lines in different situations. Sinking rates as specified by manu-facturers are best used for comparisons, much like the mileage information on new automobiles.

The following information is intended to familiarize the new angler with line types presently available and angling conditions for which each is best suited. Approximate sinking rates shown apply to lines manufactured by Cortland, Orvis and Scientific Anglers/3M.

Floating. For fishing on or just under the surface in streams or open water.

Intermediate. (Sinking rate, 1.15 - 1.75 inches per second)
This line floats if dressed and sinks slowly if not dressed. A good line in windy conditions as it sinks just far enough to escape being kicked around and drifted in surface chop.

Slow Sinking. (Sinking rate, 1.25 - 2.50 inches per second)
   For working just under the surface in shallow water or in estuaries during high slack tides when there is virtually no current and a slow drop of the fly is desirable.

Fast Sinking. (Sinking rate, 2.0 - 3.0 inches per second)
This is the original sinking line and still widely used. Good

for moderate currents and small, coastal streams with pools no deeper than five to six feet.

X-Fast Sinking. (Sinking rate, 3.25 - 4.25 inches per second)
For deep pools in medium coastal streams and swift salt-water currents where penetrating several feet under the surface is required to present a fly.

XX-Fast Sinking. (Sinking rate, 3.75 - 6.50 inches per second)
Excellent for large river pools or in salt water where getting the fly down quickly is required.

XXX-Fast Sinking. (Sinking rate, 7.0 - 10.00 inches per second) With a sinking rate like lead core and much better handling qualities, this line fills the bill for the swiftest fresh-water pools and will drive a fly down into the deepest salt-water feeding lanes of the chinook salmon.

FLY LINES FOR SALMON FISHING
(Approximate Sinking Rate — inches per second)

APPROXIMATE SINKING RATE (INCHES PER SECOND)

Manufactuer	Floating	1.25 – 1.75 Intermediate	1.75 – 2.50 No. 1 Sinking	2 – 3 No. 2 Sinking	3.25 – 4.25 X Fast Sinking	3.75 – 6.50 XX Fast Sinking	7 – 10 XXX Fast Sinking
Scientific Anglers	Level Double Taper Wt. Forward Single Taper	Double Taper Wt. Forward	Double Taper Wt. Forward Single Taper	Level Double Taper Wt. Forward Single Taper	Double Taper Wt. Forward Single Taper	Wt. Forward Single Taper	Single Taper
Orvis	Double Taper Wt. Forward	Double Taper Wt. Forward		Double Taper Wt. Forward	Single Taper	Wt. Forward	
Cortland	Level Double Taper Wt. Forward	Double Taper Wt. Forward	Double Taper Wt. Forward Single Taper	Double Taper Wt. Forward Single Taper	Double Taper Wt. Forward Single Taper	Wt. Forward Single Taper	Single Taper

Regardless of the never-ending barrage of fly line improvements that keeps pouring forth from the design and marketing divisions of tackle manufacturers, let alone the smorgasbord already set before us, no equipment chapter on West Coast fly fishing would be complete without addressing the importance and ongoing use of **lead core lines**. First used as shooting heads when there weren't standard lines available that would reach down into the dregs of a river pool or tide rip, an appropriate length of lead core line remains a very effective tool in some situations.

Since so much of our salmon fly casting is practiced in places where kelp rafts, barnacle-encrusted rocks awash in intricate currents or snag-laden holding pools, we are often reluctant to probe such places with a $15.00 shooting head no matter how good the prospects may be of tying into a salmon. This is where an inexpensive lead core shooting head becomes a genuine alternative in terms of tackle losses to herculean hangups. A drift or two through a fishy looking spot no matter how tough it may be to negotiate is pretty easy to justify with a lead core head worth a couple of dollars.

Another application of lead core is to carry several short lengths (3, 4, 5, 6 feet, etc.) with loops whipped into each end. These can be added to the front of a sinking line to ensure a gravel scratching drift of the fly through a deep pool and are quickly changed to a lighter or heavier length as needed.

Most of us who are solemnly wed to salmon fly fishing will admit to having a couple of lead core shooting heads and a few shorter lengths squirreled away in a vest pocket. Not many among us are overjoyed with the casting properties of the stuff. In fact, opinions on casting lead core range from, "Okay, if you gotta use it," to, "totally miserable." In one of his *Field & Stream* columns several years ago the late, great Ted Trueblood concisely and eloquently detailed the merits of shooting heads. He also admitted to the occasional use of lead core, then added something like, "I fear that one day when I come forward hard on a low backcast I might cut my head off." Treacherous though it may be to use though, lead core line has established a position in western salmon angling and is not likely to be displaced in the near future.

Shooting Line and Backing

Shooting line (the small diameter monofilament or level fly line attached to a shooting taper) and backing (the braided line — usually dacron — employed under the fly line for added capacity) are important items for the angler to consider. When using a shooting taper, the running or "shooting" line behind it gets a lot of work and handling. One that you can become generally comfortable with is vital because rest assured, you spend a little time at least cussing it. Backing line isn't especially critical in handling ease but with 100 yards of it stretched out between you and a brawling, hook-nosed coho salmon you'll want to be using something that really shores up your confidence.

For years the search for a perfect shooting line has been going on and as yet it remains a largely unrewarded quest. We've tried all brands of monofilament, spliced our own level lines to heads and most of us in the salmon angling fraternity have sworn off of shooting tapers completely —

several times. Harry Lemire, noted Washington angler and fly tier, at one time was impregnating 45-pound test braided dacron with hot Mucilin for use as a running line. As I recall his method worked pretty well.

All running lines have a singular problem in that when a person is handling 50 to 70 feet of it — even while employing a stripping basket — there is a tendency for it to tangle. With practice and patience this tangling is minimized but will no doubt remain at least a minor nuisance until some major breakthrough is made. The only way to find the best shooting line for your angling is to try the different ones on the market. They all work at least as well as the better homemade concoctions and considerably better than all the rest. A final note on running lines is that we certainly could use about a No. 4 sinking type for working super fast sinking shooting tapers deep in salt water or in some freshwater situations. At this time no such line is on the market.

Backing line is available in breaking tests from 15 to 36 pounds. Most widely used and adequate for most situations the salmon angler will face in fresh or salt water is 18- to 20-pound test. For really big chinook salmon found in West Coast rivers like the Kenai, Skeena, Skagit, Elk or Smith, some anglers favor backing of 27- to 30-pound test.

Running and backing lines are available from several companies and sold through most fly shops and catalog houses.

Sunset Line and Twine Co. Petaluma, California 94952.
Amnesia. Memory-free monofilament, 20-pound test, 200-foot spools. Colors, fluorescent green, fluorescent red and black. When stretched as it is pulled from the reel, Amnesia becomes very limp and pliable. Tangle resistance is good. Requires repeated stretches during a day of fishing.
Micro-X. Braided dacron backing in 15-, 18-, 27-, and 36-pound test. "Oneshot" spools, 175 yards.
Sunset backing is color-coded: 15-pound (green), 18-pound (yellow), 27-pound (orange), and 36-pound (red). This is a very handy feature for knowing what backing is on what reel.

Cortland Line Company. Cortland, New York 13045.
Cobra. Oval-shaped monofilament, 20-pound test, 150-foot spools. When stretched as it is pulled from the reel, Cobra becomes very limp and pliable. Tangle resistance is good. Requires repeated stretches during a day of fishing.
Micron. Braided dacron backing in 20- and 30-pound test. Connected 50-yard spools or 1000-yard bulk spool. Color, white.

Orvis Company. Manchester, Vermont 05254.
Orvis backing is offered in 20- and 30-pound test in spools of 50 through 300 yards or in a bulk spool of 1000 yards. Color, white.

Scientific Anglers/3M. St. Paul, Minnesota 55144.
Shooting line, a level fly line of .029 diameter, is offered in 100-foot coils. Good tangle resistance. Requires occasional stretching during a day of fishing. Colors, light green and fluorescent orange.

LEADER — THE FINAL CONNECTION

There is no magic in either buying or constructing a

Shooting line can be either small diameter floating fly line or monofilament. Backing should be braided dacron, which does not stretch, in at least 18-pound test. — Dan Berglund photo

salmon leader. We are literally never, when salmon angling, going to be faced with a situation requiring a leader precisely tapered as we would on a crystal clear spring creek, trying to place a No. 24 Jassid in front of a choosy old four-pound rainbow. Our need is for a stout leader with a tippet strength range of six to 20-pound test, depending on the conditions, fly pattern and the salmon in question. There is no need for a leader longer than nine feet and often a requirement for one of not more than three feet.

There is one rule to follow in building or buying salmon leaders and it is to be certain that the butt section is at least .023 diameter monofilament. Salmon flies are usually bulky or heavy and can cause a flimsy leader to collapse on a strong power stroke. The result is a dangerously low turnover of a fly that can hit the caster in the hand, arm, back or head with only slightly less impact than a .243 Winchester slug.

For all practical purposes, standard, off-the-rack leaders in six, seven and a half and nine foot lengths with tippet strengths of 2X through 8/5 (approximately eight to 12-pound test) will do just fine for saltwater coho from young feeders to adult fish. Chinook are more likely to be boated with tippets of 12- to 20-pound test. In fresh water, where the fly must often dig deeply, short leaders of three to four feet are the rule in tippet strengths that will match water conditions and the salmon species sought.

Excellent leaders are available from Aeon, Cortland and Orvis, to name a few. Should you decide to tie your own tapered leaders, the following table is provided:

Knotted Tapered Leaders

Type	Length	Monofilament Section Lengths, by Diameter	Lb. Test*
Stout	3 feet	.023 - 1 ft.; .020 - 1 ft., .017 - 1 ft.	20[1]
Stout	4 feet	.023 - 2 ft., .020 - 1 ft., .017 - 1 ft.	20[1]
Stout	6 feet	.023 - 3 ft., .020 - 1 ft., .017 - 2 ft.	20
Medium	6 feet	.021 - 3 ft., .020 - 6 in., .017 - 6 in., .014 - 2 ft.	14
Medium Light	6 feet	.020 - 3 ft., .018 - 6 in., .015 - 6 in., .013 - 2 ft.	12
Light	6 feet	.020 - 3 ft., .017 - 6 in., .015 - 6 in., .011- 2 ft.	9[2]
Medium	9 feet	.021 - 5 ft., .020 - 6 in., .018 - 6 in., .017 - 6 in., .014 - 2 ft. 6 in.	14
Medium Light	9 feet	.021 - 5 ft., .020 - 6 in., .018 - 6 in., .016 - 6 in., .013 - 2 ft. 6 in.	12
Light	9 feet	.020 - 5 ft., .018 - 6 in., .017 - 6 in., .015 - 6 in., .011 - 2 ft. 6 in.	9[2]
X Long & Light	12 feet	.020 - 6 ft., .018 - 1 ft., .016 - 1 ft., .013 - 1 ft., .011 - 3 ft.	9[2]

*Breaking test on tippets is approximate and will vary depending on brand of monofilament.

[1]Many experienced anglers dispense with tapered leaders in short lengths and use level sections of appropriate diameter or breaking test.

[2]Tippets can be reduced by one step (example: .011 to .009) if an extra light leader is desired.

PUTTING IT ALL TOGETHER

It was years ago on the estuary of the Dosewallups River, a small, unsullied stream plunging down from the Olympic Mountains and out through a big oyster bed to meet Hood Canal. The time was early October and an overcast I could nearly touch was dropping misty, cold rain onto the tide flat. Behind me toward the mountains, yellowing alders stood out through the low cloud cover and a couple of anglers a few hundred yards upstream, near the 101 bridge, were gray, ghostly figures casting into the Dosie.

I stood hip deep in the estuary pool, fly rod in hand, watching bright coho salmon flashing and splashing all around me. My first cast attracted several salmon to the small Fall Favorite but no takers. With a dozen more casts I was into a lively jack coho of about 18 inches. Within half an hour another five jacks had thoroughly shredded my Fall Favorite and I quickly knotted another to the leader.

On my next cast a deep-bodied coho of perhaps 12 pounds slammed into the fly, made a twisting leap and streaked down the pool toward the canal. For several minutes the battle continued and things seemed to be going my way when, on a direct, steady pull against the reel drag — the line went slack. The big coho was gone. My fly was gone as well and the tiny spring-like curls in the monofilament tippet told the story: my hastily-tied knot had pulled through.

Assembly of the components — rod, reel, backing and line — is not difficult but must be done carefully with attention given to every knot and splice. Considering that there may be six or more knots and splices between you and a trophy salmon during the course of a battle (fly knotted to leader, two or three knots in the leader, leader to fly line, fly line to backing and backing to the reel), the importance of studious effort in each and every step of tackle assembly becomes clearly defined.

During the past several years there have been many new and sophisticated splices and knots worked out by ingenious fly fishermen, making the transition of line to leader or backing to fly line sleek, strong and snazzy. The primary use for such painstakingly fashioned joins is to allow us the most delicate and splash-free presentation of our line (and fly) to a wary trout. Such delicate presentation is not essential to salmon angling, although we do indeed need smooth, stout connections that will not hang up in the rod guides or be pulled apart by an overgrown or unusually vigorous salmon. Another need is the ability to change leaders, lines or shooting heads quickly, making some of the epoxied connections that are very strong and smooth unsuitable since they are also very permanent.

In facilitating line and leader changes quickly, especially during fishing when time is all important in making the right adjustments to get a fly in the feeding lane of a salmon, one of the best methods is with a series of strong, smooth loops. Factory-made shooting heads and tapered leaders are, in fact, almost always provided with loops. Most of us have also used the whip-finished loops (wrapped by using a fly tying bobbin and varnished) but the very best loop for fly line and shooting head ends was designed by the great southern California rod designer, Russ Peak, and is called, naturally enough, the Russ Peak Loop. Another excellent

loop that is suited to connecting monofilament shooting line to shooting heads is the Spider Hitch. For attaching fly to leader by use of a loop to allow an active, fluttering action the Vic Dunnaway Knot is easy to tie and possesses good strength. It is similar to the Improved Clinch Knot, which is also a very good connection.

For those who really want to get into knots for angling there is a section on the subject in McClane's *Standard* and a very well done book on the subject by veteran Chicago-based outdoor writer Tom McNally entitled *Fishermen's Knots*. We are going to deal with the basics for setting up a fly outfit that can be taken out and fished with confidence. It is one way to do it, but certainly not the only way. There are many other knots and splices that will work and if you have some favorites that you utilize with confidence on big, tough fish, then by all means stay with them. Our information essentially presents a place to start for the novice.

Blood Knot. Used for joining two strands of monofilament when building tapered leaders or replacing a tippet.

Improved Clinch Knot. For tying a fly to the tippet or attaching backing line to a reel spool.

Uni-Knot or Vic Dunnaway Knot. A knot that can be used for attaching a fly to the leader either snugged up against the hook eye or as a loop connection for maximum action on the retrieve. When a fish hits the fly the knot is drawn up tightly against the hook eye.

Spider Hitch. For forming large loops or doubling a line. Easy to tie and strong, it makes an excellent connection for running line to shooting taper.

Nail/Needle Knot. For attaching a leader butt to fly line or attaching backing to the fly line.

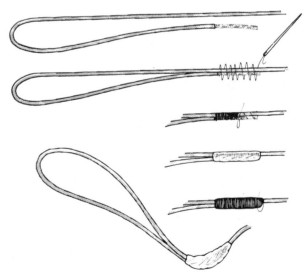

RUSS PEAK LOOP
1. *Peel back 1-1½ inches of line finish with acetone.*
2. *Sew through 7-11 times with thread.*
3. *Add layer of Pliobond and start whipping with tying thread.*
4. *Alternate Pliobond and wrapping to build a smooth splice.*
5. *After final wrapping, add last coat of Pliobond and allow to dry overnight.*
6. *A strong, flexible and long lasting loop is the result.*

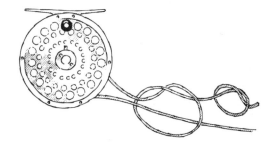

BACKING TO REEL KNOT
For connecting braided dacron backing to fly line.

BACKING TO FLY LINE KNOT
To complete this knot smoothly for easy passage through rod line guides, pull it slowly while rolling the loops back and forth between thumb and forefinger. This keeps coils of backing aligned.

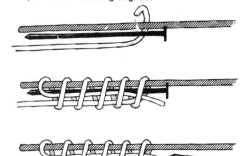

NAIL KNOT
The standard for permanent line-to-leader connection. Should be wet when pulled up tight to avoid stretching or burning the monofilament. Very strong.

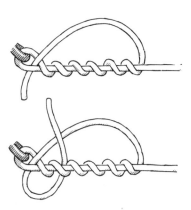

IMPROVED CLINCH KNOT
For securing fly to leader tippet. Should be wet when pulled up tight. Very strong.

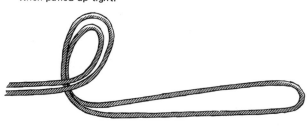

BLOOD KNOT
For connecting leader sections and tippets. Should be wet when pulled up tight.

SPIDER HITCH
Form desired length loop. Wrap several turns around thumb and pull through. A good, quick replacement knot for a broken shooting line loop. Takes a bit of practice.

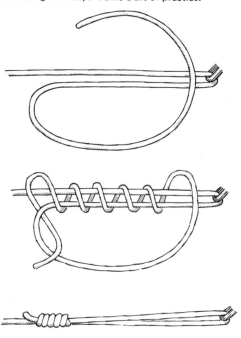

UNI-KNOT
Allows fly to swing freely for additional action in current or during retrieve. Snugs up against hook eye when fish strikes.

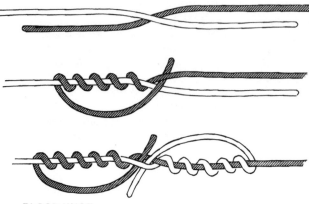

Russ Peak Loop. The strongest and most flexible loop for either end of a fly line. Designed by California rod building maestro, Russ Peak.

Fly Line-to-Backing Knot (Albright Knot). This is a quick method of attaching fly line to backing and if pulled up carefully, it is smooth and will slip through the rod guides easily.

Backing-to-Reel Knot. A simple, fast connection that snugs up against the reel spool nicely.

By utilizing a few of the basic knots illustrated, the two primary fly line setups, the standard fly line and backing rig and the backing-to-running line-to-shooting taper, are easily put together.

Leader, Fly Line and Backing. The standard for setting up all fly lines.

Leader, Shooting Taper, Running Line and Backing. For setting up a shooting taper.

ACCESSORIES AND CLOTHING

When it comes to collecting collateral equipment to supplement the activity of angling, the salmon fly fisher, while not quite as doodad intensive as the addicted trout angler, certainly finds need and consolation in gathering about him an array of knives, nippers, hemostats, fly boxes, polaroid sunglasses, tackle bags, tackle boxes, fishing vests and binoculars, to name a few of the more important items. Much of this equipment is already counted in the duffel of most fly anglers but worth a once-over for the newcomer.

Since West Coast fly fishing is a year-round activity for the truly addicted salmon angler, we can find ourselves, depending upon the season, under a blazing sun, casting into the teeth of a gale, fending off generous to overwhelming doses of rain, or occasionally facing sleet, hail and snow. A wardrobe that will repel the elements does not need to be tremendously extensive but does require careful thinking through for each item selected.

From the first nip of winter until spring we can count on needing long underwear, thick flannel shirts, heavy sweaters, flannel-lined or woollen trousers, gloves, a variety of caps and hats, perhaps a down vest — and no-nonsense raingear! From summer through autumn we need billed caps or wide-brimmed hats, poplin and lightweight flannel shirts, khaki or denim trousers, medium-weight sweaters, lightweight windbreaker — and no-nonsense raingear!

For staying warm and dry the Pacific Coast angler has traditionally relied on wool and rubber with pretty good results. The important thing about wool is that it will keep a person reasonably warm even if it gets wet and with rubber raingear we always get a little wet via condensation. Developments over the past few years have brought us new synthetic materials which are proving to be excellent for outdoor wear. Polypropylene provides warmth in very trim well-fitting turtlenecks, underwear and tee shirts. Fiber pile, a space-age, warm-when-wet material, is used for trousers and jackets and Gor-tex is already a household word as the right stuff in breathable rainwear that will allow perspiration to pass through but will not allow rain to get in. There are superb waders on the market of neoprene that fit better and are warmer than any we've had before and anyone who has spent any amount of time in traditional waders knows the limitations they place on climbing in and out of a drift boat or just getting around during a day on the river.

For extremely cold conditions, outer garments filled with goose down or high loft synthetics like Hollofil II are excellent. Often the fly caster will opt for a vest in combination with a heavy sweater for warmth and freedom of casting movement since the arms are not restricted. One thing to remember with down is that it is indeed a great insulator, but loses its loft and insulation capability when wet. The high loft synthetics, while not reported to be warm as down on an ounce-for-ounce basis, will retain warmth when wet.

Everyone seems to have slightly different needs when it comes to staying comfortable in severe weather. Most outdoor experts will advise us to think in terms of layering several light garments rather than going with a single, heavy item since it is easier to make adjustments during a day of fishing or on a trip where the weather can offer daily surprises.

Most areas of the country have sporting goods or outdoor stores that specialize in quality items for keeping us warm and dry. The people in these stores are mostly experienced outdoor folks and almost always anglers themselves. They can offer valuable guidance in choosing clothing and raingear. If on the chance that you cannot find the clothing you need nearby your home, the following firms sell complete lines of premium clothing by mail order.

Polar Bear Waders. The Avid Angler. 11714 - 15th Ave. N.E. Seattle, Washington 98125.

The Avid Angler Fly Shop proprietor, Tom Darling, offers custom-tailored neoprene waders under his private Polar Bear label. Made to Darling's design specifications, including a gravel cuff and extra strength at stress points, Polar Bear waders have established a solid reputation with West Coast Guides, waterfowl hunters and cold weather anglers.

Eddie Bauer, Inc. 5th & Union. P. O. Box 3700. Seattle, Washington 98124.

Famous for an extensive line of premium goose down garments and sleeping bags, Eddie Bauer offers a full range of outdoor clothing and raingear. Retail outlets for West Coast anglers in Seattle and San Francisco. Catalog available.

L. L. Bean, Inc. Freeport, Maine 04033.

L. L. Bean has a full line of outdoor garments, footwear and equipment. One of the low-cut models of the famed leather top/rubber bottom Maine Hunting Shoe makes an excellent after fishing, camp shoe. Spring catalog features a fly fishing section with items of interest to the western fly fisher. Retail store in Freeport, Maine only. Catalog available.

Columbia Sportswear. 6600 North Baltimore. Portland, Oregon 97203.

Columbia manufactures a complete line of outdoor garments, including cold weather parkas in several styles, special angling raingear and fishing vests — including one model of heavy cotton duck with lined hand warmer pockets which is great for cold weather angling. Good selection of accessory items also available. All of Columbia's items are well designed and constructed of premium materials. Sold under the Columbia brand name or many private labels at most outdoor stores. Catalog available.

Cabela's. 812 13th Avenue. Sidney, Nebraska 69160.

Full line of outdoor clothing and accessory items. Spring catalog has a good fishing tackle section.

Damart. 1811 Woodbury Ave. Portsmouth, New Hampshire 03805.

Cold weather undergarments in a variety of weights and styles. Made from a synthetic material called Thermolactyl. Catalog available.

Pete Grampaoli, Chico, California, enjoys an evening refreshment while awaiting dinner at Hannah's Fishing Camp after a day on the Elk River. LJ

Early Winters, Ltd. 110 PreFontaine Place South. Seattle, Washington 98104.

A variety of unusual and useful items from well designed clothing to gourmet camp foods. Retail store in Pike Place Market area of Seattle. Catalog available.

James-Scott. 356 Hillcrest. El Segundo, California 90245.

Innovators in neoprene, James-Scott offers waders, wading shoes and a wide range of unique accessory items that are very well thought out and constructed. All James-Scott waders feature a neoprene foot and zip-on gravel cuff. Retailed nationwide through better outdoor stores. Catalog available.

Orvis. Manchester, Vermont 05245.

Exceptional clothing and accessories to go along with their fine fishing tackle. If there is a one-stop shopping catalog for the salmon angler, Orvis is it. Retail store in San Francisco for West Coast anglers.

North Fork Industries. 728 South Brighton. Kansas City, Missouri 64124.

Manufacturers of a variety of items from vests to soft tackle boxes for fly storage. Catalog available.

Patagonia. P. O. Box 150. Ventura, California 93002.

Manufacturers of a broad line of polypropylene, pile and bunting garments from long johns to jackets, including raingear. Functional, trim and warm-when-wet clothing to suit every outdoor type from alpinist to salmon angler. Also, other nicely styled but utilitarian clothing for both rugged use and casual wear. Sold through most outdoor stores. Catalog available.

Recreational Equipment, Inc. (REI). P. O. Box C-88123. Seattle, Washington 98188.

Products designed for the average outdoor person on up to one planning an assault on Mt. Everest. Good selection of clothing and camping items of interest to the salmon angler. West Coast retail outlets in Seattle, Portland, Berkeley and the Los Angeles area. Catalog available.

In the Tackle Bag (or Vest)

The angler needs a multi-pocketed vest or stout canvas tackle bag in which to transport the apparatus and implements essential to the game of salmon fly fishing. A tackle box would be fine for boat fishing except that there are really none available that are designed for the fly fisher's equipment. A vest is most often used for stream and bank fishing while a bag is somewhat handier for use in a boat. Things to look for in either of these items are strong stitching reinforced at stress points, pockets or compartments suitable for our equipment, and secure closures. Some better bags and vests have waterproof inner linings, a feature cherished by those of us who have fished through a rainy day or waded a step too far and arrived home to find a camera filled with water or several boxes of flies soaked.

The gear we need in our fishing vests or tackle bags, as the case may be, is not much different than any other fly angler. A variety of boxes to hold a selection of flies ranging from small, sizes 8 through 4 shrimp and comet patterns, to bucktails and tube flies of four inches or more, can be made of metal or plastic. Keep in mind that salt water can eat up your favorite Wheatley in no time so it should be retained strictly for freshwater use. Rugged, semi-rigid plastic boxes with stainless steel or plastic hinges and snug fitting lids are the answer for saltwater patterns. Boxes meeting these requriements are offered by Cortland, Plano, Bonnand of France, Scientific Anglers, and others. A generous selection of patterns — even for an extended trip — can easily be stored in four boxes.

A leader wallet will keep a dozen or more ready-tied leaders at hand. This can be of plastic or leather, depending on how nifty we can afford to be. Six spools of leader from six- through 15-pound test will handle most tippet needs, although some veteran anglers carry 20- or 25-pound tippet material for really big chinook.

For cutting and clipping, a twosome of a hemostat and an angling clippers will handle everything from snipping leader to trimming hackles into shape. The hemostat also serves as a hook remover and is helpful in pulling knots snug when fingers are cold and uncooperative.

Additional items of importance include a leader straightener, a bottle of reel oil, a container of split shot or twist-ons and a good pair of polaroid glasses. The saltwater angler is especially well served by a pair of compact binoculars of about 7 x 21 or 8 x 30 magnification for searching out surface feeding activity or foraging sea gulls. It is a good idea to carry a small container (a 35mm film cannister will do) holding a few aspirin, antacid tablets, allergy pills and band-aids. It doesn't make much sense to let a headache, upset stomach or a bleeding finger terminate an otherwise good fishing excursion.

Finally, we need an extra reel spool or a few spare shooting tapers to handle the variety of angling condtions we're sure to face during the course of the day. And most of us have a few special flies and a conglomeration of other little items absolutely vital to a successful outing even if they only provide shoring up for our sometimes shaky self-confidence. For all intents and purposes, though, the angling vest or bag need not be an overly bulky or heavy affair, but for most of us — it will be.

CARE OF EQUIPMENT

Much has been written about taking care of equipment but it is still discouragingly common to hear a person say, "I almost had that big slug in the net when my reel froze up," or something similar. Equipment represents a significant cash investment and there is no evidence that it is ever

The relatively well-protected water of South Puget Sound is ideal for casting from a small cartop boat that can get from place to place quickly and is easily rowed for a quiet approach into casting range of feeding salmon. Les Johnson's 12-foot Jon boat provides an excellent fishing station for a lone angler but can fish two. — Peninsula Gateway photo

going to be less expensive than it is today. It pays us to take good care of what we already own so that our alloted tackle dollars can be spent to expand our equipment base, not needlessly replace valuable items that have deteriorated through neglect.

All manufacturers of quality tackle provide information on proper care of the item. Maintenance booklets or sheets will have, depending on the type of equipment, parts lists, cleaning and oiling instructions, troubleshooting tips plus information on handy knots, splices and so on. It is a good idea to keep these on file since they will almost certainly be needed from time to time.

Equipment care does not need to be difficult. What it really amounts to is washing every item of tackle thoroughly in fresh water after a day of fishing, especially if the day has been spent on salt water. A reel, for instance, may go several days in fresh water with little evidence of problems but the corrosive effects of salt water on expensive equipment can be very severe in just a short time. Be certain to follow the cleaning and maintenance instructions offered by the manufacturer. If you do not have this information, routinely apply the following maintenance program after each outing:

• Rinse a fly rod off in fresh water, occasionally employing a mild, liquid soap for an extra measure of cleaning after each angling trip. After rinsing completely in clear water, rub the rod down gently with a soft, dry cloth and let it stand out to dry overnight before storing it back in the tube.

• Strip fly line from the reel spool and rinse off thoroughly, including a good drenching of the backing. Pull the line through a soft, dry cloth as it is rewound onto the reel.

• Remove the reel spool from the frame and rinse both completely. Dry with cloth, then use a moisture displacement such as WD-40 on the frame and spool bushing, taking care not to spray the fly line. Wipe the excess oil from all metal surfaces and apply reel lube as needed. Wipe the reel frame down with the WD-40 dampened cloth and allow the reel to air dry overnight before storing away.

• Rinse off boats and motors after each use. Outboard motors should be flushed regularly with fresh water to reduce corrosion of the cooling system; they should be disconnected from the fuel tank and run totally out of gas at the end of each trip.

• Soak flies in fresh water after use and squeeze damp-dry with a paper towel or cloth. Air dry overnight, fluff them back up and store them away for another day.

When considering equipment care, just remember that the manufacturer designed and built it to last for many seasons. Our attention to the maintenance of said equipment will contribute in large measure to our enjoying it for many seasons — or replacing it early with hard-to-come-by dollars that could have been a down payment for a day on the Rogue River, or, a week on the Kenai.

BOATS FOR SALMON ANGLING

Whether down a river, across a sheltered bay or on the Pacific Ocean, we love chasing and fishing for salmon from small boats. With a boat we have mobility, thus are able to cover a lot of water during a day of angling, be it drifting a stretch of river or buzzing around on a sprawling saltwater estuary. There are times when fish are scattered and the ability to pick up and move quickly can spell the difference between a nice coho for the broiler or the skunk. It is also nice to have the option to chase down a hooked salmon that is hellbent on taking a $25.00 fly line and 175 yards of brand new backing off your reel. Then, there are always those times (hopefully rare) when we do not bring a fish fairly to net and find our solace instead by motoring around in the boat on a nice, sunny afternoon.

Western river drift boats are designed to take just about any stretch of white water an experienced, intelligent oarsman is willing to tackle. River boats are also used occasionally on sheltered saltwater spots but the rocker bottom design so very well suited for drifting rugged rivers is not truly at home on salty bays or for fast, four-mile runs to the next productive cove.

Another system gaining favor for river angling — one that can be easily transported in (or on) a compact car and

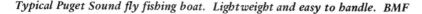

Typical Puget Sound fly fishing boat. Lightweight and easy to handle. BMF

assembled at the launch area — is a rubber raft fitted with a tubular metal frame, oarlocks and a solid, flotation-filled floor. This type of raft setup is comfortable for two anglers and handles nicely even in pretty rough water.

For fishing protected saltwater bays or river estuaries, 12- to 14-foot boats of aluminum or fiberglass are most commonly used. The best of these will have a fairly wide beam and flat floor to facilitate fly casting with at least a semblance of stability. Balanced to motors that will put them on a plane, craft of this type will fish two anglers in modest comfort for a day, provided their tackle doesn't take on expeditionary proportions.

Handling ease is extremely important in a small boat. This is to say that it must scoot along briskly under power and be able to knock down a bit of wind chop. The salmon angler also needs a dry boat, one designed to direct lumpy water away from and not into it. The boat must be maneuverable with only gentle urgings of the oars as sliding quietly into casting distance of a feeding salmon is a large part of the game in saltwater fly fishing.

Any boat that is going to be used for serious salmon angling should be rigged for "silent running." This is accomplished simply by covering the deck with pieces of indoor/outdoor carpeting and lubricating the oarlocks to eliminate squeaking. Like any other fish, salmon can be frustrating in that they'll be jumping beside your boat one minute, seemingly without fear, and spook at the slightest sound the next. The silent treatment includes securing thermos bottles, landing nets and anything else metallic that can rattle and bang against the boat gunwale, sounding an alarm a great distance through the water.

To illustrate the importance of being quiet I need only go back to the fall of 1983 during a day of fishing on Oregon's Elk River with guide Todd Hannah. The Elk was low and clear, holding the vanguard of the fall/winter chinook run. We'd hooked several fish, lost a few big ones and landed several bright jacks. After fishing a usually productive pool for nearly an hour with little success, Todd surmised that the salmon were off the bite and suggested we move to another spot and have lunch before resuming our casting efforts. I agreed, then added, "I don't think that this pool has a salmon in it."

Todd carefully pulled up the anchor and replied, "Oh, yes, there are. If there are any salmon in the Elk River, there are always a few in this pool. You just look down toward the bottom as we drift out of here." I did so just as Todd banged a metal thermos against the side of the aluminum drift boat. The bottom nearly exploded as a school of big chinook tore off upstream, whipping the water to a froth as they shot to the head of the pool. Todd smiled and nodded knowingly, "Just off the bite," he said.

Anglers who choose to fish big water such as the Strait of Juan de Fuca, Barkley Sound on Vancouver Island or the Pacific Ocean proper out of LaPush, Depoe Bay, Arcata or other coastal fishing hamlets usually opt for a boat in the 18- to 22-foot class that is fast, has plenty of freeboard, a cuddy cabin, and can handle severe weather that can come up very quickly. There are times when a run of five to ten miles offshore is required to locate schools of coho salmon but for the angler prepared to do so, the fly fishing rewards can sometimes be monumental when a rip full of foraging eight- to 12-pounders goes on the bite.

While there are many excellent small boats on the market at this time, not many are aimed specifically at the fly fisher. It is reasonable to assume that this will change as saltwater fly fishing continues to build a following. What we are witnessing since about 1977 is a rekindling of the fishing that started in the 1930s and '40s — a renaissance of the old West Coast tradition of casting from small boats for big, bright salmon. Given the potential market we represent, we can count on boat builders to provide us the proper craft to be casting from.

CONCLUSION

Fishing tackle. We all probably own too little and too much. We certainly overspend on one item and cut corners too severely on another. Then, to keep us in a muddle, the manufacturers are pumping out new goodies at a rate that overloads our faculties — and we love it! Tackle can be a curse should it fail during a battle with a once-in-a-lifetime salmon and a salvation to tinker with on weekends when winds render the bays dangerous or the rivers are running bank full. It is easy for the most cautious and reserved of our angling ranks to go a little crazy when it comes to buying fishing tackle but it is very important to keep in in perspective. We should buy the best tackle from reel to hook that we can afford and always deal with a reputable tackle shop. In doing this we'll almost always be fishing for salmon with tackle that will land a salmon. Putting want aside, we need no more and no less. For all the preceding rambling, it is just this simple.

Tod Hannah, fishing guide, tried his hand with a fly rod and came up with a bright jack chinook. LJ

9.

Future Prospects

IT IS WITH A COMBINATION OF DISMAY, acceptance of human nature and finally hope that this chapter is addressed. History provides a very clear pattern. Man, regardless of origin, behaves in about the same manner, which is, *I want mine first*. If there's a resource at stake, we as humans act like sharks, tearing at it until it's either all gone, or until we can become heros by restoring it. This latter situation somehow never occurs until the resource is at the brink of disaster. What a tragedy! To take care of a resource when it is abundant somehow seems totally outside of human capability. Can the salmon managers, and the salmon harvesters change this pattern or not? Therein lies the hope and likewise the challenge.

Over the past ten years, most major wild chinook and coho stocks have experienced marked population declines up and down the Pacific Coast. There are some promising exceptions, but the overall trend is either stability at inadequate levels or continued decline. Perhaps the only really bright spots in this otherwise thought provoking scenario are the recent record breaking runs established for sockeye and pink salmon in western Alaska.

The basic problem with Pacific salmon is that they don't stay in one place. They're travelers, and during their lifetime may pass through the political jurisdictions of several states and at least one other country.

When there is an abundance, and therefore more than enough to go around, this creates no conflict, but we're long past this point in history, by any measure. One of the greatest threats to the continuance of a viable salmon fishery, either commercial or recreational, stems from a simple fact of modern life. While the number of salmon can be increased substantially through wise management, such management is no match for the increasing mobs of fishermen utilizing more and more efficient harvesting equipment. Something has to give on this collision course. Mostly to date, it's been the fish.

As an attempt to address the issue and gain management control of the situation, one of the most important developments has been passage of the Magnuson Fishery Conservation and Management Act of 1976.

The Act extends United States jurisdiction from the three-mile limit within which the individual States have control to 200 miles offshore, thereby encompassing a large part of the salmon saltwater feeding habitat. At the same time it states that "conservation and management measures shall prevent overfishing, while achieving, on a continuing basis, the optimum yield from each fishery." Optimum yield, in this context, is further defined as follows:

"The term *optimum* with respect to the yield from a fishery, means the amount of fish:

a) which will provide the greatest overall benefit to the nation, with particular reference to food production and recreational opportunities; and

b) which is prescribed as such on the basis of the maximum sustainable yield from such fishery, as modified by any relevant economic, social, or ecological factor."

The Act established a series of regional management councils to cover the entire United States offshore area. Of these, the North Pacific and Pacific Fishery Management Councils encompass the West Coast salmon waters under federal jurisdiction.

Results of this management approach to date would seem to be mainly a slowing down of the decline of the fishery. Squabbles over allocation and the size of the allowable harvest seem to constantly interfere with maintaining and rebuilding the resource. This stems from the just quoted definition of optimum yield by which the Council members are guided, namely that relevant economic or social factors must be considered along with the biological capabilities for salmon production. Whenever a user group faces a more restrictive harvest than it had previously, it cries out in anguish. The Council listens, and if it doesn't, then the

Secretary of Commerce does. If they don't, then the affected inshore state agency responsible for allocation jumps in, the chorus being that there are lots more fish to be harvested than the biologists predicted. Unfortunately, the salmon can't talk, and the resulting overharvest goes on, year after year. In all fairness to the Councils, it is difficult to think where we'd be without the braking influence they've exhibited on the harvest. Furthermore, their most recent decisions indicate a closer attention to the impact on the salmon. They're even learning to say no.

In June 1984, the Pacific Council was asked to make an in-season increase in the allowable coho harvest off the Oregon-California coast by the commercial trollers. This, in the face of a disastrously low wild coho spawning escapement in the preceding year at 41% of the established goal. The trollers claimed that the salmon that failed to return the prior year had spent an extra year in the ocean and were, in fact, alive and well. Therefore, all those extra fish should be made available to them.

Technical observers were placed on selected vessels by the Council and numerous samples taken of the coho in that area. Results showed that there were in fact no fish a year older than normal, and that catch rates did not indicate an error in forecasts of abundance. The Council's decision was: no change in allowable catch. So, there is reason to hope that decisions in the future will be less reflective of the outcries of the downtrodden.

With this apparent swing toward decisions favoring the resource, it is fair to ask for re-examination of the potential for increased harvest resulting from such decisions. In testimony presented before the Pacific Council in 1982 for the Federation of Fly Fishers, I examined the expected results from allowing sufficient chinook and coho salmon to spawn that would fully utilize *existing* natural spawning beds in Washington, Idaho, Oregon and California, *without* any habitat improvement. The estimated outcome was astounding. In 1981 the combined ocean catch of these two species offshore from the three states involved was 2,570,000 fish. By allowing 645,000 of these to escape to spawn annually (for the most part within a five-year period), the allowable catch could be increased by 1,800,000 fish, or 70%. The challenge has not been accepted to date. What an opportunity exists, and what a lesson in short-sightedness it reveals.

. . .

The other matter of major concern confronting salmon managers is the lack of specific agreement covering appropriate spawning escapement and harvest allocation for salmon migrating through the waters of another country. For Pacific North American salmon stocks this means the United States and Canada.

Negotiations between the two countries have been conducted since 1970 without resolution. The overall objective has been to allow the country originating the runs of salmon, either naturally or artificially, to provide for proper spawning escapement, and to harvest the catchable surplus produced by that country, without unduly disrupting existing fisheries.

Pacific salmon fly fishing veteran, Al Allard, a septuagenarian who can fish longer and harder than some men half his age, works a shallow water estuary in Puget Sound. BMF

The most recent negotiations have focused on three major issues:

1. United States interception of Canadian sockeye and pink salmon generated in the Fraser River.
2. Canadian interception of United States produced chinook and coho on the west coast of Vancouver Island, the Strait of Juan de Fuca and northern British Columbia.
3. Proper allocation of salmon harvest between countries for fish spawned and nurtured in rivers running through both countries.

Fraser River

In 1913 and 1914, massive rockslides in British Columbia's Fraser River decimated the huge historical runs of sockeye. The United States and Canada agreed by Convention in 1930 to jointly finance the building of fishways to restore full upstream migration capabilities in return for one-half of the harvestable sockeye from Convention waters. These waters include the southern two-thirds of the Strait of Georgia, all of the Strait of Juan de Fuca and off the west coast of Vancouver Island between the 48th and 49th parallel, exclusive of Barkley Sound. Subsequently, in 1957, pink salmon were added to the Convention. The fishways themselves were completed between 1944 and 1966 at a cost of almost 1.4 million dollars. This investment was made equally by the United States and Canada. Management of the salmon runs under terms of the agreement has been by the International Pacific Salmon Fisheries Commission since 1940. Results have been positive with an approximate doubling of the sockeye run during that time. Response of pink populations has been even greater. However, the extremely well done Pearse Report, completed in 1982, resulting from the need to identify ways to improve

Canada's Pacific fisheries, indicates that current levels of production for Fraser River salmon of all species could be far larger with tighter adherence to optimum spawning escapement requirements. This same document indicates, overall, that Canadian declines of salmon stocks are a direct result of overfishing, with habitat destruction a substantially lesser cause.

Coastal British Columbia Catches of U. S. Chinook and Coho

Chinook salmon, and to a lesser degree coho originating in the Columbia River, coastal Washington, and Puget Sound, have become a prime target for Canadian and Southeast Alaskan trollers. Again citing the Canadian Pearse Report, the estimate of U. S. produced chinook caught off the west coast of Vancouver Island is between 70 and 90% of the Canadian harvest in this large and important area. Of chinook generated in the upper Columbia River, according to Washington reports for 1982, 63% were taken by British Columbia and 29% by southeast Alaska ocean fisheries.

This situation clearly provides little incentive for the United States to further improve their fish production or even to maintain it.

Transboundary River Allocations

Canada has raised the serious question of their proper right to harvest salmon spawned in, and provided freshwater juvenile growth, in rivers that originate in British Columbia and the Yukon Territory, but which subsequently flow into the ocean through Alaska. The Alsek, Stikine, Taku and Yukon are the principal rivers in this category. Percent of harvest due each country from these rivers has as yet to be agreed to.

A group unloads for an angling adventure at Bristol By Lodge in Alaska. BMF

A massive effort was mounted to resolve these issues by treaty, and the chief U. S. and Canadian negotiators actually signed off an agreement in December of 1982, subject only to ratification by both governments. Regretably, certain United States commercial fishing interests were able to head off presentation of the proposed treaty prior to its reaching the United States Senate. Subsequent efforts to renegotiate fell apart in January of 1984. Currently, pressure is building on both sides of the border to try once more to finalize this document of such clearly major potential impact on the salmon fishery.

. . .

The world is never static and responses to the salmon problems on the West Coast bear this out.

One of the most positive developments for marine sport salmon anglers and one of the truly major success stories in fish culture throughout the world has occurred in Washington's Puget Sound. By 1969, sport catches of chinook and coho in this front yard fishery to Washington's major population centers had declined to a small fraction of what they had been a short 20 years earlier. The excellent native resident coho fishery was only a fourth of what it had been, the resident pink fishery was all but eliminated and the resident chinook catch was well down from former levels. This scenario occurred in the face of dramatic increases in hatchery releases and adult hatchery returns. Unfortunately, these adult hatchery-reared returns were so sexually mature they had for the most part stopped feeding by the time they reached inner Puget Sound, and, therefore, were not readily available to sports fishermen.

The knight in shining armor was Frank Haw, recently retired master talent of Washington's Department of Fisheries. Faced with this problem of rapidly declining salmon for recreational fishermen, he did his homework, and developed the solution that today provides the backbone of West Coast saltwater fly fishing, and an inner Sound recreational salmon fishery equal to Washington's famous coastal sports fishery.

The "homework" consisted of observing in departmental published research done in the mid-1950s that coho tagged in their second year of life in central Puget Sound before July 1 generally were recovered in the ocean. Those tagged after July 1 tended to be caught inside Puget Sound. Haw reflected on this, and came forward with the theory that artificially delayed releases from hatcheries would produce the non-ocean-migratory salmon necessary to restore the resident sports fishery. His concept was published in the mid-1960s and tested by experimentation cooperatively undertaken by the National Marine Fisheries Service, the University of Washington's Fisheries Research Institute and the Washington Department of Fisheries. Initial releases of over a million coho composed of various test groups occurred in 1969, entering the catch in 1970. Results were spectacular. Coho retained an extra three months contributed *sixty times* more to the 1971 sports catch than normally released hatchery production fish. The answer was clearly in hand.

Subsequent experiments with chinook and saltwater pen rearing were undertaken. Ocean destined chinook are normally released following ninety days of hatchery rearing.

By increasing this time frame to over a year, with the additional time spent in saltwater pens, much the same results were obtained as for coho. Even better, since chinook live four years instead of the three for coho, the maturing, feeding chinook were available to the sports fisherman for an additional year. Instead of being four to five pounds at maturity, as was the case with resident coho, resident chinook were 15 pounds or three times as big by spawning time.

Regrettably, a serious disease problem in the form of vibriosis arose from exposure to higher water temperatures during the summer while the young chinook were in the saltwater pens. This was corrected by substituting freshwater habitat to accomplish the extended rearing.

With most problems resolved, production under this program has been consistently increased over the years to present levels. As an indication of success, the yearly sports

Jim Teeny holds up a large chinook salmon taken in November from the Trask River in Oregon.
— Jim Teeny photo

catch of salmon for inner Puget Sound has increased from 65,000 fish in 1969 to almost 200,000 in 1982. Further expansion is expected to await evaluation of the program at current production levels. There could well be natural feed and other habitat restrictions on future increases.

No one individual could accomplish the research and development required to transform his concepts into an effective, proven program without a lot of able minds working together in a coordinated framework. Washington Department of Fisheries' Ray Buckley worked closely with Haw in development of both programs. Harry Senn was instrumental in solving extended chinook rearing in freshwater. Pete Bergman co-developed the coded wire tag now used as a standard for fish tagging throughout the world, and National Marine Fisheries Service's Tony Novotny was an important contributor in the area of saltwater pen rearing. Saltwater salmon fly fishers as well as all the other Puget Sound sports anglers should mentally thank these men every time they hook a salmon in Washington's inner marine waters. Without them, there would be very few salmon with which to entertain themselves.

Perhaps most significant is the fact that this resident salmon program, which has created the very backbone of Puget Sound sport and commercial fishing, is the only major salmon production in which the State's residents reap the full benefit of the cost of their program. Until such time as the United States and Canada can agree by treaty on restricting their catch of the salmon produced by the other country, this will sadly remain the case.

. . .

Meanwhile, as the West Coast participants in the salmon fishery continue their traditional squabbling over who gets what piece of the pie, others eyed the situation as an opportunity. Clear across the world, the Norwegians have perfected techniques for mass production of pen-reared Atlantic salmon, not with trout-size fish as are being produced using coho in the Northwest, but full-blown fish of six to ten pounds that can be filleted or steaked. These are killed fresh on order and delivered by air to the customer within 48 hours.

According to the June 1984 issue of *National Fisherman* magazine, some startling trends are developing. U. S. salmon production in 1981 was around 250,000 tons, of which more than half was exported. Catch and shipments are expected to remain at about that level. That same year the Norwegians introduced just ten tons of their fresh product to this country. Their forecast for production in ten years is 100,000 tons. Japan, Scotland, Iceland, Chile, the United States and Canada are getting into the act with their own substantial programs.

Obviously, the resulting flood of production should take the heat off Pacific salmon stocks prized for the fresh fish markets. These are predominantly chinook and coho, also the most prized by the sports angler. Lower prices for troll-caught salmon may very well be the outcome, so that a still sharper contrast in economic benefits will be available between sports and commercial use of these fish. Interestingly, the summer 1984 edition of *The Atlantic Salmon Journal* points out that in 1983 the combined pen-reared production from Norway, Scotland and Ireland was over 20,000 metric tons, almost three times the combined commercial

and sport catch of Atlantic salmon worldwide (about) 8,000 metric tons). The question is, are we looking at our own future for Pacific salmon? It could be a situation that has a silver lining for the resource and for the recreational fisherman. It could also be the salvation of a lot of commercial fishermen, if they follow the Norwegian lead and become salmon farmers on their own.

Plans for Improved Salmon Fisheries

With all these issues stirring in the world of Pacific salmon, it is essential we take a hard look at what needs to be done to maintain and restore them so they can continue to be an important part of our fishery in perpetuity.

Of utmost urgency and a basic cornerstone for improvement is to complete negotiations, ratify and implement an equitable U. S./Canada Salmon Interception Treaty. Hopefully, by the time this book is published, at least negotiations will have been resumed between the two countries.[1]

A second matter that clearly needs to be addressed is that of harvesters paying the costs of producing what they catch. Based on all the wailing and gnashing of teeth at public hearings, and in the various publications, absolutely none of the participants is getting "his fair share." Nothing could be farther from the truth in almost all situations. Using preliminary figures from British Columbia and Washington in 1983, it is possible to cast some less emotional light on the subject.

British Columbia spent approximately 72.5 million dollars for the year on salmon management. During the same year, almost 36 million salmon were harvested of all species for a cost of $2.02 per fish. In return, sports fishermen paid $2.94 in licenses per fish for the 590,000 salmon taken, clearly adequately paying for their share of fish caught. For the other participants, an entirely different case is brought to light. British Columbia's commercial fishermen paid a scant $.06 per fish for the privilege of catching over 35 million salmon. In combination, the fishermen paid only five percent of the cost of providing the fish they took.

In Washington, the total Department of Fisheries budget for 1983 was 27 million dollars. Of this, an estimated 84%, or 22.7 million dollars was spent on salmon. For the five million salmon caught that year, the cost of production was $4.49 per fish. Recreational anglers took 864,000 salmon, paying $1.26 in license fees per fish. Commercial fishermen for the same year paid just $.45 per salmon for the four million fish they harvested. For the total catch, the participating fishermen in Washington paid a mere 13% of the production cost. It should be noted that the Washington catch was down materially in 1983 due to the negative impact of warming ocean temperatures known as El Nino. However, the story is much the same for 1982 when seven million salmon were caught. In that year the price paid for licenses and fish taxes still only amounted to 19% of the cost of managing and producing the salmon harvested.

If these percentages are at all representative of the situation from California through Alaska, and there is no reason to believe that they are not, then a rather basic question needs to be asked.

With so many fishermen working the resource now that few are making a decent living, wouldn't it be far more

---

[1]The treaty was signed, ratified and became effective March 18, 1985.

appropriate to increase the licenses and fish taxes to the level where the federal, state and provincial programs are self-supporting? If this were done, an important change should occur. We'd really find out how important salmon fishing is to the participants. My guess is that a significant percentage of the current license holders would decide that they really weren't very serious about it anyway. Its basic appeal to date has been the concept of getting something for nothing and that's just about the way it's been. But why should the general taxpayers of either country, most of whom have never caught a salmon nor have any desire to, pick up the tab to indulge those of us fortunate enough to have these great fish available at our doorsteps?

The result of such a change should be a far better balancing of the sustainable production of Pacific salmon with an economically attractive fishery for the fulltime troll, net and charter boat fishermen. For the sports angler it should result in a far greater opportunity to catch salmon. My suspicion is that for recreational fishers, the gap between current license fees and those necessary to pay their way is not so great as to be any real obstacle. Once people begin to look at today's cost of a tank of gas and a couple of hamburgers, it seems reasonable to assume they'll decide sports salmon fishing is a bargain by comparison and support the license hikes. Should the required jump in fees for the commercial fishermen provide an incentive to leave the industry in any numbers, there should be a clear case for review of salmon allocation between commercial and sports fisheries based on maximum economic benefit to the state or province involved. As this changes over time, so should the allocation.

It is very conceivable that for the entire coast, as the fresh salmon market is met in other ways, that at least chinook and coho should and will be harvested entirely by the recreational fishery, with the exception of fish allocated under law to the treaty Indian tribes. After all, in 1983 there were over 700,000 sports fishing licenses sold in Washington and British Columbia combined, while there were only 31,000 commercial licenses issued. Sooner or later, this issue must be addressed in a rational way.

By now it is becoming increasingly apparent that we have gone too far down the path of expecting hatchery production to solve all problems. Instead, this single-mindedness has created problems of its own. In my opinion, we need to manage wild and hatchery stocks as separate entities in order to maximize the benefits of each.

Wild stocks offer great genetic diversity and special adaptation to the river systems in which they occur. We can't afford to lose this in our quest for more fish on the table. We have only to look at the huge size of the world-famous chinook from the Kenai River in Alaska, and Rivers Inlet in British Columbia to demonstrate the point. Besides, given the basic protection they require, these stocks provide us with the least expensive production.

Their undoing has been sharply accelerated by the traditional mixed stock fishing which takes place, especially in the offshore ocean harvest, but which also occurs in the inside fishing up to the point where the individual stocks separate before heading up their individual spawning rivers.

Differences in reproduction requirements are at the heart of the problems. Wild stocks require an average 30 to 50%

The salmon hatchery at Rowdy Creek, Smith River, California. This hatchery, operated by the Smith River Kiwanis Club, operates on private donations, producing fall chinook salmon and winter steelhead. The hatchery uses brood stock only from the Smith River to protect and perpetuate the extremely large fish native to the Smith River watershed. LJ

A nice coho that hit a fly at Neah Bay, Washington. — David Wands photo

of total run size for adequate spawning escapement, while hatchery stocks, with their more protected reproductive environment, need only five to ten percent of the run for the same purpose. Until very recently, this simple fact has been ignored in setting offshore fishing regulations. Most of the time seasons and quotas have been established based on hatchery egg take requirements only. The inevitable result has been clearly demonstrated, with the wild runs, for the most part, getting weaker and weaker.

My proposal is that all ocean and inside harvest on mixed natural and hatchery stocks, whether recreational or commercial, be restricted to a level that allows the natural runs to pass through to their spawning grounds in sufficient numbers to bring full utilization of existing spawning and nursery areas. Since the life cycle of most salmon is five years or less, this should be accomplished in a five-year period. At the very most it should not extend beyond two cycles, or ten years. Longer rebuilding periods for wild stocks are nothing more than passing this politically hot potato on to the next generation. There is no need for it. The very foundation of our salmon management should be full production of our wild runs. Any other commitment can only lead to their ultimate demise.

Hatcheries, and the characteristics of their stocks, are most useful as supplements to wild production, and as mitigation for loss of natural runs due to dams and other permanent loss of freshwater habitat. Historically, most hatchery stocks seem to have been bred solely to provide the highest number of released fish at the least cost. This always looked good in annual reports, if not to the fisherman. But then, since he was essentially getting a free ride,

he really didn't have much of a right to say anything.

The time has come to pay our own way, as I stated earlier. Once having done so, then it seems very appropriate to take a sharp look at hatchery practices, and expect changes to be made to reflect the change in harvest timing already recommended to maximize wild production.

Whether for commercial or recreational purposes, we need to take a fresh look at the specifications making our quarry most desirable to us as consumers. What do we want from these hatchery salmon? A list is easy to prepare, keeping in mind these fish will be harvested either in terminal saltwater areas off individual rivermouths, or downstream in fresh water from hatchery facilities. A laundry list of desired characteristics would certainly include the following:

1. Large size for the species.
2. Bright, silver color for extended period.
3. Hard fighting.
4. Willing biter.
5. High quality flavor and firm flesh.
6. Extended run arrival.
7. Run arrival during weather favorable for harvest.
8. Runs spaced throughout the year to serve fresh markets over the full 12 months.
9. Run timing not to overlap significant natural wild runs in the same area.
10. Minimum straying to alernate spawning sites, to preclude diluting genetic characteristics of wild stocks.

Not so surprisingly, these are the very characteristics wild fish had that were most marketable, historically. Certainly, with all our current technical ability, we can restore them in our hatchery fish. Initial stock selection and subsequent attention to individuals selected for spawning can provide the large size. We have had a reverse process going on for decades with our selective harvest of the larger fish, leaving mostly runts to return to the hatcheries. A bright, biting, hard fighting fish of top quality eating characteristics arriving over an extended period of time merely describes a wild, immature fish, characteristically destined for spawning in a large river, therefore requiring a long freshwater trip to the spawning beds.

For years, hatchery managers have tried to accomplish just the opposite. What they wanted was a fish that arrived at the hatchery fully mature, ready to spawn, with the entire run present in as short a time frame as possible. This fish had stopped feeding, was dark in color, fought poorly, and because of its nearness to spawning had rapidly declining firmness and flavor. In other words, they succeeded. For them, it reduced the time to hold salmon in the hatchery ponds while they matured, and reduced the cost for extra labor to artificially spawn the salmon since they all arrived at a predictable, uniform time. This was probably all right when most of the fish were harvested much earlier in the cycle, but it is no longer appropriate with the proposed change in harvest timing. Care in selection of stocks initially should address the other desirable characteristics in an effective way. The hatchery challenge needs to be made. The results can be spectacular.

Pacific salmon of all species and strains are beautiful beyond measure in their streamlined, silvery, simplicity of form. They have shown themselves to be amazingly tenacious in the face of massive attempts to eliminate them, whether by consumption or destruction of their habitat. They can be a continuing and increasing part of our enjoyment and sustenance. We have the knowledge at hand to maintain and restore their numbers. It's entirely up to us whether we choose to do so. I, for one, am counting on our good judgment.

Members of the Sacramento Fly Casters working the Chetco River just above tidewater for fall chinook salmon. This southern Oregon stream is well-known for large salmon. LJ

10.

Ethics

FLY FISHING ETHICS AS IT RELATES TO salmon fishing is really a code of individual conduct, which, when put to use by all participants, assures that the pleasures of the sport are maintained for all to share.

If you are the only one fishing, there really is not much of a problem except for obeying the fishing laws, respecting private property, and commiting yourself to sound conservation practices to insure that there'll be salmon there next year and the year after that. Most of our difficulties arise from the fact that more and more of us want to fish in the same place at the same time. Add to this a rather finite number of fish, and you have the basis for open warfare. The trick is to find a way for each of us to enjoy our fishing without interfering with the enjoyment of other fishermen.

In fresh water, care should be taken to approach the water carefully so as not to spook the fish that someone else is already working on. It also means waiting your turn quietly in the background until the fisherman already there moves on. Conversely, if you are the one already fishing, there is an obligation not to stay on the prime water indefinitely, but to move on after a reasonable period of time. If you're in a boat, then it stands to reason that you would quickly and quietly drift through an area where others are bank fishing, keeping as much distance as possible between you and them, and keeping your line out of the water to avoid tangles. Besides, with your mobility, you have much water to fish that they don't. If you encounter another boat, either slow down enough so you don't crowd his fishing or ask if you can pass around him and fish ahead only after allowing enough room between boats so fish you are working have a chance to settle down before he gets there. If someone hooks a fish close by, reel in at once and give him room to play and land his salmon. In other words, think of the courteous way to resolve people problems on the rivers, and act accordingly.

Appropriate saltwater conduct has not been as clearly defined, but it's apparent from crowding that's beginning to take place in the more popular areas that it is more than time to do so.

The problem is that courteous fishing practices covering the traditional ways of catching salmon in salt water, namely mooching and trolling and even casting buzz bombs and other lures with spinning and level wind outfits, don't necessarily apply to fly fishing. Let's face it, surface disturbances may not bother a salmon 60 feet down, but in the more normal fly fishing depths of ten feet or less, those disturbances count. Careless boat operation can put the salmon down for anywhere from a half hour to the rest of the day. This is important to consider when most saltwater fly fishing is done out of a boat.

Late last winter, I had searched several miles of normally good salmon water to no avail, and had taken hours to do it carefully. Finally I located a school of feeding coho in a shallow cove, and was congratulating myself on my good fortune after catching and releasing several in a row. About that time a boater, out joy riding with his family, roared up alongside and asked me how the fishing was. I rather caustically replied, "It was just great until you made all those waves and noise racing over to see how I was doing." His apology and quiet retreat couldn't undo the damage. Not another fish showed that day, although I fished through until total darkness.

The number one rule of conduct is to respect the other person's fishing space. Don't race in, motor wide open, when you see someone else hook a fish or see another fisherman just working an area. Instead, slow down and detour around so you're sure you won't put his quarry down. And if the other fisherman is on shore, be doubly courteous and give him an even wider detour since he has far fewer productive places to go.

There's an awful temptation to snuggle up to the successful fisherman. Don't! This is clear water fishing over spooky fish, and they're easy to put down. A good fly caster will put out close to a hundred feet of line. If you're doing the same, casting at the same fish from opposite directions, you'll need 200 feet between you, and that's a good rule of thumb to follow — 200 feet between you and the next boat. If you start drifting closer, either put out an anchor (quietly slipped over the side instead of thrown), row out of his casting area, or start your motor at slow speed and ease out of his way. It's amazing how many people can fly fish over a moving pod of salmon if they'll follow these procedures.

My friend Bill Matthaei put it this way, "Don't rock my boat, stay out of my casting range, and we'll get along okay."

The point is, we have a spectacular new fishery developing which can provide us with not only the pleasure of beautiful surroundings, but also the joys of fishing alongside and with courteous fellow fishermen. We can lead the way towards this goal, and should view the development and widespread adoption of responsible fly fishing behavior as equally as important as the development of new tackle or techniques. It is the essence of the fishing experience.

A trio of stocky, fly caught coho salmon taken from Alaska's Togiak River. BMF

Appendix I
Fishing tackle shops

There are well-stocked, professionally staffed tackle shops nearby most good Pacific Coast salmon fishing areas. In addition to handling rods, reels, flies and other essentials, tackle shops are excellent resources for securing guide services and focal points for the latest fishing information. Here are a few that we have visited, or know by reputation:

ALASKA

Mountain View Sports Center
134 So. Park Street
Anchorage, Alaska 99504
(907) 277-9733.

CALIFORNIA

Eddie Bauer, Inc. (Jon Ray)
220 Post St.
San Francisco, California 94108
(415) 986-7600

The Fly Shop (Brad Jackson & Mike Michalak)
4140 Churn Creek Road
Redding, California 96002
Toll Free 1-800-535-3474 (Calif.), 1-800-533-3474 (Out-of-State),
(916) 222-3555.

Greenwater Tackle
P. O. Box 566, 4 Pacific Woods Road
Gualala, California 95445
(707) 884-3075

Orvis
166 Maiden Lane, Union Square
San Francisco, California 94108
(415) 392-1600

Tirne Flies (Larry Simpson & Mac Stuard)
716 - 9th St.
Arcata, California 95521
(707) 822-8331

OREGON

Brookings Sports Unlimited (Lew Sapp)
P. O. Box C, 625 Chetco Avenue
Brookings, Oregon 97415
(503) 469-4012

The Caddis Fly Angling Shop (Bob & Kathy Guard)
131A E. 5th Avenue
Eugene, Oregon 97401
(503) 342-7005

Don's Tackle Shop (Don & Lola McClain)
7622 S. E. Foster Road
Portland, Oregon 97206
(503) 774-5270

Kaufmann's Streamborn
12963 S. W. Pacific Highway (99W)
Tigard, Oregon 97223
(503) 639-7004

The Silver Sedge Fly Shoppe (Jerry Kime & Rusty Randall)
138 S. E. "H" Street
Grants Pass, Oregon 97526
(503) 479-4430

WASHINGTON

The Avid Angler (Tom Darling)
11714 - 15th Ave. N. E.
Seattle, Washington 98125
(206) 362-4030

The Greased Line Fly Shoppe (Mark Noble)
5802 N. E. 88th Street
Vancouver, Washington 98665
(206) 573-9383

Kaufmann's Streamborn
15015 Main Street
K-Mart Shopping Center
Bellevue, Washington 98007
(206) 643-2246

The Morning Hatch Fly Shoppe (Garry M. Sandstrom)
11011 "C" Occident Street S. W.
Tacoma, Washington 98499
(206) 582-6650

Prichard's (Debbie & El Willy)
2106 Kalama River Road
Kalama, Washington 98502
(206) 673-4690

South Sound Anglers (Randy L. Frisvold)
1151 Black Lake Blvd.
Olympia, Washington 98502
(206) 943-2532

BRITISH COLUMBIA

Bob's Sporting Goods
4150 E. Hastings Street
Burnaby, British Columbia V5C 2J4
(604) 298-8551

Appendix II
Taxonomic list of baitfish species

Scientific Classification	Common Name	Scientific Classification	Common Name
Phylum Chordata		Family Osmeridae	
Sub Phylum Vertebrata		Genus *Thaleichthys*	
Class Osteichthyes		Species *pacificus*	Eulachon
Order Clupeiformes		Genus *Allosmerus*	
Family Clupeidae		Species *elongatus*	Whitebait smelt
Genus *Clupea*		Genus *Hypomesus*	
Species *harengus pallasi*	Pacific herring	Species *pretiosus*	Surf smelt
Genus *Sardinops*		Genus *Mallotus*	
Species *sagax*	Pacific sardine	Species *villosus*	Capelin
Family Engraulidae		Order Perciformes	
Genus *Engraulis*		Family Ammodytidae	
Species *mordax*	Northern anchovy	Genus *Ammodytes*	
Order Salmoniformes		Species *hexapterus*	Pacific sand lance

Appendix III
Taxonomic list of invertebrates identified from zooplankton samples and stomach contents

Scientific Classification	Common Name
Phylum Cnidaria	Coelenterates
Class Hydrozoa	
Genus *Velella*	"Purple sailor"
Class Scyphozoa	
Class Anthozoa	
Phylum Ctenophora	
Phylum Nematoda	Round worms
Phylum Mollusca	
Class Gastropoda	
Order Mesogastropoda	Snails
Genus *Littorina*	
Order Thecosomata	Sea butterflies
Class Bivalria	Clams, oysters
Class Cephalopoda	
Subclass Coleoidea	
Genus *Loligo*	Squids
Genus *Octopus*	Octopus
Phylum Annelida	Segmented worms
Class Polychaeta	
Subclass Errentia	
Family Syllidae	
Genus *Autolytus*	
Family Nereidae	
Genus *Platyneris*	
Subclass Sedentaria	
Family Spionidae	
Family Opheliidae	
Phylum Arthropoda	
Class Arachnida	Spiders, mites
Order Araneae	Spiders
Class Crustacea	
Subclass Branchiopoda	
Order Cladocera	Water fleas
Genus *Podon*	
Subclass Ostracoda	Mussel or seed shrimp
Order Myodocoda	
Subclass Copepoda	Copepods
Order Calanoida	Calanoids
Genus *Calanus*	
Genus *Evcalanus*	
Genus *Paracalanus*	
Genus *Aetidius*	
Genus *Metridia*	
Genus *Epilabidocera*	
Genus *Acartia*	
Genus *Candacia*	
Order Harpacticoida	Harpacticoids
Order Cyclopoida	
Genus *Oncaea*	
Genus *Corycaeus*	
Order Monstrilloida	
Order Caligoida	
Subclass Cirripedia	Barnacles
Suborder Balanomorpha	Sessile barnacles
Genus *Balanus*	
Subclass Malcostraca	
Order Mysidacea	
Family Mysidae	Opossum shrimp
Genus *Boreomysis*	
Order Cumacea	
Genus *Cumella*	
Order Tanaidacea	
Order Isopoda	
Suborder Epicaridea	
Suborder Flabellifera	
Order Amphipoda	
Suborder Hyperiidea	
Genus *Parathemisto*	
Genus *Hyperia*	
Suborder Gammaridea	Sand fleas, scuds
Genus *Calliopius*	
Genus *Corophium*	
Genus *Anisogammarus*	
Genus *Paraphoxus*	
Genus *Accedomoerra*	
Suborder Caprellidea	
Genus *Caprella*	
Order Euphausiacea	Krill
Family Euphausiidae	
Genus *Euphausia*	
Genus *Thysanoessa*	
Order Decapoda	
Suborder Natantia	Shrimps, crabs
Section Penaeidea	Shrimps
Section Pleocyemata-Caridea	
Family Hippolytidae	
Genus *Heptacarpus*	
Family Pandalidae	
Genus *Pandulus*	
Genus *Pandalopsis*	
Family Crangonidae	
Genus *Crangon*	Sand shrimps
Section Macura	
Family Callianassidae	
Genus *Callianassia*	
Genus *Upogebia*	
Section Anomura	Crabs
Family Poecellanidae	
Family Paguridae	Hermit crabs
Genus *Pagurus*	
Section Brachyura	True crabs
Infrasubsection Brachyrhyncha	
Family Cancridae	Cancer crab
Genus *Cancer*	
Family Pinnotheridae	Pea crabs
Infrasubsection Oxyrhyncha	Decorator crabs
Family Majidae	
Class Insecta	Insects
Order Ephemeroptera	Mayflies
Order Isoptera	Termites
Order Plecoptera	Stoneflies
Order Psocoptera	Lice
Order Homoptera	Aphids
Family Psyllidae	
Order Neuroptera	Alderflies
Order Diptera	True flies
Family Chironomidae	Midges
Order Hymenoptera	Ants, bees, wasps
Phylum Chaetognatha	
Genus *Sagitta*	
Phylum Chordata	
Class Larvacea	
Genus *Oikopleura*	

Appendix IV
Federation of Fly Fishers

The Federation of Fly Fishers is an international organization of individuals and clubs who are bound together to:

Provide a voice for fly fishers,
Promote the sport of fly fishing, and to

Protect our fishing environment for future generations.

For additional information, write to: Federation of Fly Fishers, P. O. Box 1088, West Yellowstone, Montana 59578; telephone (406) 646-9541.

Appendix V
International Game Fish Association

Specific rules for fly fishing have been adopted by the International Game Fish Association (IGFA). These must be followed explicitly for the catch to qualify as an official world record. An important consideration is that the motor on the boat must be out of gear when casting and retrieving the fly. Trolling is NOT permitted.

For complete details, contact the International Game Fish Association, 300 East Los Olas Blvd., Fort Lauderdale, Florida 33316 - 1616.

Appendix VI
State fish and game agencies

State and provincial agencies charged with the management of salmon resources provide fishing regulations and license information on request. Some may also offer visitors' literature and fishing maps, either free or for a small fee. Always check current information well ahead of the time you plan to embark on a salmon fishing trip to avoid problems such as tackle restrictions, changes in season opening and ending dates or even area closures. For information, write:

Alaska Department of Fish and Game
Box 3-2000
Juneau, Alaska 99802

State of California Department of Fish and Game
1416 Ninth Street
Sacramento, California 95814

Oregon Department of Fish and Wildlife
P. O. Box 3503
506 S. W. Mill Street
Portland, Oregon 97208

Washington State Department of Fisheries
115 General Administration Building
Olympia, Washington 98504

Province of British Columbia
Ministry of Recreation and Conservation
Fish and Wildlife Branch
Victoria, British Columbia, Canada

Appendix VII
List of Recommended Reading

There are a great many excellent books available to the salmon fly fisher that provide information on salmon and other anadromous species. Subjects include applicable fishing techniques, flies and fly tying, tackle, geographic data and general information. Our recommendations probably already line the library shelves of veteran West Coast anglers and should be considered a good starting list for the aspiring collector of angling volumes.

Pacific Northwest Fly Patterns by Roy Patrick.

Flies of the Northwest by the Inland Empire Fly Club.

Steelhead Flies and Fly Fishing by Trey Combs.

Sea-Run — The Complete Guide to Fishing Sea-Run Cutthroat Trout by Les Johnson.

Pacific Salmon by R. J. Childerhose and Marj Trim.

Streamer Fly Tying and Fishing by Joseph Bates.

Universal Fly Tying Guide by Dick Stewart.

Fly Casting With Lefty Kreh by Lefty Kreh.

Fisherman's Knots by Tom McNalley.

McClane's New Standard Fishing Encyclopedia by A. J. McClane.

The Atlantic Salmon by Lee Wulff.

Fly Patterns of Alaska by the Alaska Fly Fishers.

Bibliography

Alaska Flyfishers, 1983. Fly Patterns of Alaska. Portland: Frank Amato Publications.

Anadromous Salmonid Environmental Task Force, 1979. Freshwater Habitat, Salmon Produced, and Escapements for Natural Spawning Along the Pacific Coast of the U. S. Portland: Pacific Fishery Management Council.

Anderson, J. M., Summer 1984. Taming the Leaper. Atlantic Salmon Journal.

Bergman, P. K., 1984. A New Management Structure for Anadromous Salmon and Steelhead Resources and Fisheries of the Washington and Columbia River Conservation Areas. Report of the Salmon and Steelhead Advisory Commission. Seattle: National Marine Fisheries Service.

Bohn, B. R. and Stockley, C. E., 1981. Columbia River Fish Runs and Fisheries 1957-1979. Oregon Department of Fish and Wildlife, Washington Department of Fisheries.

Caras, R., 1975. Sockeye, The Life of a Pacific Salmon. New York: The Dial Press.

Champion, E. D., August, 1979. Catching Coho With Flies. Anchorage: Alaska Magazine, Alaska Northwest Publishing Co.

Chaney, E. and Perry, L. E., 1976. Columbia Basin Salmon and Steelhead Analysis. Pacific Northwest Regional Commission.

Childerhose, R. J. and Trim, M., 1979. Pacific Salmon. Seattle: University of Washington Press.

Crutchfield, J. A., Jr. and Schelle, K., 1978. An Economic Analysis of Washington Ocean Recreational Salmon Fishery with Particular Emphasis on the Role Played by the Charter Vessel Industry. Seattle: University of Washington.

Ellis, D. V., 1977. Pacific Salmon Management for People. Victoria: University of Victoria.

Fisheries Research Institute, 1961. Pacific Salmon — Selected Articles from Soviet Periodicals translated from Russian. Washington, D. C.: Israel Program for Scientific Translations, Ltd. through Office of Technical Services, U. S. Department of Commerce.

Foerster, R. E., 1968. The Sockeye Salmon, Bulletin 162. Ottawa: Fisheries Research Board of Canada.

Forrester, C. R., 1981. Statistical Yearbook 1977. Vancouver, Canada: International North Pacific Fisheries Commission.

Fredin, R. A., Major, R. L., Bakkala, R. G., Tanonaka, G. K., 1977. Pacific Salmon and the High Seas Salmon Fisheries of Japan. Seattle: National Marine Fisheries Service.

French, R., Bilton, H., Osako, M. and Hartt, A., 1976. Distribution and Origin of Sockeye Salmon in Offshore Waters of the North Pacific Ocean. Bulletin 34. Vancouver, Canada: International North Pacific Fisheries Commission.

Fresh, K. and Caldwell, R., 1979. Salmon-Herring Predator/ Competitor Interactions (Phase I). Olympia: Washington Department of Fisheries.

Fresh, K. L., Caldwell, R. D., and Koons, R. R., 1981. Food Habits of Pacific Salmon, Baitfish, and their Potential Competitors and Predators in the Marine Waters of Washington, August, 1978 to September, 1979. Progress Report 145. Olympia: Washington Department of Fisheries.

Godfrey, H., Mason, J. E. and Tanaka, S., 1965. Salmon of the North Pacific Ocean, Bulletin 16. Vancouver, Canada: International North Pacific Fisheries Commission.

Godfrey, H., Henry, K. A. and Machidori, S., 1975. Distribution and Abundance of Coho Salmon in Offshore Waters of the North Pacific Ocean. Bulletin 31. Vancouver, Canada: International North Pacific Fisheries Commission.

Hart, J. L., 1973. Pacific Fishes of Canada. Ottawa: Fisheries Research Board of Canada.

Haw, F. and Bergman, P. K., 1972. A Salmon Angling Program for the Puget Sound Region. Olympia: Washington Department of Fisheries.

Haw, F. and Buckley, R. M., 1973. Saltwater Fishing in Washington. Seattle: Stan Jones Publishing Co.

Jacobson, J. and Davis, K., 1983. Federal Fisheries Management. A Guidebook to the Fishery Conservation and Management Act. Eugene: University of Oregon Law School.

Jensen, A. C., 1979. Wildlife of the Oceans. New York: Harry N. Abrams, Inc.

Major, R. L., Ito, J., Ito, S., and Godfrey, H., 1978. Distribution and Origin of Chinook Salmon in Offshore Waters of the North Pacific Ocean. Bulletin 38. Vancouver, Canada: International North Pacific Fisheries Commission.

Marriott, R. A., and Logan, S. M., 1971. The Coho Salmon in Alaska. Juneau: Alaska Department of Fish and Game.

McClane, A. J., 1974. McClane's Standard Fishing Encyclopedia. Holt, Rinehart and Winston, Inc.

McPhail, J. D., and Lindsey, C. C., 1970. Freshwater Fishes of Northwestern Canada and Alaska. Bulletin 173. Ottawa: Fisheries Research Board of Canada.

Neave, F., Yonemori, T., and Bakkala, R. G., 1976. Distribution and Origin of Chum Salmon in Offshore Waters of the North Pacific Ocean. Bulletin 35. Vancouver, Canada: International North Pacific Fisheries Commission.

Netboy, A., 1973. The Salmon, Their Fight for Survival. Boston: Houghton Mifflin Company.

Netboy, A., 1980. The Columbia River Salmon and Steelhead Trout. Seattle: University of Washington Press.

North Pacific Fishery Management Council, 1978. Final Fishery Management Plan and Environmental Impact Statement for the High Seas Fishery off the Coast of Alaska East of 175 Degrees East Longitude. Anchorage: North Pacific Fishery Management Council.

Pacific Fishery Management Council, 1978. Final Environmental Impact Statement and Fishery Management

Plan for Commercial and Recreational Salmon Fisheries off the Coasts of Washington, Oregon and California Commencing in 1978. Portland: Pacific Fishery Management Council.

Pacific Fishery Management Council, 1983. Proposed Plan for Managing the 1983 Salmon Fisheries Off the Coasts of California, Oregon and Washington. Portland: Pacific Fishery Management Council.

Pacific Fishery Management Council, 1984. Final Framework Amendment for Managing the Ocean Salmon Fisheries Off the Coasts of Washington, Oregon and California Commencing in 1985. Portland: Pacific Fishery Management Council.

Pearse, P. H., 1982. Turning the Tide — A New Policy for Canada's Pacific Fisheries. Ottawa: Department of Fisheries and Oceans.

Public Law 94-265, 1976. Fishery Conservation and Management Act of 1976. Washington, D. C.: U. S. Government Printing Office.

Repine, J., 1977. Fishing Alaska. Anchorage: Wilderness Publishing.

Roskelly, F., 1979. Flies of the Northwest. Spokane: Inland Empire Fly Fishing Club Publications.

Salmon Industries of the United States, 1974. The Pacific Salmon — A Unique Problem in Ocean Resource Management. Seattle: National Marine Fisheries Service.

Schmitt, W. L., 1965. Crustaceans. Ann Arbor: University of Michigan Press.

Secretariat, INPFC, 1979. Historical Catch Statistics for Salmon of the North Pacific Ocean. Bulletin 39. Vancouver, Canada. International North Pacific Fisheries Commission.

Smith, D. L., 1977. A Guide to Marine Coastal Plankton and Marine Invertebrate Larvae. Dubuque: Kendall/Hunt Publishing Company.

Straight, L., 1980-81. B. C. Angling Guide, Vol. 8. Vancouver, Canada: Lee Straight Publications.

Strickland, R. M., 1983. The Fertile Fjord. Seattle: University of Washington Press.

Takagi, K., Aro, K. V., Hartt, A. C., and Dell, M. B., 1981. Distribution and Origin of Pink Salmon in Offshore Waters of the North Pacific Ocean. Bulletin 40. Vancouver, Canada: International North Pacific Fisheries Commission.

Van Hulle, F., 1972. The Sockeye Salmon in Alaska. Juneau: Alaska Department of Fish and Game.

Verhoeven, L. A., 1974. Migratory Fish Resources of Northwest Coastal Streams. Portland: Crown Zellerbach Corporation.

Washington, P. M., 1977. West Coast Recreational Fisheries for Salmon: Seattle: National Marine Fisheries Service.

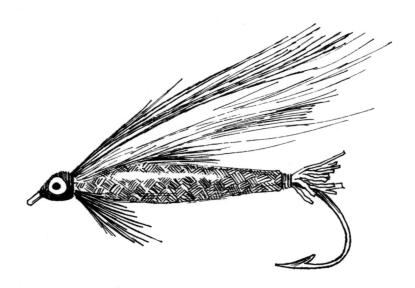

Index